Americana
MUSIC

John and Robin Dickson Series in Texas Music
Sponsored by the Center for Texas Music History
Texas State University
Jason Mellard, General Editor

Americana
MUSIC

Voices, Visionaries & Pioneers
of an Honest Sound

LEE DAVID ZIMMERMAN

Texas A&M University Press | College Station

This paper meets the requirements
of ANSI/NISO Z39.48–1992 (Permanence of Paper).
Binding materials have been chosen for durability.
Manufactured in the United States of America

Library of Congress Cataloging-in-Publication Data

Names: Zimmerman, Lee, author.
Title: Americana music: voices, visionaries, and pioneers of an honest sound
/ Lee David Zimmerman.
Description: First edition. | College Station: Texas A&M University Press,
[2019] | Series: John and Robin Dickson series in Texas music |
Identifiers: LCCN 2018028762 (print) | LCCN 2018035044 (ebook) | ISBN
9781623497026 (ebook) | ISBN 9781623497019 | ISBN 9781623497019
(cloth: alk. paper)
Subjects: LCSH: Americana (Music)—History and criticism.
Classification: LCC ML3512 (ebook) | LCC ML3512 .Z56 2019 (print) | DDC
781.640973—dc23
LC record available at https://lccn.loc.gov/2018028762

Unless otherwise indicated, all photographs
are courtesy Alisa B. Cherry.

Portions of this book have previously appeared in the
following publications: Bluegrass Situation, Blurt, Country
Standard Time, Glide, Goldmine, M Music and Musicians, Miami
and Broward New Times, *and* No Depression.

To my wife, Alisa,
for her love and ongoing belief in me,
and to my parents

Contents

Galleries of images follow pages 82 and 226.

Acknowledgments

This book would not have been possible without the support and encouragement of key individuals who played a major role in my creative and writing process. Thanks go out to Alisa B. Cherry for her wonderful photographs. To the editors and publishers of the magazines, newspapers, and websites who so generously allowed my stories and interviews that were originally part of their respective publications to be repurposed here. To Tamara Saviano for graciously introducing me to my wonderful publisher, and all at Texas A&M University Press for their help, support, and efforts in bringing this book to life. Last but not least, very special thanks and acknowledgments go out to my friends and family, who were so supportive throughout the entire writing process—and to Mom and Dad, who I know would be proud of me.

Americana
MUSIC

Introduction

I've been writing about music for well over twenty years. It suits me well. I'd like to say my ability is due in part to the communications degree that I earned at the University of Miami, but to be honest, that would be little more than an excuse to justify the thousands of dollars my parents poured into that institution in the form of tuition they paid on my behalf. In all honesty, it's owed more to the fact that despite my best efforts, I've never had the talent to play an instrument, even though I always dreamed that somehow I'd be up on stage. I even wrote a song once called "I Wanna Be a Rock Star" (not to be confused with the Byrds' similarly titled anthem "So You Want To Be a Rock 'n' Roll Star"). Nevertheless, I'm obsessed with music, and have been ever since hearing echoes of Elvis and Buddy Holly back in the late fifties. Then came those first Beatles albums, followed by discs by the Stones, Herman's Hermits, and all the other architects of the British Invasion. I can still recall when I acquired my first taste of the so-called new music—either bought at local record stores just beyond the fringes of my college campus, or given to me by my parents or my kind Uncle Dick.

Somehow it always seemed to find its way to my radar.

In the fifty years since, I've been obsessed with collecting records, first in the form of vinyl and nowadays via CDs. I always had the largest collection of all my friends, prompting gasps of wonderment even now. Today my entire basement is given over to rows and rows of albums and compact discs—so many, in fact, I've lost count. Here's a little tip for all you would-be music writers. Writing pays squat. But the perks are really cool. No streams or downloads for this guy. The actual disc becomes my real takeaway.

Naturally, then, music makes for good topics of conversation. After all, there's no one who doesn't have an opinion about the sounds they either love or disdain. And when they find out that I'm, well, what most people would refer to as a critic, they rarely shy away from asking my opinion.

The problem is, when people ask me what kind of music I lean toward, I inevitably say Americana. "What's that?" they ask, a look of bewilderment etching their features. That's the thing; the definition isn't easy to describe. It's a large umbrella that encompasses roots rock, country rock, gritty rock and roll, and R&B. Not everything made in America can be considered Americana, and yet it's a style that brings together the wellsprings of American music. It's a sound that reflects its traditions, its dichotomy, the sound of people sharing their hopes, their dreams, their values. It's everyman music, but music with a deep personal perspective.

"Ah, it must be country then," people reply, latching on to the fact that much of the music comes from Nashville, Austin, Appalachia, Bakersfield, Memphis, or distinct rural environs. "No, it's a kind of a new twist on country, maybe country rock, but not of the cowboy hat variety," I tell them, trying to couch my answer so as not to differentiate between their assumptions and my own musical standards. It's not the thing you'll hear on the radio, I insist—at least not on the commercial country stations. That's more like frat rock these days. No, Americana is mostly a sound that resides below the surface of what the tastemakers consider commercial. Remember those Southern California singer-songwriters of the early seventies? Folks like Jackson Brown, James Taylor, the Eagles? They could be considered forebears of Americana, I tell them, doing my best to cite some established standard. Bob Dylan. He's Americana. Willie Nelson. He is too. The Nitty Gritty Dirt Band, Poco, Gram Parsons . . . they were all Americana before the term was even coined.

As the great singer-songwriter Jim Lauderdale is prone to say when pointing to a guest artist at an event or on his radio program, "Now *that's* Americana!"

Still, for all my efforts at interpretation, I've always found it difficult to come up with a precise definition, something that people can get a handle on. So that's where this book comes in. It's not my only reason for writing it, mind you. My desire to become an internationally known author and authority has something to do with it too, but hopefully that comes later. First comes the challenge of encapsulating a style that's so broad and yet so special and significant it's ultimately subject to interpretation. It's like trying to describe what it's like being in love. Or the color yellow. Or that feeling in both head and heart when you sense that you have realized your dreams and there's no turning back.

Therein lies the challenge.

It's best then to find a frame of reference. While Americana is a burgeoning genre these days, its origins go back to America's infancy, when newly arrived immigrants from England, Ireland, Africa, Scotland, and places south of our border planted their seeds in the backwoods of Kentucky, the early settlements of Virginia, and the rural reaches of Texas, Tennessee, and the Carolinas. It's a sound borne from tradition and, furthered by a reverence for those roots, one that pushes forward while expanding its parameters.

Consequently, the term "Americana" covers a wide gamut of sounds and styles. In its strictest sense, it's a blanket term for bluegrass, country, mountain music, rockabilly, soul, and the blues. By a broader definition, it can encompass all the trails and side routes that lead on from there. Hank Williams, Johnny Cash, Carl Perkins, and Tom Petty can all lay claim to extending the range of Americana, but so can Kinky Friedman, Elvis Costello, Solomon Burke, and Jason Isbell. It's both new and old, classic and contemporary, trendy and traditional.

Americana Music: Voices, Visionaries, and Pioneers of an Honest Sound will attempt to define that trajectory by first taking a look at Americana's origins, and then through interviews with those who were responsible for taking it forward, providing essential context while exploring new directions that led toward the present and future.

And Now, Forward into the Future

While the intent isn't to narrow things down or define this genre too specifically, it's hoped that this book will instill an understanding of the wide reach of the music it embraces. In so doing, we can then appreciate how these sounds continue to shape and influence the vast sphere of popular music as a whole, both in the United States and abroad.

To be sure, not every significant voice is accounted for here. This is a selective sampling at best. However, those artists that do share their voices in these chapters represent many of the most influential and authoritative individuals of the past and present—musicians who played a major role in guiding that transition from the homegrown music of yesteryear to the merger of rock and country that first produced what was once called "country rock" and then helped forge Americana and the sounds we celebrate today. The firsthand insights of those whose stories help shape that sound—people like Ralph Stanley, John McEuen of the Nitty Gritty Dirt Band, Chris Hillman of the Byrds and the Flying Burrito Brothers, Rusty Young of Poco, Kinky Friedman, David Bromberg, Lyle Lovett, Jay Farrar of Wilco, and so many more musicians integral to its evolution—will help provide a history of how Americana originated, how it reached a broader audience in the sixties and seventies, and then became music that could claim populist appeal in the new millennium.

Enjoy . . .

1

Back to the Beginning

1

··

Routes and Roots

One of the earliest threads of Americana and one rooted in more rustic realms, bluegrass has in fact seen a consistent surge in popularity, thanks to artists who have taken the music's traditional trappings and moved them toward the mainstream. It's clearly not your father's bluegrass anymore.

John McEuen witnessed that rise in popularity firsthand during his tenure with the Nitty Gritty Dirt Band, one of the bands responsible for forging the connection between the old and the new. Some might consider him a purist, not because he eschews modern methods—far from it—but rather because as a loyal bluegrass devotee, he helped spur its popularity early on.

Today's music lovers are tapping a tradition once nourished by Bill Monroe, Hank Williams, Lester Flatt, Earl Scruggs, Ralph Stanley and the Stanley Brothers, the Osborne Brothers, Elvis Presley, Buddy Holly, Johnny Cash, Howlin' Wolf, Muddy Waters, B.B. King, Chuck Berry, Willie Nelson, Bob Dylan, the Band, and scores of other artists who brought bluegrass, folk, blues, rockabilly, and roots their initial popularity in the forties and fifties. An offshoot of the folk music brought to Appalachia by early immigrants from the British Isles in the late eighteenth century, Americana's origins began with traditional tunes that could be plucked, picked, and played on banjo, guitar, fiddle, and mandolin. By incorporating shared vocals and multipart harmonies, it evolved into a uniquely American musical form, a sound initially dismissed simply as "hillbilly music."

Americana, especially in its primary incarnation as Bluegrass, can claim Appalachia as one of its places of origin. Yet in no time, the impetus and inspiration spread elsewhere as well. To North and South Carolina, to Tennessee—and places like Nashville, Memphis, and Knoxville—down south to Alabama and Mississippi, to New Orleans and the Mighty Delta and the Big Bayou, through to Texas, the southern border and beyond, up the mighty Mississippi to places like St. Louis and Kansas City, and then all the way to Chicago and Detroit and the Midwest, to Colorado and eventually out to California by way of Bakersfield, LA, San Francisco, and Joshua Tree, to Arizona, Portland, and Seattle, up through Canada and then back east, through the Great Plains, to Toronto and the Maritimes, and of course into New England and the Big Apple. Thanks to the early haunting grounds of Emmylou Harris, we can also include the nation's capital as well.

It was bands like the latter-day Byrds, the Everly Brothers, Bob Dylan and the Band, the Flying Burrito Brothers, Poco, the Nitty Gritty Dirt Band, New Grass Revival, and the Grateful Dead— many of whom began taking their cues from bluegrass innovators like the Dillards, David Grisman, John Hartford, the Kentucky Colonels, and Del McCoury—who introduced that music to adventurous audiences in rockier realms. Let's not forget Glen Campbell, Dolly Parton, Emmylou Harris, Linda Rondstadt, Rodney Crowell, or Gram Parsons, either. They furthered a crossover drawn on those anything-goes artists' irreverent attitudes and edgier material that appealed to a contemporary crowd.

2

The Instrumental Essentials

Oh Susanna! don't you cry for me
I come from Alabama with my banjo on my knee . . .
—STEPHEN FOSTER, "OH SUSANNA"

Let's continue our journey from past to present with a history lesson. And no, you won't be tested later. But to fully appreciate the transition to Americana, it may prove valuable . . .

Championed early on by Bill Monroe, Lester Flatt, Earl Scruggs, the Stanley Brothers, and scores of lesser known but no less innovative artists, homegrown American music found its first wave of popularity in the 1940s and 1950s as an offshoot of the traditional folk music brought to Appalachia by immigrants from England, Ireland, and Scotland, who originally had settled in those mountains during the late eighteenth century. Early ballads like "Cumberland Gap," "Pretty Polly," "Barbara Allen," and "Cuckoo Bird" were transplanted and transformed over the decades, adapted into tunes that were played on banjo, guitar, fiddle, and mandolin, creating a sound ideally suited for communal gatherings on back porches in the company of neighbors, friends, and family. With multipart harmonies and shared vocals tossed back and forth, this new form of folk music evolved into a uniquely American musical form, an original root of Americana, a popular offshoot of both folk and country, as well as a style tagged as hillbilly music due to its specific demographic appeal.

With that evolution, the fiddle came to the forefront of that sound. An instrument that's essential to folk, country, and bluegrass, it isn't limited to any specific genre. Indeed, its origins are tied to European tradition, and specifically to the violin, which first originated in Italy during the mid-sixteenth century. Even now, the names Norman Blake, Vassar Clements, Richard Greene, and Byron Berline are all synonymous with this early American music—particularly its essential element, the fiddle. Doug Kershaw and John McEuen amplified the fiddle's image by bounding across the stage like madcap musicians, exuding exhilaration and enthusiasm. Alison Krauss, Rhiannon Giddens, and Sara Watkins take a more measured approach, but regardless, their virtuosity is never in doubt.

The initial evidence of bowed instruments dates to approximately 900 AD. However, the term "fiddle" is first thought to have been used in the twelfth century, and it eventually came to define an array of classical stringed instruments even before the formal emergence of the violin. These days, fiddles and violins are mostly interchangeable, and the two instruments remain indistinguishable from one another, even despite their varied applications and array of different genres.

Modern fiddle music is generally considered to be an outgrowth of Irish tradition, given that it always remained an essential element in Ireland's folk music evolution. It was especially apt for dance tunes, thanks to its lively sound when played at a rapid pace. The so-called tin fiddle—a less expensive version of the traditional wood fiddle—was manufactured in massive quantities throughout the nineteenth century, continuing the cultural connection that prompted one seventeenth century Irish scribe to note, "In every field a fiddle, and the lasses footing it till they were all of a foam."

It's little wonder then that when those first settlers emigrated to America's shores in the 1600s, they brought their fiddles with them. The early popular standards included such songs as "Soldier's Joy" (with lyrics penned by poet Robert Burns), "Flowers of Edinburgh," and "Tamlin," songs that shared both Irish and Scottish origins. However, once those migrants expanded their settlements southward, other styles began to take root. The Celtic music that characterized the Canadian Maritimes and, to a lesser extent, northern New England, morphed into the rural back porch sounds of Appalachia, and from there, into the more familiar fare associated with classic country music. It also took hold in blues realms, inspiring guitarists like Lonnie Johnson, Big Bill Broonzy, and Clarence "Gatemouth" Brown to adapt the fiddle as a second set of strings.

In the origins of bluegrass, as envisioned by Bill Monroe in particular, the fiddle literally took center stage. Chubby Wise, Byron Berline, and Richard Greene were heavily influenced by Monroe's archetypical approach, and both Berline and Greene helped imbue the instrument with a contemporary sensibility. Berline later lent his skills to the Rolling Stones and the Flying Burrito Brothers, among others, while Greene moved on from an apprenticeship with Monroe to his band Seatrain, a counterculture combo infused with folk's tradition and trappings. Doug Kershaw made the fiddle indistinguishable from zydeco and Cajun country music, helping advance its populist appeal into similar rocky realms.

Likewise, the fiddle became an intrinsic element in the development of Western swing, a move that brought it front and center. Bob Wills and the Texas Playboys hung many of their melodies on a decided fiddle finesse, both as a melodic ingredient and as a way to rev up the rhythms. Johnny Gimble and Buddy Spicher are credited for pushing its potential, while Mark O'Connor helped assert a certain virtuosity.

By the mid-twentieth century, fiddle music was firmly entrenched in the musical mainstream. The popular standard "Orange Blossom Special" helped spur its popularity by reimagining the instrument as a means of replicating the sound of a rapidly moving culture, or in this case, a fast moving train. Charlie Daniel's oft-covered standard "The Devil Went Down to Georgia" went even further, turning an old backwoods fiddle tune penned by Vassar Clements into something akin to a contemporary classic. Expounding on a theme originally developed by bluesman Robert Johnson—one having to do with an encounter with the Devil—Daniels whipped the music into a whirlwind and used his fiddle to create an incendiary sound as potent as any riff played on lead guitar.

Nowadays the fiddle is a lingering musical staple, not only in bluegrass but in country music as a whole. Indeed, it's often the fiddle player who emerges as the band's showstopper and the individual who draws most of the audience's awe and applause. That's particularly true with bands like Steep Canyon Rangers, Alison Krauss and Union Station, Old Crow Medicine Show, Carolina Chocolate Drops, Town Mountain, and the Punch Brothers, all of whom have built their reputation primarily on live concerts and populist appeal.

• • •

OK, enough fiddling around. We'd be remiss if we also didn't credit the banjo with helping establish the Americana template in the nineteenth century. Where once it was denigrated as the instrument of choice for toothless hillbilly pickers and the occasional cross-eyed character—who can forget the kid that was perched up in the tree during that strange cultural encounter in *Deliverance*—it's now a frontline instrument in any number of mainstream ensembles. From bluegrass to ballads, the banjo plays a specific role in the musical mix.

Nevertheless, like many of our early traditions, the banjo's origins can be traced to non-American sources. In this case, the first instrument that can be said to have any similarity to the banjo originated in Africa. It consisted of animal skins that were tacked on to a hollowed-out half of a gourd and then fitted with three to five strings stretched over a stick. Other early instruments of similar construction could also be found in places as diverse as Japan, Morocco, Senegal, Persia, Mali, Guinea, and the Caribbean. It was in the latter realms where the banjo's ancestors took a major step forward with the addition of fingerboards and tuning pegs.

Variously referred to as "bangies," "banjers," and "banjils," the banjo may have derived its name from the African word "mbanza." Other researchers suggest it came from the Spanish word "bandurria" or the similar-sounding Portuguese term "bandore." An early mention of an instrument with a similar sounding handle can be found in documents dating back to 1678, where the author makes mention of a "banza." An English musical reference book refers to an instrument played in the British West Indies in 1763 that was known as a "banshaw." A few years later, future president Thomas Jefferson took notice of an instrument played by his slaves, which he called a "banjar."

Banjos were first introduced to the New World with the slave trade in the 1600s and subsequently became popular among those who toiled on the southern plantations during the centuries that followed. It wasn't until the 1830s that the white populace began taking note, thanks in part to an entertainer named Joel Walker Sweeney, who picked it up from the slaves on his father's farm. Sweeney and his group, the Virginia Minstrels, capitalized on the instruments' novelty and, donning blackface, began performing their so-called minstrel shows up and down America's East Coast. A decade later, Sweeney's group became an international sensation when they introduced the instrument during a tour of Great Britain. Eventually the popularity of the banjo graduated from minstrel shows to the broader public arena, finding audiences in upper crust hotels, racetracks, and drinking establishments— the latter of which offered appreciation from enthusiastic and/ or inebriated patrons.

The Civil War helped further the banjo's popularity, as the playing style graduated from the rhythmic technique adopted by slaves and the white performers who followed, to a picking method that emphasized the sound of individual strings. Entire regiments took up the instruments to provide entertainment during lulls in fighting on the battlefield. Even so, the banjo was frowned upon by guardians of public taste. One Boston newspaper described it as "the depth of popular degradation" and an instrument best reserved for "the jog-dancing lower classes."

Nevertheless, the instrument found increasing popularity in the postwar years thanks to a boom in banjo production and the publication of instruction books that taught technique. Thousands of banjos were produced throughout the late 1800s as the instrument began finding favor in various forms of musical expression, including jazz, classical recitals, and entertainment enjoyed by the masses, from waltzes and recitals to marches and music made in the family front parlor.

The international tension that preceded the outbreak of World War I also helped nourish the banjo's popularity here at home, as increasing American isolationism fostered a desire for anything that was regarded as intrinsically American. The banjo became an integral part of the big bands that flourished both before and after the war, first as part of the so-called tango craze and later with the beginnings of swing and the big band era. Nevertheless, the stock market crash of 1929 put a damper on anything with a celebratory shine . . . which meant that by the very nature of its exuberant sound, the banjo fell out of favor with the sad city folk.

For the next fifteen years or so, banjos practically disappeared from the entertainment spectrum. Not only had public tastes changed; banjo strings themselves became hard to find. However, in the postwar years following World War II, a new generation of musicians, most of whom hailed from the heartland—the mountains of Appalachia, Tennessee, Kentucky, and the Carolinas—adopted it again, along with their rediscovery of the traditional music brought to this country by their European ancestors. Bill Monroe added banjo to his band, paving the way for a succession of players who would get their start in his lineup and later go on to greater glories of their own—David "Stringbean" Ackeman, Earl Scruggs, and Pete Seeger among them. Along with Ralph Stanley, Doc Watson, Mike Seeger, Doug Dillard, and Burl Ives, Scruggs and Seeger would help bring the banjo back into prominence during the fifties and sixties as the so-called folk revival filtered onto college campuses and took focus during hootenannies and folk concerts, leading to its eventual reemergence into popular culture. As the sixties progressed, West Coast "country rock" bands like the Byrds, the Nitty Gritty Dirt Band, and Buffalo Springfield, along with British folk rock groups such as the Incredible String Band, Strawbs, and Fairport Convention, all integrated the banjo into their repertoires. Nevertheless, it took NGDB's landmark 1972 album *Will the Circle Be Unbroken* to bring the traditional musical vanguard together with a younger generation of musicians, providing the banjo with further acceptance and appreciation from the musical mainstream.

With the widespread revival of bluegrass and traditional music in the last couple of decades, the banjo's back in the vanguard, its popularity heightened by such high profile players as Bela Fleck, Dolly Parton, John McEuen, Eric Weissberg, Tony Furtado, Abigail Washburn, the Avett Brothers, and the Steep Canyon Rangers (with and without Steve Martin). Happily then, the sound of the banjo's pluck and strum is clearly here to stay.

3

....

Mississippi and the
Birth of the Blues

Mississippi, you're on my mind . . .
—JESSE WINCHESTER

If one is inclined to start at the roots of Americana music, the fertile soil of Mississippi is the ideal point of origination. It was there that slaves made music and rhyme to accompany their backbreaking work, picking cotton and tending to crops in the brutal southern sun.

It all began with the blues.

"What they call Mississippi sound migrated to Chicago, and the people got more slick and educated on what to play and how to play and then learned to play better," reflects bluesman Bobby Rush. "Now they talk about Chicago Blues . . . but that's only a guy from Mississippi that learned to play better. Chicago Blues ain't nothing but Mississippi blues, but it's elevated to another level. You have your New Orleans Cajun kind of a sound, but it's a modification. Making love, being in love, being up, being down, being broke, having heartaches and pain . . . they all relate the same way. All blues is pretty much the same. It's in the approach and how it's played. That's why Mississippi is so strong. It all started here. This was the root of it all. You have Blind Lemon, Muddy Waters, B.B. King, Fats Domino, Robert Johnson . . . and all the guys I can think of in my time, before my time, and even before my daddy's time. They were speaking and singing the blues."

"There is a Mississippi sound," eighty-four-year-old blues legend Leo "Bud" Welch agrees. "It's rural and raw. The emotion is felt in the music, and that's what Mississippi is all about."

"The Mississippi sound is all about soul," Luther Dickinson adds. "It's about the roots of American music. It's about gospel music, about people in the fields, people singing to themselves and sharing it with others. It's about community. It inspired Elvis Presley and Johnny Cash. It's all about the American dream and about the different cultures. Even though they were separated by segregation, the music brought people together and it became a beautiful thing. It created rock and roll, and R&B and soul music, and it turned gospel music into a sexy, secular phenomenon."

Dickinson should know. The founder of the North Mississippi Allstars, along with his brother Cody, he can claim those muddy roots as part of his DNA. And as the son of Jim Dickinson, one of the most influential producers in the annals of Americana, he's well aware of the heritage that accompanies the state they called home.

Indeed, Mississippi's musical legacy is among the richest and most resilient in the nation—one that rivals Texas, Tennessee, California, the Northeast, and every other place that's a well-spring of American music. It's a history that goes back to the early eighteenth century, borne from hardship, but offering hope and opportunity for those who found music a path forward toward liberation and eventual opportunity.

Early on, the music that evolved into the blues was birthed in the muddy fields of the Mississippi Delta, where slaves and laborers chanted in rhythm and shared their sorrows, express-ing their misery and finding strength for their toil. After the Civil War, as slavery gave way to the Reconstruction, that rudimentary music developed form and structure, eventually coalescing into rudimentary songs. Traces of early African rhythms, brought to America through slave trade, remained a prominent part of the mix, but for all intents and purposes, it was the fields of southern Mississippi that became the breeding ground for the blues, well before it moved north to Chicago, Memphis, and New Orleans, and subsequently gained populist appeal.

"It's all a part of our history," says Garrad Lee, one of the own-ers of Mississippi music label Homework Town Records, as well as a principal in the Jackson, Mississippi, production company Elegant Trainwreck and a local deejay. "All American music can be traced back to the plantations. Work songs, spirituals, chants and the rest gave birth to the blues, and everything branches off that. What makes Mississippi so fertile is the history behind the music and the broad tastes of the people in the state who consume the music."

"Mississippi is midway between Memphis and New Orleans, two cities that are rich in southern culture," notes Dickinson, whose solo album *Blues and Ballads* celebrates that sharing of traditional tunes from one generation to another. "The connection between them is Mississippi. I always maintain that it's the people that make a place great, and it's the people that have passed the tradition down, person to person, hand to hand."

Indeed, the list of those who championed the music early on— Charlie Patton, Son House, and Robert Johnson among them— became key proponents of this evolving musical form, laying the foundation that fellow Mississippians such as Willie Dixon, B.B. King, Howlin'Wolf, Muddy Waters, Mississippi John Hurt, Sonny Boy Williamson, Fred McDowell, Elmore James, Bukka White, John Lee Hooker, Albert King, Junior Kimbrough, Big Joe Williams, Otis Clay, Big Bill Broonzy, Otis Spann, Hubert Sumlin, Furry Lewis, and James Cotton would build on decades later. Immortalized in song, the names Clarksdale, Rosedale, Vicksburg, and Biloxi became familiar signposts that would eventually become known to the rest of the world as well.

The blues has always thrived in Mississippi, from its formal beginnings in the 1890s, through to its prime in the twenties and thirties. Roadhouses—or as they were known locally, "juke joints"—began to spring up along the state's highways and byways and in countless small towns, providing gathering spots for itinerant musicians and places to share their songs and techniques. And although the lure of the big city would eventually claim King, Dixon, Wolf, Lewis, James, and others—many of whom would later be signed by Chicago's iconic Chess Records—the influence of these Mississippi masters left an indelible imprint on the entire trajectory of American music.

Singer Johnny Rawls can attest to that. Born and raised in Mississippi, he recalls what it was like growing up in its vibrant musical scene. "I could walk down the street and hear people singing their hearts out," he remembers. "There were blues bands and soul bands everywhere. I never realized what a blessing it was. It was so natural, like putting your shoes on. It was nothing special to me then, but now I look back and realize how blessed I was to be able to witness some of the greatest singers who ever walked the earth. I look back and think, 'Wow! Who would ever get an opportunity like that?'"

It was an opportunity, but Rawls also knows it was something more. "It's spiritual," he suggests. "It was nothing that was planned. It came out of hardship and oppression. There were people there that you may never have heard of, but they had the real deal when it came to their sound. You can't really explain it. They just have it. You can't find it anywhere else but there. They inherited it from the land, from the earth, from their struggles."

Still, Mississippi can claim credit for more than the birth of the blues. In many ways the music that it fostered became a wellspring for a sound that would eventually sweep the nation—the phenomenon that became known as rock and roll.

"Mississippi is a conundrum wrapped in an enigma," adds singer-songwriter Jimbo Mathus, whose album *Band of Storms* reflects that multihued tradition. "It's this very mystery, always held close to the vest by its initiates, that has created the legacy born of the suffering known as the blues. The blues had a baby and they named it rock and roll. Visionaries such as Sam Phillips had the wisdom and fearlessness to behold the vision, use the white man bwana bwana to make recordings translatable to the masses and—voila—Elvis. The eternal boogie, hoodoo and [author Eugene] Faulkner all play equally in true Mississippi music."

Ah, Elvis. Born in tiny Tupelo, he remains the state's most famous son, the man that brought rock and roll to the masses and forever changed the course of modern music, and with it paved the path for Americana. However, he's hardly the only Mississippian to cast an eternal influence. Musicians as diverse as jazzman Mose Allison; composer John Luther Adams; producer/songwriter Glen Ballard; gospel singers the Blackwood Brothers; rock and soul fusionists the Chambers Brothers; rocker Delaney Bramlett;

tropical troubadour Jimmy Buffett; rock and roll pioneer Bo Diddley; country stars Bobbie Gentry, Charlie Pride, Conway Twitty, Marty Stuart, Jimmie Rodgers, LeAnn Rimes, Faith Hill, and Mickey Gilley; soul singers Jimmy Ruffin and Thelma Houston; studio stalwart Lloyd Green and Burrito Brother Chris Etheridge; gospel great Mylon LeFevre and former Supreme Mary Wilson are a few of those who can claim a Mississippi birthright. Happily, many of those native sons and daughters remain an integral part of the state's musical legacy.

Dickinson concurs. "If you look back through recorded history, you have Robert Johnson, you have John Lee Hooker, you have Charlie Patton, you have the Mississippi Delta. The hill country blues changed my life. It's primitive modernism and that's why I love it. That's what rock and roll is all about. It's young white dudes playing the blues and turning it into rock and roll. It's American poetry that goes back from generation to generation, all open to interpretation. You keep it permanent, but you do your thing and hopefully that will allow Mississippi music to live on."

In the seventies and eighties, the Mississippi music scene reinvented itself, and while blues still remained as vital as ever, the infusion of pop, roots rock, and other more contemporary sounds began to take increasing hold in the musical firmament. Bands like the Hilltops, Blue Mountain, and the Windbreakers hinted at a greater diversity than ever before, each outfit also making their mark on the national scene to varying degrees.

The Hilltops, featuring University of Mississippi graduate John Stirratt, his sister and Louisiana transplant Laurie Stirratt, and her husband Cary Hudson, were an original Americana outfit who toured extensively throughout the southeast. Later John Stirratt would join the still nascent Wilco, leading to the Hilltops' demise in 1990. Sadly the band only recorded a single album, *Big Black River*, before calling it quits, but Laurie and John would later release *Arabella* in 2003, their first collaboration in a dozen years.

In the meantime, Laurie and her husband Cary kept their collaboration intact, making Oxford Mississippi the launching point for a new band, Blue Mountain, soon after the Hilltops folded. With Cary Hudson on guitar, Laurie Hudson on bass, and drummer Matt Brennan (replaced by Frank Crouch in 1995), the group went on to release eight albums throughout their combined career. Five years after their initial breakup in 2002, they reunited in 2007, by which time their reputation had grown, both in alt-country circles and among those who recognized them as one of Mississippi's foremost musical ambassadors.

The Windbreakers, a power pop duo helmed by Tim Lee and Bobby Sutliff, were something of an anomaly. Their music had no direct link to the state's musical traditions, but their early series of albums and EPs—*Meet the Windbreakers* (1982), *Any Monkey with a Typewriter* (1983), *Terminal* (1985), *Run* (1986), *A Different Sort* (1987), and their postreunion efforts *At Home with Bobby and Tim* (1989) and *Electric Landlady* (1991) established a penchant for riveting rock and roll with a determined edge and a melodic undertow. Today Lee lives with his wife and musical collaborator Susan Bauer Lee in Knoxville, Tennessee, where they helm the band Bark. Nevertheless, their ties to their native state remain intact.

"The people that have come along and made great music have all been aware of their roots and tied into their roots, whether they were beholding to them or not," Tim Lee observes. "They know the tradition because it's part of their DNA. The roots are there, but they're not making music that imitates them. There's a melding of cultures that you don't necessarily get everywhere. It's a fertile breeding ground, no matter what kind of music there is. People think of Blue Mountain as this alt country band, but there's every bit as much Robert Johnson in that music as there is Hank Williams. That's what makes it special."

Current Sounds and Styles

Nowadays, Mississippi's music isn't limited to any one particular style. In fact, its diversity has become a defining element, as expressed through nationally known acts like the North Mississippi Allstars, Steve Forbert, Jimbo Mathus, John Murry, and the Weeks, as well as indie acts like Passing Parade, Dead Gaze, the Squirms, Swamp Babies, the Vibe Doctors, the Water Babies, the Neckbones, Ming Donkey, and Laurie Stirratt's new band, Teardrop City. They're also helping to turn cities like Jackson, Oxford, and Hattiesburg into thriving centers of artistic activity. Likewise, hip-hop has become a vibrant part of the state's musical mix as well, with acts such as 5th Child, James Crow, Silas, and DJ Young Vernon contributing to the increasingly varied palette.

"I can't pinpoint a particular sound," Garrad Lee admits. "I work mainly with hip-hop artists, and that's huge here. Blues, of course, is still huge, especially electric blues. And I think we have a better indie scene than most people realize. We've put out albums from bands that I think are absolutely genius."

"Mississippi is the worst thing that ever happened to me," says the quirky Ming Donkey. "In the best way possible."

Homegrown Support

Ming Donkey's disclaimer notwithstanding, many artists agree that there is ample support for homegrown music and a growing number of venues where original music is played and even encouraged. Still the situation isn't necessarily ideal. Indeed, local musicians offer conflicting views.

"I grew up in Jackson, and back then, there really weren't bands that played original material exclusively," Tim Lee remembers. "You had to play four sets of Beatles songs before you could play any of your own tunes. So it didn't take me long to start rebelling against that and trying to make other things happen. It's interesting to me how Jackson is today . . . there's a very fertile scene going on there. There's a lot of support. There were people who liked live music thirty years ago, but they just wanted to dance to stuff they knew. Nowadays, the scene there is a lot more supportive, and there's a lot more interaction between the rock acts and the hip-hop acts. It's a really impressive thing to see."

"For a musician who knows the folk, blues and country cannon, and who isn't that concerned with money, playing opportunities are almost limitless," Jimbo Mathus suggests. "Then again, if I play 'Dixie' at the catfish house, hundred dollar bills start flying!"

"Music is everywhere," Garrad Lee maintains. "Pretty much anywhere you go, someone is playing some kind of music. I book shows at Offbeat, a comic book / record store in Jackson, and at coffee shops, art studios, and venues like Hal and Mal's, Martin's, and Big Sleep's, to name a few. . . . On a Thursday night in Jackson you can hear a singer-songwriter at Hal and Mal's while you eat dinner, then go to the art museum and hear some hip-hop on the green space outside, and maybe later go to Martin's to see a national touring act and end up at F. Jones Corner for late night blues."

For his part, the Weeks' Sam Williams cites Duling Hall in Jackson and Proud Larry's in Oxford as places where live music can be found. "There may not be an unanimous championing of the arts, but the people that do support it more than make up for the rest," he insists. "When it comes to the fans though, they're responsive and vocal and downright nutty over their music. It's a beautiful thing."

"There's a lot of places to play, but not as many as there used to be," Rush laments. "Where the cotton fields and clubs used to be, you now have casinos. Where there used to be twenty or more juke joints, the casinos put them out of business, leaving maybe two or three. But even the two or three are suffering because people are spending all of their money at the big casinos and leaving the mom and pop places high and dry. Many of the blues entertainers have to go out of state to continue to work because they can't find enough work in Mississippi. The people here didn't even embrace Elvis until he made it big."

"The state has come a long ways in embracing its music as a tourist attract," Mathus adds. "Most of the time, I end up entertaining at picnics, political rallies, crawfish boils and the like . . . in the same social stratum as the help. It's humbling but strangely freeing, being an entertainer and still working in the medium of social music—real people doing real-life things and having music a part of that very fabric of life. It's the Mississippi way. Luckily, they tolerate their eccentrics nowadays."

A Seminal Sound

These days, a definitive Mississippi sound is hard to identify. Some may assert it's the blues, and indeed, early on that was clearly the case. However, given its growing diversity, and the fact that the music scene has been burgeoning over the past thirty years, no such generalization can suffice.

"Obviously, Mississippi music tends to be influenced by the

blues," Stirratt says. "But the main difference is that it's got a gut-bucket, rootsy, dirty quality. That said, there is not a singular Mississippi sound."

"I think there is a Mississippi feel more than a Mississippi sound," Williams of the Weeks suggests. "Something in the mud promotes this uninhibited raw expression that really doesn't come from anywhere else. There is a feeling in Mississippi music today that evokes the history of the blues and soul and country, but never feels contrived."

Ming Donkey sees it as something deeper. "It's starting to seem like a free-for-all again, at least from my experience," he muses. "People think there is a Mississippi sound, and plenty of people can make a buck off that theory. But if you're willing to walk into the dark, there are plenty of other audio experiences to be had that give general meaning to our tag as the birthplace of American music."

Garrad Lee agrees, and given the diversity of sounds that he works with, he's quick to recognize the bigger picture. "Mississippi is such a unique place, and there is a shared experience we all have from living here that I tend to hear flowing through the music. I think that is what ties it all together. But to be honest, I wouldn't want to place those lofty ideals on any artist or their work. I think it's fair to say that most of the music is made by people who are just doing their thing. And I guess that's all anyone of us in this state can do."

"There's such a long tradition of music, starting with the delta blues," Tim Lee reflects. "You hear stories about guys coming down and working in the cotton fields and learning to play guitar from Junior Kimbrough, and then it all kind of culminates with Elvis, this white guy who sounds black. The blues traditions and the country tradition and the folk tradition all kind of came together, and it became a perfect melting pot. It's been fertile for a long time."

"Mississippi is rural music, country music, and soul," Dickinson concludes. "It can be about Jimmie Rodgers or Mississippi John Hurt or Charlie Feathers."

Jimbo Mathus sums things up succinctly. "The world boogie train is coming," he says. "So board up here."

4

....

Bluegrass Breaks Out

We continue our journey into definitive Americana via one of its seminal styles, segueing from the blues into bluegrass. While it's still replete with banjos, fiddles, guitars, and mandolins, those elements have expanded into other areas as well, merging and mutating as "nu-grass," jam band music, or just plain rock and roll. Whatever it's called, the breakdown in boundaries is attracting attention. What's more, that overarching appeal has been nourished by a host of instrumental insurgents—Yonder Mountain String Band, Leftover Salmon, Steep Canyon Rangers, the Deadly Gentlemen, String Cheese Incident, Alison Krauss and Union Station, Greensky Bluegrass, the Punch Brothers, Railroad Earth, and the Infamous Stringdusters—all of whom owe a debt to the nu-grass mentality.

"Many musicians of my generation were exposed to bluegrass through Old and in the Way, and the music of Jerry Garcia and David Grisman initially," says Phil Barker, a member of the up-and-coming bluegrass band Town Mountain. "Through Grisman, I found the Del McCoury Band and then first generation guys like Bill Monroe, the Stanley Brothers, Jimmy Martin, and others. Leftover Salmon definitely exposed bluegrass elements to a lot of folks in the jam band crowd, myself included. Now when folks see a band with a banjo, they're not as likely to pigeonhole it."

"Bluegrass is a respectable word now," observed Sam Bush, formerly a member of New Grass Revival, a band consistently credited with bridging the stylistic divide between traditional and progressive bluegrass. "Forty years ago, you could tell people you played bluegrass, and they didn't really know what you were talking about. It was always interesting to me that when we played to a rock audience, they take one look at us and they would call us a bluegrass band. And at the same time, if we played a blue-grass festival, the bluegrass audience would think we were a rock band. In that way we were kind of a good group to introduce this audience to this music they hadn't heard before."

"This music was never just 'backwoods music' to me," David Grisman maintains. "Traditional bluegrass music is a perfectly crafted idiom, deeply rooted in several cultures. It is also a truly American art form, like jazz and rock and roll, reflecting many aspects of our cultural heritage."

Vince Herman of Leftover Salmon points out that bluegrass started as a radio-friendly, commercial form of old-time moun-tain music. "Bill Monroe wanted something snappier and more focused than the music he grew up with to use on radio perfor-mances. Once he made it to the Opry, that music was broadcast to most of the population of the eastern US. Though it certainly was something rural folks could identify with, it was in ears all around the country."

Sixty years later, Herman's assertion finds broader meaning. The jam band world and its populist perspective have helped bring a new generation of free-spirited music aficionados into the fold, fans who have found the fast-paced picking and upbeat rhythms in tune with their rowdy, devil-may-care sensibilities. The popularity of best-selling soundtracks for relatively recent films like *Cold Mountain* and especially *O Brother, Where Art Thou?* also helped bring this music to the masses. Furthermore, the rising popularity of the Telluride Bluegrass Festival, the Strawberry Music Festival, MerleFest, Bonnaroo, RockyGrass, and the Mountain Song at Sea cruise have attracted scores of nu-grass musicians and their dedicated fans.

Still, not all of this sits well with Grisman: "What is popular now and referred to as bluegrass might be too influenced or polluted by the commercial aspects of the entertainment business for me to consider it as an important part of American musical history."

Phil Barker, noting that true bluegrass is one of the most ener-getic and engaging live music genres, agrees that the original form "stands in strong contrast to the mass-appeal, formula-fed nature of what's considered 'pop' music these days."

Nevertheless, astute observers credit the commercial success of bands like Mumford and Sons, the Avett Brothers, and the Lumineers—outfits that purvey bluegrass's communal quality, replete with banjos, traded vocals, and a distinct down-home sensibility—with helping to further ignite the bluegrass flame. "If people want to call them bluegrass, that's great," Bush agreed. "They have a large audience, and it can only help the rest of us."

Bands like Mumford and Sons, although not traditional bluegrass bands, use bluegrass instruments and have helped spread the popularity of bluegrass. "They sell hundreds of thousands of records and have won Grammies going up against pop artists," Charles Humphrey of Steep Canyon Rangers says. "By using banjos and acoustic instruments in their music, they broaden the appeal of bluegrass."

"Traditional bluegrass is appealing because it's organic," Humphrey adds. "You can grab an instrument and play without the necessity of amps and electricity. Some people love the hot picking and some love the harmony singing. If you know the traditional songs, you can jump in a jam with people you've never met and play together instantly. Bluegrass is its own language."

The musical conversation between the players and the fans impacts bluegrass as well. Yonder Mountain String Band makes their music with their fans in mind, ensuring the crowd's interest and involvement in the process. "That wall between the band and the crowd goes down," Jeff Austin, a one-time member of Yonder Mountain String Band suggests. "You pick up on that vibe that's been given to you and oftentimes it's wholly unexpected." Yonder Mountain bassist Adam Aijala agrees, saying, "Their contribution is essential to what we do. You feel it, and it makes you go bigger and bigger, and makes you want to be better and better."

Greensky Bluegrass, among others, actively attract novices to bluegrass. "I remember when we were doing shows at home in Michigan and I felt like we were really converting people," mandolinist Paul Hoffman recalls. "I was booking the band back then, and I'd tell the club owners, 'Don't worry, they're going to like it.' We weren't their normal kind of band, so I'd have to really convince them. After the show, people would come up to us and say, 'I really like bluegrass! You guys are really cool!'"

Just as the Greensky guys have been known to toss occasional covers into their set to further enhance their accessibility—at one point, they were known for tackling Prince's "When Doves Cry"—banjo virtuoso Béla Fleck has been credited as much as anyone with expanding bluegrass parameters and appeal by fusing it with jazz, classical, and other idioms. "Bluegrass is a relatively simple form," Fleck insists. "And I've learned from classical music that simple music is easiest to develop."

Still, one has to wonder if while he and others can be seen as breaking down boundaries, purists might label it heresy. "Tony Trischka, who was my teacher, really took a whipping for being so progressive," Fleck recalled. "New Grass Revival also took some amazing crap, but they got their due and ended up at the top of the scene."

Nu-grass proponents see stretching the boundaries as a valid, longstanding tradition in music in general. "My favorite musicians are individualists who push into new territory," Fleck muses. "I figured it was just what you were supposed to do."

Indeed, with today's bluegrass, everything seems possible. And just as certainly, there's an Americana audience eager to embrace it.

5

Talking with a Legend

Dr. Ralph Stanley

I am a pilgrim and a stranger
Traveling through this wearisome land
—MERLE TRAVIS

Few artists were there at the beginning and then able to figure in that long, tangled path that would parallel the evolution of Americana music. One of those that was happened to be the late and legendary Ralph Stanley. A father of modern bluegrass, he remains an American icon—one who helped bring banjo music and the sound of Appalachia into the modern era. Like Mississippi, it was a place that figured prominently in the evolution of Americana. And for that, Ralph Stanley could take much of the credit.

After briefly considering a career as a veterinarian, Stanley changed course and became a musician instead, forming his first group, the Clinch Mountain Boys, with his brother Carter in 1946. That led the two of them to go on and form the group that would soon become known as an archetype of bluegrass, the outfit simply known as the Stanley Brothers. Along the way, he developed a unique style of playing known as the claw hammer banjo style (a three-fingered technique distinguished by a rapid fire "forward roll" that's played close to the banjo's bridge) that kept him innately involved with traditional mountain music in the decades after. His accolades and honors came mostly later in his life—his inductions into the Grand Ole Opry, the International Bluegrass Music Hall of Fame and the International Bluegrass Music Hall of Honor, along with his receipt of a National Medal of the Arts, recognition as a Library of Congress Living Legend, and the Grammy he won in 2002 (for Best Male Country Vocal Performance for his rendition of the traditional dirge "O Death" from the best-selling soundtrack for the film *O Brother, Where Art Thou?*).

When I interviewed him, it was the day before his eighty-seventh birthday, and speaking by phone from his lifelong home in rural southwest Virginia, he appeared to be taking his celebration in stride. "I won't be doing too much," he replied when asked how he would spend the day. "Just hanging out around the home folks."

Humble and unassuming to a fault, Mr. Stanley—make that Dr. Stanley, courtesy of the honorary doctorate of music degree awarded him by Lincoln Memorial University in 1976—was equally humble when it came to the aforementioned milestones, but it was clear that his recognition from the Opry was the prize that remained closest to his heart. "I'm thankful that I done well and all that," he said in his typical low-key manner. "I'm real proud of that. That was something I always wanted for several years because that's a very big thing. When you get there, you've reached the top."

Indeed he had. Few other musicians could consider themselves on a first-name basis with another bluegrass legend, Bill Monroe. "Carter, my brother, sung awhile with him," he recalled. "And the two of us did a lot of things together too. We became very close friends and always helped each other out. I recorded a lot with Bill, ya know. We were the best of friends and we saw a lot of things alike."

Apparently so. Likewise, over the course of his eighty-nine years, Dr. Stanley helped foster a lot of up-and-coming talent as well, among them future bluegrass champs Ricky Skaggs and Keith Whitley. "They started with me when they were something like fifteen or sixteen," he remembered. "Both of them joined me and became famous. I certainly saw their talent immediately. Keith stayed with me six or seven years, and Ricky stayed maybe two or three years, but he was with me a couple of different times."

Although he wasn't able to play banjo with the same fluidity in his later years, his passion and purpose remained right intact up until the end. "I don't play the banjo much anymore," he told me at the time. "Just a little bit of claw hammer sometimes. I have arthritis and my fingers aren't exactly what they was back years ago. I figured I'd quit, because I didn't want to mess up. There are plenty of people that play just like me, and I can always get someone to play those parts. There's always someone wanting to record with me."

Indeed, the prospect for a new recording was always a possibility. "I haven't thought much about it, but if someone comes along and thinks it's worth doing, then I'm happy to do it," he remarked. "I couldn't tell you at this point one way or another. If things come around the right way, and I feel like I can do it justice, then it could happen . . . or it could not. It's been sixty-seven years I've been doing this. I'm still going good, and if I ever wanted to, I could do another album right now. If it ever comes natural, why, I might record again, but like I said, I might not. You never know what might come around."

His final album, *Man of Constant Sorrow*, credited to Ralph Stanley and Friends, was released in January 2015, a year and a half before he passed away. Yet, even at the end, Dr. Stanley insisted he wasn't ready to retire.

"As long as I'm able, I'm glad to do it," he maintained. "I still play with the Clinch Mountain Boys and we still work regular. We go out and work a week or two and then come home and stay five or six days. That makes a pretty good life, to be able to express yourself like that. I'm well pleased with it. I don't think my voice has faded any, and that's something I'm real thankful for."

In the end, Dr. Stanley himself served up his best possible epitaph. "I'm proud of it," he said of his legacy. "I'm really thankful that the good Lord kept me around and shown me what to do and all. I'm real proud of that."

As for that early idea about becoming a veterinarian, suffice it to say he never looked back. "I guess I was crazy at one time," he chuckled. "I thought of that a little bit, but I'm glad I didn't do it."

So are we, doctor. So are we.

6

························

The Nitty Gritty Dirt Band
Completes the Circle

I knew a man Bojangles and he danced for you
—JERRY JEFF WALKER, "MR. BOJANGLES,"
AS RECORDED BY THE NITTY GRITTY DIRT BAND

"Do I feel occasionally that we are disrespected or overlooked? Sure. But on the other hand, we've had this great career. I don't know what it is. It could be that we're a moving target musically. We cover a lot of stuff. We get bored just sitting still."

That's Jeff Hanna's response when asked if his group, the Nitty Gritty Dirt Band, has been denied due credit for helping to extend the arc of Americana.

Indeed, if the Nitty Gritty Dirt Band had done nothing more than instigate the unprecedented summit of country music's old guard and the new with 1972's epic three-record set *Will the Circle Be Unbroken*, they would have already ensured their iconic status. The album broke new ground by paying tribute to those who had paved the path that the Dirt Band and their contemporaries followed. It was about much more than finding common ground between two generations; it was, in a very real sense, a cultural connection that cut through the alienation and distrust between the insurgents of the sixties and those that touted tradition. To find the royalty of bluegrass, master musicians like Jimmy Martin, Roy Acuff, Mother Maybelle Carter, Doc Watson, and Earl Scruggs, sharing studio time with this bunch of former folkies from Orange County California was in itself a revolutionary concept.

Indeed, if anyone is looking for that crucial link in the Americana trajectory—that point where past and present fused to become the future—they need only look to *Will the Circle Be Unbroken*.

The chemistry flowed naturally, but then again, the Nitty Gritty Dirt Band weren't nearly as radical as most of their West Coast brethren. While their musical origins were similar to bands like the Dead, the Airplane, Buffalo Springfield, and other outfits that had evolved from traditional trappings, they hadn't strayed all that far from the influences that inspired them early on until the Uncle Charlie album. The band's first four albums—their eponymous debut and its followups *Ricochet, Rare Junk*, and the live effort, aptly titled *Alive*—reflected the sound of an eclectic bunch, one that mixed a love of old-time music with a penchant for both the frivolous and the profound. They also had a sense of the sounds that were echoing out of Laurel Canyon as well.

"What set us apart was that we didn't have a steel guitar player," Hanna reckons. "We leaned a little more on a Cajun influence with a rock steady beat and added in the bluegrass element as well. That's where we carved our niche."

"We were a jug band in overdrive," McEuen adds, with banjo, mandolin, and fiddle supplying the icing to the musical cake.

Formed in 1966, the band originally included singer/guitarist Jeff Hanna, singer/drummer/harmonica player Jimmie Fadden, bassist/mandolin/singer Les Thompson (who had been in a bluegrass group previously with John McEuen—the Willmore City Moonshiners), John McEuen, and guitarists Bruce Kunkel and Ralph Barr. All were under twenty years old. (Though there for the first four or five jobs, seventeen-year-old Jackson Browne soon left to pursue his own music when John McEuen joined in July of 1966.) This early incarnation of the band made the first album and managed to score a regional hit with "Buy for Me the Rain." Soon after was their part in a major motion picture, Paramount Pictures' *Paint Your Wagon*, which found them sharing screen time with Clint Eastwood and Lee Marvin for four months on the Oregon set.

Chris Darrow drifted in—and out—through that time, eventually achieving fame for his own enterprises. Jeff Hanna broke the band up after *Paint Your Wagon* in 1968, but after running into John at a Poco show in early 1969, they decided to put the band back together and came back with a vengeance courtesy of *Uncle Charlie and His Dog Teddy*. Now down to a core of Hanna, McEuen, Fadden, Thompson, and newer recruit, singer/guitarist Jimmy Ibbotson—they got their first national top-ten hit with the Jerry Jeff Walker composition "Mr. Bojangles," and several other chart contenders, including covers of "House at Pooh Corner" and "Some of Shelley's Blues," all of which put them on firm commercial footing.

"The Uncle Charlie album started our career in real time," McEuen suggests. "It was a collection of eclectic tunes, some original, some bluegrass, a classical banjo piece, and radio songs. It was an entertaining set of music where every song was a surprise. It had the perfect blend of singing and song choices . . . And it was what led to the *Circle* album—Earl and Doc had heard it too!" McEuen's approach with strings with guitar, banjo, mandolin, and fiddle made him one of the group's great assets.

"John and I went in 1971 to see the Earl Scruggs Revue playing at this club in Boulder," Hanna recalls. "So when he was driving Earl back to his hotel after the gig, John kind of popped the question. 'Would you . . . uh, uh, uh . . . do a record with us?' And Earl said, 'I'd be proud to.' A couple of weeks later, Doc Watson played the same club, and John went back with the caveat that we were doing a record with Earl Scruggs. Earl was our magnet. And from that point on, it kept evolving."

"Not many other groups would risk their entire career by doing an acoustic album after having hits like we had done," McEuen suggests. "If the *Circle* album hadn't succeeded, we would have been dead in the water."

Nevertheless, from that point on they proceeded steadily, if somewhat surreptitiously. Thompson and Ibbotson departed in the midseventies, replaced by a rotating shift of temporary additions before keyboard player Bob Carpenter joined the fold in 1979. Ironically, the "Nitty Gritty" portion of their moniker was dropped soon thereafter, allowing them to subsequently refer to themselves as the Dirt Band for the next decade.

"That was a mistake," McEuen insists. "Why would you take fifteen years of marketing and making records and then change the name of the group? They said, 'Well everyone calls us the Dirt Band.' I remember we were getting on a plane and the stewardess asked us if we were in a band. And Jimmy said, 'Yeah, we're the Dirt Band.' And she said, 'Is that anything like the Nitty Gritty Dirt Band?' It was the next day that everyone decided to change it back."

More hits came later, including the single "American Dream," written by Rodney Crowell and featuring a shared vocal with Linda Rondstadt. However, it was their appearance (as the "Toot Uncommons") backing up pal Steve Martin as he mugged his way through his novelty hit "King Tut" on *Saturday Night Live* that also thrust them back into the spotlight. Likewise, their groundbreaking goodwill tour of the Soviet Union in May 1977 not only gave them the distinction of being the first American band to tour that country, but allowed them to again break barriers.

Indeed, the eighties proved to be a productive period for the band, particularly in country music realms thanks to such songs as "Fishin' in the Dark," "Dance Little Jean," "Long Hard Road (The Sharecropper's Dream)," and "Modern Day Romance." McEuen left and was temporarily replaced by former Eagle Bernie Leadon. A sequel to the *Circle* album, *Will the Circle Be Unbroken: Volume Two*, was released in 1989, reuniting the band with some of the participants from the original recordings as well as contemporary colleagues such as Emmylou Harris, Johnny Cash, John Prine, John Denver, Roger McGuinn, Chris Hillman, John Hiatt, and Bruce Hornsby. It brought the band a pair of Grammys as well as nods from the Country Music Association for Best Country Vocal Performance and Album of the Year.

"Some of the rock intelligentsia and some even some of our rock star friends kind of dismissed us, but the folks in Nashville thought we were cool as shit," Hanna maintains. "And we thought, yeah, that's even better. Today, Americana is one big tent. It's so inclusive. You just don't have those turf wars that existed even ten or fifteen years ago."

While a world tour early in the early nineties brought them further attention, ironically, it was a shout-out by President George H. W. Bush that helped bring them notoriety by default. During an awards ceremony in Nashville, Bush bungled their name by referring to them as the "Nitty Ditty Nitty Gritty Great Bird."

McEuen rejoined the band in 2001, and the following year, the group put out their third and final *Circle* sequel, *Will the Circle Be Unbroken: Volume III*, with a new group of guests that included veterans of both the first and second *Circle* albums, as well as Tom Petty, Dwight Yoakam, Del McCoury, Sam Bush, and two of the band members' offspring, Jonathan McEuen and Jamie Hanna. It reached the top twenty in the country charts, but by this point, interest in the band, at least from a pop perspective, seemed to be waning. So far, only two albums of original material have been released in the new millennium, *Welcome to Woody Creek* and *Speed of Life*, the latter in 2009.

Nevertheless, the band continues to tour at a steady pace, spurred on as a result of their fiftieth anniversary celebration. Yet apart from a live CD and DVD *Circlin' Back*, recorded at the Ryman Auditorium in Nashville ("The Dirt Band's tribute to itself," McEuen says), an anthology, and a greatest hits, no new studio albums appear to be on the horizon. McEuen released his own effort, *Made in Brooklyn*, a collection of traditional songs reimagined along with special guests David Bromberg, Matt Carsonis, Jay Ungar, David Amram, John Cowan, John Carter Cash, and longtime pal Steve Martin. Like the original *Circle* album, it offers another example of McEuen's reverence for his roots. A revisit to "Mr. Bojangles" adds new eloquence and assurance, while covers of such classics as "She Darked the Sun," "I Still Miss Someone," "Acoustic Traveler," and Warren Zevon's "My Dirty Life and Times" applied an authentic acoustic tapestry to the album's revered standards.

"The intent was to take the best elements of the *Circle* album and the things that I've learned by being in this band, and create a recording where the listener is taken on a musical journey," McEuen. "I told the other players that this was going to be like us making our own *Circle* album."

Nevertheless, McEuen says any other parallels to his "day job" are negligible. "Most of this *Made in Brooklyn* music are songs I've wanted to record for years, but nobody with NGDB was interested in it. I'll just say this, 'Guys, I wish we could have done this with all of us.' But one guy in the band can't say, 'Hey, I've got fifteen songs I want to do on our next album.' I'm not saying it's good or bad—it's just what it is—but within the structure of the band, I did about a fourth of what I'm capable of. It was very restrictive. I didn't get to produce, arrange, or suggest what parts they should play. All of that is important to me. It's a privilege to record. I'm really glad I can, and I just had to. That's our job, making things for people. That's our purpose—my purpose—in life."

For his part, Hanna expresses some hesitation about making another record. "The sales were pretty soft on our last album," he remarks. "That was disappointing. We are our own record company, so when we make records, we're footing the bill. It's expensive. We have to wonder if anybody really gives a shit about albums these days. I think they do, and at some point you have to do it. I'm hoping that when we shut down after this tour that we'll get in the studio and cut some tracks. Maybe just an EP. But making an album just sounds like such a big undertaking now."

"Where many groups would quit because they weren't on the radio or they find touring to be more of a grind, the Dirt Band still survives, if not thrives," McEuen replies when asked about the secret of the group's longevity. "We could have quit, but thanks to Jeff and Jimmy's ability to pick good songs, the support of our fans and record company, we were able to persevere."

As does Americana.

Byrds, Burritos, and Changing Times

So you want to be a rock and roll star
Well listen now to what I say . . .
—THE BYRDS

Indeed, it was the Nitty Gritty Dirt Band and John McEuen specifically who came up with the landmark 1972 album *Will the Circle Be Unbroken*, which still ranks as the primary document that tied together all the strains of true American music.

In Part 2, we hear from other early artists who effectively cultivated a crossover that allowed the axis to shift from rock to country and back again. These are the voices of those who helped coax country music into the mainstream and laid the foundations for country rock in the process.

It was the late sixties and early seventies, and although no one knew it yet, a new genre—later to be named Americana—was about to be born.

7

....

David Crosby

A Byrd's Timeless Flight

Along with Bob Dylan, the Byrds played a crucial role in the transition from folk music to rock and roll, helping to coin the expression "folk rock" in the process. That in itself became a key turning point in the Americana trajectory—one which brought the genre all the more evident in its imprint on modern music. The term hadn't yet entered the lexicon, at least as far as popular culture was concerned, but there's no denying that by adapting traditional music to the modern sounds brought over from the UK, the Byrds were responsible for a significant shift in music's form and function.

As much as Roger McGuinn, David Crosby could claim credit for that transition. A devoted folkie early on, he brought a unique melodic quality to the band's music, imbuing it with an idyllic imagery and freewheeling sensibility that allowed the group to explore new terrain, from folk and country to experimental sounds that defined the group in all its many stage.

It's little wonder then that many so indelible images of Crosby come to mind over the span of his more than fifty years in the musical spotlight.

There's the beaming young man in the cape with the mischievous look in his eyes who gazed with a kind of beatific innocence from the covers of those early Byrds albums. The fearless rebel in his signature fur hat who raged onstage at Monterrey, insisting there was a hidden conspiracy that killed President Kennedy.

The lion-maned man in a fringed buckskin jacket sharing an abandoned couch for the cover of the first Crosby, Stills and Nash album. The defiant druggie clenching a joint wrapped in rolling papers resembling an American flag. The emaciated-looking man, ruined from the ravages of drugs, who pleaded from the pages of *People* magazine that if you ever loved him or his music, please come to his rescue. The immobile, glassy-eyed singer onstage with partners Crosby and Nash. The newly shorn individual beaming on his release from prison. The snowy-haired troubadour with eyes closed, wholly immersed in harmony. The steely-eyed elder statesman who can now afford a knowing smile.

However, today on the phone, it's a different, far less intimidating Crosby—or "Croz" as his friends refer to him—who practically seems to beam as he shares reflections from his home in Santa Barbara on the eve of his first solo acoustic tour in, by his own estimation, some thirty years. Earnest, affable, and animated, he's so friendly and down to earth that two minutes into the conversation, you abandon any obligation to call him Mr. Crosby and settle instead for just plain Dave. Despite any preconceptions to the contrary, he's clearly willing to share his anecdotes and reflect on a mostly joyous half century of making the music that's largely become a soundtrack for many people's lives.

Your songs have always carried such vivid imagery. How do these images appear in your imagination, and what inspires you to put them in song?

I'm not really sure how it works. A lot of it just comes to me. I've been a sailor all my life. . . . That has affected my songs. A lot of them are connected to the ocean. Some of the lyrics in my best songs, such as "Guinevere," were written while riding our bikes through Coconut Grove and taking out the rental boats at night. That's part of the lyrics in that song.

After a half century of making music and achieving such legendary and influential status, are you ever able to step outside yourself and appreciate all you've done?

The temptation is there because of the Byrds, and because of CSN and CSNY, but the truth is, I try very hard not to look at myself the way other people do. I know secretly inside myself what a dirty person I really am. That's a healthier place to look at it from. If you start looking at yourself from the way the press may do, or your fans may do, you get a grandiose version of yourself that's not really true to life. It's healthier to look at myself and say, "OK, Dave, you put your pants on like everyone else, one leg at a time, and you're not made out of solid brass. You're just a guy and you've been given a talent and you're lucky, that's what you are, and you can't let your ego get out of hand." Because I see all the time friends of mine who buy their own press and think they're larger than life, and it turns into being a disaster for them. So I try not to stand up there and say, "Gosh, I'm significant!" [*laughs*] It's a lot healthier to sit back and think of myself as a lucky goof-ball. [*laughs*]

Still, does the music you've made over the years set a high bar that's sometimes intimidating when you're mulling over something new?

That's one of the reasons you don't look back at your body of work. I've spent almost no time looking backward at what I've done with my life. I put almost all of my attention on looking forward, but one of the reasons I do that is that you're not intimidated by what you've done and it doesn't overshadow what you're doing today. My interest is in what I can do today, what I might be able to do tomorrow, and what I can do next week, or next month, or the rest of this year. That's where my whole focus is . . . 99.9 percent looking forward on what's possible and what I can still do. If you keep looking back over your shoulder, you're going to end up running smack dab into a tree. It doesn't really help to sit back and rest on your laurels.

Certainly no one would blame you if you did.

Maybe not, but it's not a healthy thing, and it doesn't lend itself to writing new music. That's the thing. I put the focus forward on what I can do, what I will do. It's a way healthier place for me.

You still seem to love making music.

It's a thrill for me and I love it. I really have a blast when I do it. I get involved in it very fully and let myself go. I don't know of anything else that's that much fun that you can do with your clothes on, really. [*laughs*]

You were once considered a bit of a rascal . . .

I was a scoundrel! [*laughs*]

I didn't want to say that. But out of curiosity, are you still harboring any of that mischievousness that you were once known for?

I'm still a mischievous person, yes. But I'm quite different from the person I was back then. I don't do hard drugs and I don't drink and I don't mess around. I've been married thirty-eight years, and I don't fool around at all. So I'm a lot different guy then I was back then. I had a lot of fun, but I do regret the time I wasted being stoned on hard drugs. Those things just destroyed me. But once I got free of those things, my life took a very good turn, and I'm pretty happy the way I am now. For the last few months I haven't even been smoking pot. I've been completely sober because I've had this writing surge and I really need to pay attention.

Some people say a little smoke can enhance creativity.

Well, I know, but it does disorient me. Which isn't always so bad. It's great for walking on the beach or making love or listening to music, but it's not so great for working. And creative writing is work because you have to focus. So I haven't been doing that. And it's been twenty-five years since I've had anything else. Maybe close to thirty. I'm a pretty happy guy now, and I think that's the key to this creative surge. I have a great family, I have this great life, and I'm alive. And at one point that was a pretty iffy situation, just being alive.

8

···································

Chris Hillman

The Byrds and Beyond

If David Crosby can claim a significant role in the transition to Americana, then credit former band mate Chris Hillman for taking that mutation several steps further. It's not a difficult case to make by any means. In fact, all it takes is to sample only a single one of the bands that Chris Hillman has been affiliated with— the Byrds, the Flying Burrito Brothers, Souther-Hillman-Furay, McGuinn Clark and Hillman, Stephen Stills's Manassas, and the band that he's been associated with on and off over the past twenty-five years or so, the Desert Rose Band—to understand Hillman's essential role in the evolution of Americana.

Despite a humble start as a teenager playing mandolin in a succession of southern California bluegrass bands—the Scottsville Squirrel Barkers and the Hillmen in particular—Hillman's stock rose rapidly when he joined the Byrds, where he became a prime mover in the band's musical development. An increasingly prolific songwriter (he helped pen the classic "So You Want To Be a Rock 'n' Roll Star"), he and later recruit Gram Parsons eventually spun off into the Flying Burrito Brothers, continuing the country crossover the Byrds had begun with *Sweetheart of the Rodeo*, an album that's now considered pivotal in the crossover from rock to country.

Notably, Hillman remains as passionate as ever about making music. At the same time, he's also deeply committed to his ideals, especially those having to do with his Christian faith and his politics, both of which tend to distance him from those with whom he came of age in the rebellious sixties and seventies.

When we caught up with him prior to a new run of shows with a stripped down version of the Desert Rose Band—an acoustic quartet consisting of Hillman, guitarists John Jorgenson and Herb Pedersen, and bassist Bill Brysin—he was gracious, friendly, forthright, and all too willing to share his memories and reflections on a life well lived.

You've had such an amazing career and been a part of so many amazing bands . . . it's hard to know where to start here.

You're very kind. I'll tell you something. I've always loved music, but I didn't really seek out to be a rock star. I was shy, so I didn't really set out to do that. I don't know if I was just lucky—I wasn't the greatest writer or player or singer—but I had a great time. I think I survived by not seeking out that stardom. It came to me later. I had some great groups. I don't look back in any negative way. I really don't do that in my life. I got to do what I was supposed to do. Maybe I could have done it better [*laughs*], but I'm still playing and that's a joy. It's a blessing, I gotta tell you. As long as I can still sing and play, and somebody wants to hear me, I'm good. That's a good thing. I worked with some wonderful people.

What is the state of the Desert Rose Band these days? That band has been around in some shape or form for just about twenty-five years, correct?

It's been dormant for awhile, but it rises now and then. Occasionally we will get together. And why? Well, we parted company when we finally put it out to pasture, but we remained friends. When we were playing together in the eighties, we never had any baggage, not baggage in the sense of giving into areas that were bad—drug abuse, for example—or this or that. It was a consistent professional situation. Our consistency was 90 percent on stage, and after all these years, I'm in a band that I'm basically heading up, writing the songs and singing lead. But besides that, I'm in a band that's really professional, that knows how to go out there and do a show, and we remained very good friends. So that's a good thing. So we go out as an acoustic quartet or trio, and then once in awhile we do the entire band, as with the Norwegian gig. And this is the funny thing—the Norwegians love the Desert Rose Band. We're like the Beatles over there. I don't know why that is or what that's all about, but they go absolutely insane, and it's mostly guys that are going crazy. I don't know what that's all about either. . . . They're so into that kind of country music that they'll even get rhinestone jackets made and wear them to the show. It's like a Grateful Dead thing over there. I don't know if we'll play again after this July. I don't know. It's just a day-to-day thing, and we'll have to see what happens.

Are you ready to resume your solo career?

The way the technology is today with Pro Tools, if I wanted Emmylou Harris to be on my album, all I'd have to do is send it down to her in Nashville. If I wanted McGuinn's twelve string, all I'd have to do is to send it to him. In fact, Roger and I had written a song at the end of McGuinn, Clark, and Hillman in the late seventies, and we did it one time on stage—one time in Long Island. And I listened to this song the other day and it sounds like a 1966 Byrds song, and so I really want to tackle that. That just might negate everything I just said to you. [*laughs*] I'd want drums, and I'd put the bass on it and send it to Roger to put the twelve string on it. It's not going to be the Byrds, but it just has that feel to it.

And if you wanted to do some recording with Roger—and it sounds like you have a good relationship there—if you did do something, inevitably people would say, "It looks like the Byrds are getting back together." So maybe there would be a Crosby factor?

Well, that won't happen. That just will not happen, at least not as a planned out thing. Roger's not interested in having that happen. I don't know why, but I respect it. That's OK.

I read a recent article in which Crosby said McGuinn is the sticking point as far as any reunion is concerned.

He is. I get along with both of them. My communication with Roger is via email. Crosby I speak to because he's about fifty miles away from me. I don't really have any issues with anyone who's still around. What's the point?

You say it will never happen, but never say never, right? As long as you guys are still around, who knows what might happen.

You're right. There's been offers that would astound you for us to get back together, but it's not going to happen. And I'm OK with that. I respect Roger, and he really loves what he's doing now. We're all getting older. We're all lucky that we're still working. David just made a really good album. He's singing great and it's different, and he's coming up with some really interesting stuff that's out of left field. And that's refreshing.

How about a Hillman-Crosby album? I'm just tossing this out there now.

I think I'd rather do a Hillman album and have friends guest on it. That's the best way to approach it. [*laughs*]

Actually, we could suggest all kinds of combinations, given all your past affiliations. Personally, we loved the Souther-Hillman-Furay Band.

We actually sat down together not long ago, and I don't who it was—maybe Richie's manager—suggested we put it back together and go out on the road together. Playing, not recording, but maybe a short tour opening for someone else perhaps. And I said we need to listen to those songs again. I don't know if I like them, and I was being honest. I love everybody's individual songs, but I don't know if I liked what we did together. So I don't know how we would approach that. It never got off the ground. Once again, both of those guys are incredible musicians. Richie is one of the great entertainers, and Souther is one of the better songwriters, but as a group we never got off the ground. But

I hear that from people—that love for Souther-Hillman-Furay. I just don't hear it myself. It had some moments. Let me put it that way. But I don't think any one of us ever do any of those songs in our individual sets.

The first album was amazing, a classic. The second album, maybe not so much. It's just a shame though that those tunes from the first record won't ever be heard live.

Well, yeah, but to quote you, never say never. Maybe some kids in England will do them. You never know.

And of course there was Manassas, your band with Stephen Stills. Any talk about reconvening that ensemble?

Nah. They put out an album of outtakes called *Pieces*, and I tried to talk Stephen into recutting some of those songs or cutting some new songs as a marketing tool to bring more attention to it. But he didn't want to do that, so OK. To me, that album is OK, but it sounds more like a rehearsal. Whatever. You gotta make something look really great to make it enjoyable. You can't put a gun to someone's head and say, let's get the Byrds back together. It's like you can't march some poor guy on drugs into rehab at gunpoint. If they're going to clean up, it's got to be their idea. They have to come up with some kind if epiphany where they think, "Oh, that's a good idea." I'm happy doing what I'm doing, to be honest with you. There's not much more I really want. Like I said earlier in the conversation, I'm totally blessed to be able to do what I do. I would like to do another album.

You've left an incredible legacy you left in your wake . . . that must be incredibly gratifying.

Well, I'm—excuse the corny cliché—I'm really blessed. I had a great job, just to be able to do what I wanted. I got to do what I love and I survived. I made stupid mistakes like everybody else, but I never went over the line of decency. If I had, I wouldn't be talking to you now. It was really great. If everything stopped tomor-

row, I'd have had a wonderful time. I'd say, "Thank you very much.
I got to do what I love. I don't have animosity toward anyone."
No, I'm not some perfect being that you're talking to. I still have
areas where I try to get better all the time. Bucket lists? There's
some stuff I'd like to do, but it's narrowing. I'd like my kids to be
successful. I'll tell you one thing, and this is kind of left field, but
it ties everything in. Everything that my generation in the sixties [was] going on about—f'ing on traditional values—well boy,
were we ever wrong. Everything that we were stepping on were
the things that held civilization intact for thousands of years. And
we're reaping the benefits of it now. I'm not at all like my peers.
I'm very conservative. I wasn't a fan of the Obama administra-
tion at all. I'm more Libertarian if anything. That lends itself to
some interesting conversations with David Crosby.

Point/counterpoint.

[*Laughs*] I say, "Let's put it this way, Crosby." I say, "Ted Nugent
and I are on the same page. He and I are one side of the fence
and all the other guys are over there. Anyway, it's just a joke.

**There are certain people you've known who sadly aren't
with us anymore. People like Gene Clark, like Gram
Parsons. Are they still present in your mind and consciousness? How often do they enter your thoughts? Are they
still present in any way to you?**

I think of them all the time. I think of them in a good light. I
never think of them with anything bad. I had two great years
with Parsons when we hired him in the Byrds. There was about
six months with him there.

**And then you went on to play with him in the Flying
Burrito Brothers.**

Yes I did, and the first year was really good. Then we lost him.
We lost him to excess, and I had to part company with him. I just
remember the good times. He was funny. He was bright. He was

great to write songs with. And Gene was a great guy. Even after the Byrds, I would work on some of his projects. I liked the guy. I always respected him, even when I didn't like him. I also miss Mike Clark, the drummer. In the early days, when we were just getting together, Mike and Gene and I lived together. Gene would write four or five songs a week, and we would use maybe three out of five. That's how prolific he was. So we'd sort of work them up, and then we'd share them with David and Roger. Gram gets a little more attention now than Gene, but it doesn't really matter. They both died tragically. And that sort of enhances the legend.

You likely saw the best and the worst of those people.

I don't know why I'm talking about all this, but I guess the point is, we blow these people up to some mythical proportions, whether it's a musician or an actor. Look at Phillip Seymour Hoffman. Look at how much press he got. What a great actor! So you say, wait a minute, all these guys we just talked about—Gram, Gene—they're all good, They were all gifted and talented. What is that? I could get into a basic spiritual take on it all. I do believe this—that place you get when you find that success. Everything you do, it's almost like the Devil opens this door and says, "Great, come on in. I got more stuff to show you." It's very rare that someone that talented maintains that stability. What helped me was I figured out when to leave the fantasy behind and cross the line into reality.

9

·······························

Richie Furay Remembers

Seminal Member of Buffalo Springfield, Poco, and Souther-Hillman-Furay Shares His Story

Ask most music scholars to name the most influential American bands of the past five decades, and more than likely they'll include Buffalo Springfield in their top ten. Suggest they name the groups that spearheaded the country rock crossover, and chances are Poco will show up prominently as well. If they're also well informed, they'll single out Richie Furay as the common link between the two outfits and a major contributor to the music that eventually helped spawn a genre broadly defined as Americana—a vast umbrella perhaps, but certainly a sound that resonates throughout many forms of popular music today.

Still, despite a career that reaches back over fifty years and his solid standing in Buffalo Springfield, Poco, and supergroup of sorts the Souther-Hillman-Furay Band, it could be well argued that Furay himself has yet to get his due. It's a dilemma Furay himself has struggled with over the years.

Ironically, the credit that Poco should have received for bridging the country-rock divide is often attributed to the Eagles. "We started a whole new genre of music which became the biggest kind of music there is. Americana music," Furay surmises. "I love it when people say, 'Oh you sound like Glen Frey.' Really? I remember when he was sitting on my living room floor when I was coming up with Poco. You have this backward. When I saw the Eagles, they would mention Buffalo Springfield being an influence but they wouldn't mention Poco."

From the beginning, Furay has sought that recognition in ways large and small. Rightfully so. His career has paralleled many of the trends in modern music over the course of several generations, beginning with his decision to join a folk group while attending Oberlin College in Ohio.

"Folk music was the thing," he recalls. "We would 'go down the road,' as they referred to it, and entertain sororities. I joined the acapella choir and yet it was quite an amazing thing because I don't really read music. I stood with my ear trained on whoever was singing. I had never done that before. I won a contest for singing 'They Call the Wind Mariah,' and that's how I got in."

Furay's next stop was an ad hoc hootenanny group called the Au Go Go Singers, a nine-piece ensemble that modeled itself after the Kingston Trio; Peter, Paul, and Mary; and the various other outfits that were turning folk songs into top 40 hits.

"When we got to New York, we started knocking on doors and we got to play at the famous folk club, Cafe Wha," Furay explains. "We thought it was a big deal, but we were scheduled during intermission, while they were turning the crowd over."

One of Furay's fellow singers was a similarly inspired young man named Stephen Stills. With the two of them in tow, the band began to get a fair number of bookings and eventually made an album for Roulette Records. They even did a television show, *Rudy Vallee on Broadway Tonight*. However, after a tour of Texas, the group ground to a halt.

The end of the Au Go Go Singers brought Furay to a crossroads. Eager to find a job, he rang up a cousin who worked at airplane parts manufacturer Pratt and Whitney. "He asked me if I'd be there for the gold watch," Furay remembers. "I didn't know about the gold watch, but I had to put food on the table, so I took the job."

Ironically, it was another soon-to-be icon that put him back on course. "Gram Parsons lived across from me in New York and he brought me the Byrds's first record," Furay muses. "It was like, 'Oh my gosh, I've got to get out of here.' So I called Stephen. The only contact I had was through Stephen's dad, who was in import-export in El Salvador. So I sent a letter off to him and it came back with not enough postage. I had to send it again. Eventually I got the call from Stephen, and he said, 'Come on out to California. I've got a band all together and all I need is another singer.' So I said I'd be there."

As it turned out, there was no band. Even so, he moved into Stills's tiny apartment, and the two would sit face-to-face practicing harmonies and learning new songs. They would famously run into Neil Young weeks later after Young headed west, also in search of Stills.

"We were on Sunset Strip outside our little apartment and Neil was ready to get on the 405 and head to San Francisco in his old '53 Hearst," Furay says. "Stephen recognized the Hearst and somehow or another we all stopped, made our way to this parking lot across the street that belonged to Ben Frank's restaurant, and that was the beginning of Buffalo Springfield."

The band soon enlisted bassist Bruce Palmer and eventually drummer Dewey Martin. However, Palmer's problems with substance abuse led to a steady string of difficulties. He also had immigration problems. Furay notes that in nine years, there were nine people in and out of the band. "It made it very difficult for us," he admits. "It was like one step forward and three steps back."

Regardless, the band's popularity quickly accelerated, although to the band members, who were struggling to pay the bills, the progress initially seemed slow.

"Then suddenly, we played at the Whiskey a Go Go with the Doors," Furay reflects. "We played on a double bill with Love and the Seeds, and we're doing concerts with the Turtles and the Beach Boys. It was an amazing time. When we started at the Whiskey, nobody knew who we were. But after we became the house band and had played there six weeks, people were lined up around the block. I don't know what they caught on to, but they caught on to something."

That "something" was the band's newfound confidence and a stockpile of superior songs that made them one of the most prolific outfits around. "We actually felt like our only competition was the Beatles," he says in retrospect. "That's how we looked at our music. We were on a mission. Neil and Stephen were definitely insightful as to what was going on. I was just happy to be there."

Sadly, after two albums, their eponymous debut and the classic *Buffalo Springfield Again*, the band began to splinter. During their famous appearance at the Monterrey Pop Festival in 1967, Young opted not to show, and his place was taken by David Crosby. The band was so fractured by the time they recorded their swan song, the aptly named "Last Time Around," that Furay and engineer/guitarist Jim Messina had to cobble it together from the members' individual contributions.

"There were all these people in and out in two years and it was very, very difficult," Furay says woefully. "Every time you tried to learn a new song, it became a whole new process. You couldn't start where you left off. You had to start over again. I said in my mind, "I'm there as long as Stephen's there." He was the heart and soul of the Buffalo Springfield, so when he went off to do the *Super Session* album with Mike Bloomfield and Al Kooper, that was it."

Still, Furay and Messina were determined to keep things going, and the demise of Buffalo Springfield led directly to the formation of Poco. "We both had country-ish backgrounds and we wanted to lean toward country music that could be embraced by both rock fans and country music fans alike," he explains. "Gram Parsons was doing the same thing. So with the *Last Time Around* record, we decided we wanted to put a steel guitar on there and see how it works. A road manager of ours said he knew the best steel guitar player in the world, but he lived in Denver. That was Rusty Young. So sight unseen, we brought him out and there it was. We asked him if he wanted to be in the band and started looking for drummers and bass players, and Rusty suggested George Grantham. I'm not real sure who hooked us up with Randy [Meisner] and Timothy [Schmit], but they both auditioned on the same day."

Interestingly enough, Gregg Allman also tried out for Poco early on. "I don't think the chemistry would have been right," Furay observes. "But Duane called him before we had a chance to really get together and said, 'You got to get back down here because we have something going on.'"

In that case, the "something" was, of course, the Allman Brothers.

Despite their popularity with the college crowd, Poco never achieved all Furay has hoped for. He insists that Columbia label head Clive Davis never really understood what the band was all about. When Poco's superb single "Good Feelin' to Know" failed to reach the higher strata of the charts, Furay became frustrated and decided to venture out on his own. It was especially irritating that the Eagles had come along afterward and emulated their success, and yet they were clearly soaring while Poco seemingly couldn't get off the ground.

Furay points to one missed opportunity in particular that may have helped seal their fate. The band was invited to play Woodstock, but their manager, not recognizing how big the festival would become, suggested he had a better gig for them and booked them instead at a high school outside of Washington, DC. "That could have changed everything," Furay maintains. "Just about everybody that was on that stage had an opportunity to show their wares. It could have really changed the entire trajectory of the band."

He made up his mind that the only way to succeed was to venture out on his own. "I was driven at that point in my life," Furay reflects. "It wasn't necessarily a good time for me. It was a tough decision to leave Poco, but I was so driven. I'd seen Stephen and Neil get their success. I'd seen Timmy Schmit and Randy Meisner with the Eagles. I said, 'Wait, there's something out there.' I was basically blinded by that idea. I called agent David Geffen after 'Good Feelin' to Know' failed to chart."

Furay knew what he wanted and shared his goal with Geffen. "I knew radio could take you to a different level. You needed a hit single. A hit single launched you into different venues. It put you on the radar. You could go anywhere in the country and perform. It was a difficult thing for me. It was four albums down the road with Poco, and when it didn't happen, it felt like it was never going to happen. I was driven for the hits, so that's when David mentioned J. D. Souther and Chris Hillman were available. He told me, 'Let's put together another supergroup and we'll be on our way.' David said SHF would take us to another level, and so I'm looking at him and thinking, 'Wow, I've been at this thing for six years now and maybe that's all there is to it.'"

Unfortunately, the SHF band didn't bring the good fortune he had hoped for. Their excellent eponymous debut led to a less than successful follow-up, the ironically dubbed *Trouble in Paradise*. Furay himself fully accepts responsibility. He was, he says, "in one of the deepest moments of my life during the making of the second album. Nancy and I had been married for seven years, and at that time we had been separated for seven months. We recorded the album three miles from my home up at the Caribou Ranch with Tommy Dowd, and yet I don't even remember the experience. I just wasn't in touch with what we were doing. My family was living down the street from me and I wasn't even connected. I was disoriented at that time, and I wasn't even there."

Several years went by between the last SHF record and Furay's initial solo foray, *I've Got a Reason*. "My main focus was to put my family back together," he declares. "I had also become a believer. I was taking a little walk on the beach one day in St. Petersburg, Florida, and I said, 'OK Lord, you've made a commitment to me, so now let's talk about how I can serve you.' And at that point, everything became clear. I had to make a decision. Do I want my family, or do I want my name up there on the marquee at Carnegie Hall? I chose my family. I eventually met some people in California and went into the studio with them, even though music was the furthest thing from my mind. I thought we made a really fantastic record. David Geffen called me up and said, 'You're not going to give me any of that Jesus music, are you?' I told him I thought he was really going to like the record. 'You don't have to worry about that,' I said. 'Jesus isn't on the record anywhere.' It was all about my wife Nancy and me, and the struggle of getting it back together."

Unfortunately, more frustration would follow. David Geffen was leaving the label he had helped found, Asylum, which had signed Furay as part of SHF. A new president, Joe Smith, took over. "We did not have a rapport," Furay insists. "When *I Got a Reason* was done, I went in and recorded *Dance a Little Light*, but we hardly got any support from Asylum. It was very disappointing. When we played at the Roxy, I was hoping the record company would come and try to turn things around. But instead, they walked right in and said, "When's the next record?" And we had just released *Dance a Little Light*. We weren't too much down the road with that record. At that time, you could work a record awhile. It was like, 'Oh man.'"

Furay returned to writing and recorded what would become *I Still Have Dreams*, but he wasn't pleased with the initial results.

At the suggestion of the local Asylum rep in Denver, he went to LA to rerecord the album with the famous studio band the Section. The title track went to number thirty-nine on the charts, but his dismal experience with the label led to a parting of ways.

"When it was over, it was over and done with," Furay insists. "I threw up my arms and said 'Lord, what do you want me to do?'" The answer came in the form of a new mission—to become a minister at a church he and wife Nancy helped found in Boulder, Colorado. He remained there thirty-five years until his retirement. He also turned his attention to recording religious music, beginning with his initial independent release, *Seasons of Change*.

Two more devotional albums followed several years later: *My Father's House* and *I Am Sure*. However, he wouldn't discard secular music entirely. *Heartbeat of Love*, released in 2006, found him reunited with old friends Stephen Stills, Neil Young, Paul Cotton, and Rusty Young, as well as other musical pals like Mark Volman of the Turtles and Jeff Hanna from the Dirt Band. The record was well received, but got little exposure due to lack of record company backing.

There were other indications that Furay was willing to look toward the past as well. A later eighties reunion with Poco yielded an album entitled *Legacy* and a hit single in "Call It Love." Nevertheless, it left him with a bittersweet aftertaste. "It was a challenge for me," he confesses. "Our personalities had changed over time and I was a little more conscious of what I wanted to project. I didn't want vulgarity. It was pretty common then. Not that we were going to do it, but it was evident it was there even while recording the record. If you would have heard the original lyrics to 'Call It Love,' you would know what I mean. They were pornographic. So that was my first debate. I said, 'I'm not singing on it. I'm not playing on it.' I had to draw a line. So Jimmy [Messina] sat down with the guys who wrote it in Nashville and came up with something that was acceptable. Our manager at the time was trying to push us into another genre. And it wasn't us. It wasn't Poco, and it wasn't me, and at that point in my life, I was a pastor. They made a video and I figured we'd have artistic approval, and so I was waiting and waiting to see the video. When I saw it, I was a little more critical than maybe I should have been, but there were girls in T-shirts with everything showing that could be shown. I'm thinking, 'You've got to be kidding me.' I said, 'You can't release this.' We went to Nashville for RCA's national convention and I was up in my room at the hotel, and I get a call saying, 'Richie, we've got to talk. We're going to release this video to VH1.' We were supposed to play three hours later, but I went to the airport and flew home. You can talk so much. If talk doesn't work, you have to take action. So I left. The song did become a pretty good hit, but it wasn't necessarily Poco.

These days, Furay is where he wants to be. An upcoming tour will mark Poco's fifty-year anniversary. His 2015 release, *Hand in Hand*, was received with stellar reviews. It's not only a love letter to Nancy, his wife of fifty years, but also a nostalgic look back at his life and the indelible impression he helped instill in modern music. The leadoff track "We Were the Dreamers" sums it up succinctly, a wistful reflection of the sound he helped carve that continues to resonate through Americana music today.

"I was just living my life and making my music and trying to figure out what I wanted to do," he says now in retrospect. "I do think about it a little bit now. I tell myself, 'You paved the way.' When we did the Buffalo Springfield reunion a couple of years ago, I really needed that. I needed to know I didn't ride into the Rock and Roll Hall of Fame on Stephen and Neil's coattails. And that it had a lot to do with my contributions at the time. And doing those reunion shows satisfied me that I finally got the recognition. Standing onstage between Stephen and Neil, it was a great moment. It was important to me, because even though they were the primary writers, I don't want to think that my contribution was any less important . . . for my own self worth. I needed to know that what I did then was pretty cool."

10

·····························

Poco Primes Country Rock

Born from the wreckage of Buffalo Springfield, Poco can rightly claim the distinction of being among the very first bands to make the crossover from rock to country. While the term "Americana" had yet to take hold, in 1968, when pedal steel player Rusty Young, singer/guitarist Richie Furay, singer/guitarist Jim Messina, guitarist Randy Meisner, and drummer George Grantham made their bow at LA's trendsetting club the Troubadour, the idea of a group melding down-home sentiments with an upbeat attitude was still somewhat revolutionary. Nevertheless, Poco proved the precursor to bands like the Eagles in particular (who twice drafted two of Poco's members—Meisner and later Timothy B. Schmit) and a host of others who scaled the charts by mining the same populist appeal.

Over the years, members came and went—most recently, singer/guitarist Paul Cotton, a veteran of the band for the past four decades. That left Young, Poco's sole constant since the beginning, to take the reins and steer the band's legacy. Indeed, Poco's legacy has languished at times, taking them from being the darlings of the college crowd to all but ignored to significant hit-makers ("Crazy Love," "Heart of the Night") in the late seventies, to a band whose appeal to its devoted fans (referred to as "Poconuts") still brings them a revered status. Their latest album, *All Fired Up*, recorded with the latest incarnation of the band (Young, bassist Jack Sundred, drummer Jack Lawrence, and keyboard player Michael Webb) marked another career highlight. Sadly, though, as Rusty Young—the group's only member to have played every gig since their inception—indicates in this interview, it may also be their last.

We understand you're working on a book. Is this your memoir about the early days of Poco?

Yeah, it is. It's about what happened during those years. A lot of the most interesting stuff is about the seventies. The business isn't like it is now. People didn't have all the security around them. You'd be able to hang out backstage. You'd be able to walk in the studio and watch Dean Martin or Barbra Streisand record, as well as the other rock and roll acts like Dan Hicks and the Hot Licks [*chuckles*] or Stevie Wonder. So it's all these stories about things that I think of as life lessons that I learned in music. We played with Jimi Hendrix and Janis Joplin and Eric Clapton. . . . I have a great Keith Moon story, and one about Elton John early on. So all these anecdotes have little lessons in them, and if I can pass that on . . . it would be nice. Pretty much in every book I've read they sugarcoat things so much, and I decided I didn't want to do that. I'm probably going to make a lot of enemies, but I'm intent on telling it like it really is. It's almost finished, so it will probably take me only a couple of months to wrap it up.

You were there at a crucial juncture, prior to Poco's formation, in the final throes of Buffalo Springfield. Was that as divisive a time as it has been described? What do you remember of those sessions that they hired you to play on?

I played on a song called "Kind Woman," and because we got the notion that we wanted to start our band, I hung out and was there for a lot of it. Anytime you have Neil Young involved in anything, there's going to be chaos, and there was chaos then and there will continue to be as long as Neil Young is involved in it, I suspect. They had to finish that record because they were contracted to Atlantic Records to give them one more album, and so they had to do it. But nobody really wanted to, I don't think. I certainly got that impression. And Neil—just like he did with Crosby, Stills, Nash and Young—when he recorded with them, he would go off and do his own thing with his own musicians and just bring it in and say, "Here it is." That's the way he works, at least with Crosby, Stills, Nash and Young. So he wasn't there. I only saw him one day when he came in and heard the final mix on "Kind Woman." Stephen (Stills) was in a studio down the hall doing his stuff by himself, and Richie (Furay) and Jimmy (Messina) were by themselves working on their material. David Crosby was across the hall producing Joni Mitchell's first album, so there was a lot of interaction between those guys. It was an interesting time, yeah.

Was your original intention to carry on with the Springfield's legacy, but with the country rock element?

Richie had done it with "A Child's Claim to Fame" and "Kind Woman." That was the country part of the Springfield where Neil and Stephen were way more rock and roll. You have to remember that in 1969, there weren't synthesizers, so if you actually wanted a certain sound, you had to have a real musician playing. So that's why I got involved, because I could play steel guitar and dobro and banjo and mandolin, and pretty much all the country instruments, except for the fiddle. So I added color to Richie's country rock songs, and that was the whole idea, to use country-sounding instruments. Also, I pushed the envelope on steel guitar, playing it with a fuzz tone, because nobody was doing that, and playing it through a Leslie speaker like an organ, and a lot of people thought I was playing an organ, because they didn't realize I was playing a steel guitar. So we were pushing the envelope in lots of different ways, instrumentally and musically overall.

Today, the term "Americana" is such a widely used term, but Poco were really the pioneers of that whole genre, along with the latter Byrds and the Burrito Brothers. Do you think that Poco truly got credit for that?

Not really. It's confusing. I find that with journalists, if someone tells a journalist something, whether it's true or not, and a journalist writes it down, and other journalists borrow it from that journalist, pretty soon, if a lie is told enough times, then it becomes the truth. So the whole thing about Gram Parsons and the Byrds becoming the whole country rock band . . . it's just not really so. But you kind of had to be there to understand how that whole

notion got started. I think things went the way they were supposed to go. We did have a big hit in 1978, and if it hadn't been
for Richie leaving the band, and Timmy leaving the band, and
Jimmy leaving the band, I never would have been a songwriter
or a singer, so those things had to happen for my life to be the
life it is. So I'm really pleased.

**What was it like when Richie in particular left the band?
That must have been traumatic, no?**

When Richie left the band, we flew out from Colorado to Los
Angeles, and we had a meeting in David Geffen's office. I heard
that Richie was leaving the band and he was going to do something with Chris Hillman, and so we pretty much knew that was
going to happen. So I asked Richie and he said, no, that wasn't
going to happen. So we fly out to this meeting with management,
and Richie goes into Geffen's office, and Geffen comes out and
says, "OK, Richie's quitting the band." There were four of us sitting on the couch there in the waiting room and he starts with Tim
and says, "Now Tim, you write songs and sing, don't you?" And
Tim says, "Yes." So he says, "Well don't you worry about Richie
leaving, you'll be fine. And he looks at Paul, and he says, "You play
guitar and sing and write songs, don't you?" And Paul says "Yes."
So he says, "Don't you worry, you'll be fine, don't worry about it."
Then he looked at me and George, and he looked me in the eye,
and he said, "Now you don't sing and you don't write songs, do
you?" And I said, "No, I don't." So he said, "Well, you're in trouble." And that was the day I became a singer-songwriter, and if it
weren't for David Geffen saying that to me, it never would have
happened, and I owe him greatly for that. And if it wasn't for
Richie quitting, I never would have done that, and my life would
be totally different from what it is now.

**Speaking of which, what happened with Paul Cotton? He
was in the lineup for a very long time.**

He got married, and his wife is his manager, and she decided he
was better off as a solo artist.

In the late seventies and early eighties, Poco had some chart hits with "Crazy Love" and "Heart of the Night." Was that a deliberate plan, to remake yourselves into a radio-ready hit-making band?

No, I've just always written songs. What happened in 1978—actually the end of '77—Timothy left the band to join the Eagles, and of course that was a really cool thing, because how many times do you get to join a band like the Eagles? So that left me and Paul, and the record company was going to drop us. So we had written some songs—I had written "Crazy Love" and Paul had written "Heart of the Night"—and our management decided to invite the people from our label down to a rehearsal studio, and we played those songs for them. We said, "These are the songs we want to record, and we think we will do well with them." And they agreed, so we went into the studio and recorded them, and "Crazy Love" became number one on Billboard for six weeks. It was our first hit record, our first gold album, our first platinum album, and all that kind of stuff. The band didn't need another singer-songwriter when Richie and Jim were in the band. My job was to play steel guitar and make the music part of it. So when my job changed, it opened up a whole lot of opportunity for me. So I liked the way things went.

Were you pleased with the reunion album in '89?

It was the very beginning band, which was Randy Meisner, Richie Furay, Jimmy Messina, me, and George. I think that [Legacy] was a great record. Of all the records we've done, if I had to say one was overlooked, [this would be it]. Even though it went gold, I think it should have been bigger and more appreciated. On that one album, you have the Eagles via Randy Meisner, you have Loggins and Messina with Jimmy, and you have Poco with me. So here, on one album, you have three or four of the biggest bands in America that came from one band, Buffalo Springfield. These are the guys that started out playing at the Troubadour in 1968. I can't think of another band that has that heritage. I think that was a great record that we made. . . .

Agreed. But out of curiosity, was there any thought at that point about doing another album or keeping the reunion going?

Not really, because people don't change. The same reason that the band didn't make it even through the very first album we made, the same reason that it ended after that record is that people don't change. All the same bugaboos come flying back.

And then you had that reunion gig at the Stagecoach Festival a few years back.

Yeah, we did five or six shows, and that was one of them.

So there was no thought given into going back into the studio at that point?

No, not really. It's that same old thing. You call up Timothy and say, "Hey can you drop that Eagles thing?" That's not going to happen. It's a personality thing, a love/hate thing. They love each other, but they have a hard time working together. And they all have their own thing. Richie has his family band. Jimmy's doing well as a solo artist and he's doing his own thing, and Poco has been great for me over the years. But for me, it's time to stop. I'm going to be sixty-eight in February . . . and I think for me it's kind of silly to carry on. People say, "Well look at Mick Jagger or Paul McCartney." But the difference is those guys have a private plane, a limo that takes them to the airport. They stay at a five-star hotel; they go down to the gig and everything's set up for them. . . . I have to load up all my gear, drive to the airport, get on a Southwest Airlines flight, drive all my gear to the hotel, and then drag all my gear from the hotel to the stage, spend all day setting it up, play a show, tear down all the gear, drag it back to the hotel. . . . If I lived the life that Mick Jagger lived, then I might consider playing on further, but not with the kind of touring that we have to do.

In 2017, you transitioned from Poco into a solo album, your first individual effort in your more than fifty-year career. So what finally made you decide to go it alone?

Everything has its time, and we had our time and it was great. I just really want to end on top, and for me we are ending on top, because our band is really, really good. It's one of the best Poco bands we've ever had, and maybe even the best. So I feel like we're going out on top. That final Poco album, *All Fired Up*, was a work I'm really proud of, and I think it's the record to end on. It's time.

11

....

Timothy B. Schmit

From Poco to the Eagles, Still Flying High

If Timothy B. Schmit was any more prolific, then Webster's Dictionary would have to come up with an entirely new word to describe his remarkable work ethic. Then again, his first band was called the New Breed, a name that readily suggested an auspicious introduction. Although their one single of note, 1965's "Green Eyed Woman," didn't exactly ensure immortality, the band did evolve, changing their name to Glad and releasing their first and only full length recording, *Feelin' Glad*, three years later.

Of course, the most important shift in Schmit's career would come later, beginning with Poco and later the Eagles. Schmit first auditioned for Poco in 1968, only to lose out to Randy Meisner, who had rejoined the band he originally helped found. Schmit finally got the gig when Meisner left for good to join the Eagles. Ironically it was Schmit who again took Meisner's slot, this time in the Eagles when Meisner gave that group his notice in 1977.

With both bands, Schmit was able to make his presence known immediately. He contributed the song "Keep on Trying" to Poco, and later helped propel the mega hit "I Can't Tell You Why" to the top of the charts for the Eagles. He continued to play an integral role in the Eagles until their initial breakup in 1980, and subsequently rejoined them when they reconvened again in 1994.

Still, those two groups represented only part of his trajectory. Schmit's session work has occupied a significant portion of his career, and like Woody Allen's enigmatic Zelig, he regularly appears in the most unexpected places. He appeared on three Steely Dan albums (*Pretzel Logic*, *The Royal Scam*, and *Aja*), as well as signature songs by Firefall ("Just Remember I Love You"); Andrew Gold ("Never Let Her Slip Away"); Bob Seger ("Fire Lake"); Boz Scaggs ("Look What You've Done to Me"); Toto ("Africa," "I Won't Hold You Back"); Don Felder ("Heavy Metal"); Crosby, Stills and Nash ("Southern Cross"); Richard Marx ("Should've Known Better"); Jars of Clay ("Everything in Between"); and fellow Eagle Don Henley ("Dirty Laundry," "You Don't Know Me at All"). In addition, he's toured with Jimmy Buffett's Coral Reefer Band (it's said he actually termed the phrase "Parrotheads" to describe Buffett's rabid fans), Ringo Starr, and Dan Fogelberg.

He is, in short, one prodigious individual.

Surprisingly, though, Schmit's individual efforts happen to be in relatively short supply. In a career that spans some fifty years, he's only released six solo albums, including his latest, *Leap of Faith*, his first offering in almost seven years.

That said, Schmit appeared anxious to give the new record the attention it deserves. In 2016, he made a rare appearance at the Americana Music Festival in Nashville for a few showcases and press appearances. Charming to a fault, still boasting the shoulder-length locks that have become his identifying trademark and a quiet speaking voice that gives way to his upper register in the studio, he graciously consented to a one-on-one interview in the hosting hotel's lobby. As always, he was thoroughly engaging.

Your first album of note was with a band called Glad. Whatever happened to those guys?

I see those guys all the time. They're my best friends. Whenever I go to Sacramento—which is where I'm from and where we got together in high school—we always get together and at least have lunch. We actually played together at our last high school reunion.

OK, let's fast-forward. Please give us some background on the new album.

I like to write songs, and whenever I have a song or a few songs, I turn on the mother ship and start recording. And I've been doing that for quite a few years, especially for this record. This album took awhile for a couple of reasons. For one, I'm not a particularly fast writer. I take my time. And then, of course, I was out on the road with the Eagles, so I would come home, write, record, and do it all in between tours. So the album actually spans several years of work.

You've had a long and prolific career, but not a lot of actual solo albums. So is it a matter of limited time?

I said this recently—I finally feel like I'm getting the hang of things and learning how to do it. It's really a great feeling to have some new energy as you get older. It's really good. Plus, this album is self-penned. All the songs are mine. I've collaborated in the past, but it's always a bit of a compromise because you're working with other people. When I went back and listened to my earlier solo albums, and I listen to the songs I wrote myself, I actually prefer those. They sound truer because they come from me. So on my last two albums, I chose to write all the songs myself, and it's much more satisfying to me.

Where are you based?

I live in Los Angeles. That's where I recorded this album. I have a separate studio on my property and that's where I work.

You set a high bar with your early work, and even if you were to quit tomorrow, your reputation would still be assured. When you do a solo project, are you cognizant of the fact that there's a certain level of expectation and that you have to meet a high bar?

The only bar that I have to meet is really just for myself. I'm not trying to be profound, but my solo stuff is very personal and it's my own thing. It's not being scrutinized by others. I can do what I want. I don't have anyone saying, "No, you shouldn't do that."

It's very freeing and very nice. The other situation that I've been in, like with Poco and the Eagles, were different, but it was also helpful to me to work with some of the greatest songwriters ever. Real professionals. I learned a lot, and I take all that with me. I'm still learning. I feel like I'm starting to be a real songwriter, even though I've been writing songs for a long time.

You say this album is very personal. Can you give us an example of why that is?

It's really just what's going through my head, and in some situations, what's going on in my life. On a good portion of these songs, whether it's alluded to or not, I direct my thoughts to my wife, my greatest friend. There's only one sort of direct love song on this, but there's kind of a mention of her here and there. Like I said, it's just what's going on in my head. I try to keep my eyes open, to be aware of life situations, and face the many challenges. I've done really well professionally, but you can't escape the normal life quagmires and problems and situations that you wish would never happen. There's even a song on the record called "Slow Down" that's really just about stepping back and asking what's important. Why am I going so fast? We're all heading in the same direction, but we need to try to keep our eyes open and not even hedge toward the dark side. It's about that kind of thing.

Do you have a bucket list?

I've traveled all over the place, but there are some places I'd still like to visit. Maybe some Third World countries. I don't know. I've been so fortunate. I've had such a great life that if it all ended, I would still have a pretty full ship.

So we have to ask—are the Eagles still intact? Are things on hold or are there plans going forward?

Well, right now, not really. Glen [Frey] has only been gone nine months. Everybody's out doing other things. Henley's on the road and Joe's been out as well. We've only gotten together once recently, and that was at our manager's wife's birthday party. It was really great to see each other a few months after Glen's passing. But nothing's really been talked about. Honestly, I can't really see calling it the Eagles anymore. The Eagles are over. That whole thing was really spearheaded by Don and Glen. They were the principal writers. Glen was a huge part. I suspect something will happen someday, but I'm not hiding anything when I say nothing's been talked about. I suspect at some point, when we decide what we want to do, if it's time, we'll do something together, but for right now I'm just concentrating on the present and on this new album.

12

················

The Eagles' One Time Wingman Don Felder Shares His Story

It's 9 a.m. California time, and though Don Felder sounds surprisingly cheery, when asked how he's doing, he admits to being a little drowsy. "It's too early to tell," he sheepishly admits. "I'll let you know after my second cup of tea."

A rocker who arises at 9 a.m.? And gets energized with a cup of tea? It's certainly a far cry from the wild and reckless existence he was accustomed to during his twenty-seven year tenure with the Eagles ("where you're going to bed at sunup and going back into the studio at sundown . . . a dark, Dracula lifestyle"), the band that brought him fame, fortune, and no shortage of conflict and controversy until he was abruptly terminated in 2001. It was a difficult time, Felder contends. He not only found himself unemployed for the first time in his career, but also going through a divorce from his wife of twenty-nine years. "Everything I knew just changed," he reflects. "My career, my friends—or the people I thought were my friends—my marriage . . . everything."

Nevertheless, the Eagles were the band that brought country rock its commercial credence. Little wonder then that after an extensive period of self-examination and reflection, Felder would offer his own insights on the band and the role he played in its success via his 2008 memoir *Heaven and Hell: My Life in the Eagles* (1974–2001). Little surprise as well that the book became a *New York Times* best seller.

"Who would have thought that a student who so poor in English would become a best-selling author?" he laughs. "I was raised in the Deep South. I still have the scars and calluses from being dragged into church and Sunday school for years, but once I was in the Eagles, I was drugged—not dragged—into all sorts of promiscuity and drugs and everything that was not part of my upbringing, and I realized how that had influenced my life and made a sharp detour away from all the morals and ethics that I was raised with. I wondered how I ever got there. I wanted to understand the process that had taken me from being raised dirt poor to now being a multimillionaire, from the values of the church to a life of sin."

Out of that process, Felder began focusing on music again, performing gigs with a band that includes his son Cody on percussion and daughter Leah helping with harmonies, and writing songs borne from his life experiences, both the triumphant and the troubling. "I'd be in the studio for three or four days and then go right back on the road so my production time was limited. I'd be writing lyrics on airplanes on the way to shows or figuring out guitar parts between gigs. So the whole process stretched out over two or three years. It was a very cathartic experience to take those life episodes and write them into songs and be able to play them for people who might relate to those same sort of feelings."

His efforts eventually gelled into *Road to Forever*, Felder's first solo album in thirty years and only the second individual effort in his entire career. While the songs are emotive and reflective, Felder's guitar play is rich and robust, bringing to mind the razor-sharp licks he contributed to the Eagles. Yet though his presence his unmistakable, he's also enlisted an all-star supporting cast, including pals David Crosby, Graham Nash, Tommy Shaw, Steve Lukather, and Stephen Stills, who he first played with as a teenager in band called the Continentals in his hometown of Gainesville, Florida. Ironically the band also included his future Eagles band mate Bernie Leadon. Likewise, the first musicians he performed with when he relocated to LA were Crosby and Nash. It was Nash himself that recommended Leadon for the Eagles.

"A lot of people that are on this record were brought in, not because they're high profile musicians, but because they had something to add. It wasn't a matter of just having some names on the record."

Then again, contributing to sessions has been Felder's forte. The list of musicians with whom he's collaborated is nothing less than a who's who of musical icons—a list that includes Barbra Streisand, the Bee Gees, Bob Seger, Michael Jackson, Alice Cooper, Stevie Wonder, Elton John, Paul Simon, and dozens of others of similar stature.

"I really enjoy that," he effuses. "It's allowed me to throw myself into these projects, and though they might not have been my rock and roll forte, they've forced me to adapt to other styles, from bluegrass to jazz to country and everything in between. It forces me to not only rely on things I have in my arsenal but to reach out for new fresh things as well."

At the moment, however, Felder's happy to focus on himself. "In trying to continue to raise the bar higher and higher, the Eagles got to a point Glenn called the 'hardening of the artistry,' where it's hard to beat yourself and rise above what you accomplished and to make that leap of faith and write and play or be creative. But once I was out of the band and I didn't have the restriction on me to write for a specific cast of characters, I found I could write and play to my strengths and my experiences, without having to consider the Eagles format per se."

Despite all the problems and petulance, Felder still speaks well of his former colleagues. "A lot of the disputes that took place in that situation were for the best of the band, for the best record, the best songs, the best singing. When the motivation was not to produce mediocrity, it tended to raise the bar higher on ourselves. There were bound to be disputes. There were five guys in this band that could write and sing and play. When you get that much talent and that many egos, there's bound to be conflict. So I always took a great deal of that contentiousness with a large grain of salt. Instead of really digging in and fighting wholeheartedly for something, I'd back off and make concessions. You have to take the good with the bad, the heavenly with the hellish."

These days Felder remains friendly with other ex-Eagles Ber-

nie Leadon and Randy Meisner and says he still has fond feelings for later recruits Timothy B. Schmit and Joe Walsh. As far as
Don Henley and Glenn Frey are concerned, Felder says he has
no relationship with either. Although he won't comment about
their reaction to his book, it seems clear those Eagles had their
feathers ruffled.

"I've tried to reach out several times, but the only response I
get back is from their lawyers," he says sadly. "That's their choice,
not mine. I wish the guys could reach the point where we could
have some sort of empathetic understanding or amicable relationship, but unfortunately at this time, that doesn't exist."

13

....

Graham Nash

Past but Present

It would be difficult, if not impossible, to single out a musician that's accomplished more in his career than Graham Nash. Suffice it to say, he's helped paved the foundation of modern rock, and by extension, Americana, beginning with his initial efforts with the Hollies to his definition of the term "folk rock," as expressed through Crosby, Stills, Nash, and (sometimes) Young.

"Yes, I've been around quite a long time," he says simply, while acknowledging the implications.

Still, apart from a brief one-off reunion in the early eighties and mentions in 2013's autobiography *Wild Tales: A Rock & Roll Life*, Nash has rarely revisited his Hollies legacy. On the other hand, his devotion to CSN and CSNY has never wavered. He oversaw the release of *CSNY 1974*, a sprawling CD/DVD combination box set that documents the band's legendary victory tour encompassing stadiums and arenas throughout the United States and Europe. Notably, too, Nash has also produced career spanning retrospectives for his CSN band mates Crosby and Stills, an act of camaraderie that's impressive in its own right. And then there's his tours with that band, an ongoing venture that continued with little let-up, from their formative years in the late sixties to their live stage appearances in the present millennium. Nash's contributions to the band's canon—songs such as "Teach Your Children," "Our House," "Marrakesh Express," and "Just a Song before I Go," among many—makes him an intrinsic part of that conglomerate, even though it sometimes comes at the expense of maintaining his personal projects.

Even so, for all his time spent in retrospect, Nash remains very much a part of the present while also investing substantially in the future. His solo outings have continued unabated, albeit at wide intervals. His reputation as a renowned photographer has helped him broaden his reach into other artistic realms, while his company Nash Editions, specializing in printing, scanning, commercial photography, and reproduction, has made him a highly successful entrepreneur. And even though his double induction into the Rock and Roll Hall of Fame was made possible by his affiliation with his two keynote ensembles—the Hollies and Crosby, Stills and Nash—he can still pride himself on the fact that his efforts gained him entry not once, but twice . . . a formidable accomplishment for any journeyman musician.

"It all hit home when I was standing in front of the Queen of England and she asked me how the Hollies were," Nash recalls when asked about how fame has affected him. "I thought, oh my God. She was awarding me the OBE, the Order of the British Empire, and I was thinking about my mother and father and how proud they would be to find me standing in Buckingham Palace and talking to the Queen . . . I said, 'The fact is, Your Majesty, I've been gone from England for almost fifty years, and quite frankly, I'm very honored with this award you're giving me, but I didn't think anyone had noticed.' And she said, 'Well now you know' and shook my hand, and that was the end of that."

Nash's *This Path Tonight*, released in early 2016, marked his first new solo effort in nearly fourteen years. Its cover pictures him huddled against the cold, trudging through a snowy woods, his frosty white hair blending seamlessly with the frozen landscape.

In a sense, the album implies the fact that indeed Nash is looking back. That's especially evident, given song titles like "Golden Days," "Back Home," and the title track itself.

"Yep. That's it. I'm not getting any younger," he muses. "However, these songs are all very recent. They were written in just a month by me and my friend Shane Fontayne, who was the second electric guitarist in the Crosby, Stills and Nash band. We shared a bus going around the country, and we wrote twenty songs in a month. And then we recorded them in just eight days. My life is going through incredible changes, and my music reflects my life, as it's always done."

That said, how does he account for the long lapse between his individual efforts? "The truth is that when you have two or three other partners, you're always doing things with them," Nash says about the long lapse between his individual efforts. "I'll go on tour with David, la la la. . . . I like being a member of a band. I like being a solo artist of course, but I really enjoy being in a band."

Given his storied past, one would think that the past is always present. "I just get on with what songs I'm working on," Nash counters. "You know, it's like, 'Here I am. This is what I'm doing now.'"

Unfailingly polite ("I don't like to keep people waiting," he says, having called precisely on time for our phone interview) and still betraying a hint of his English accent even after forty-eight years of living in the States, Nash insists that laying on his laurels is not something he could ever consider.

"I'm not a relaxing guy," he insists. "The truth is, when you write songs, the first thing you want to do is play them for your partner, play them for your family, and then go out and play them for the public. That's what we do. We're communicators. We're writing songs about life that we feel people need to listen to."

So what becomes a legend the most? "I think, and I hope, that my music will resonate," Nash answers. "I think I've managed my life fairly well, and maybe touched a few hearts in the process. I think I'm an honest musician and I've done my job well."

14

....

Dwight Yoakam Goes Back to Bakersfield

One of today's most prominent procurers of the Bakersfield sound, Dwight Yoakam, not only helped bring Bakersfield back to prominence, but actually paralleled the trajectory taken by Americana. The early eighties, when Yoakam first appeared on the scene, were a transitory time for American music. After the deconstruction of rock brought on by punk and the seismic shift toward disco in the mid- to late seventies, the playing field was wide open for new and, as yet, unimagined insurrection. Not surprisingly, it didn't take long for it to take root, especially in the teeming nightlife of LA, where new and innovative outfits like X, Los Lobos, Green on Red, the Long Ryders, and the Blasters were finding fertile ground for their unlikely blend of insurgent attitude and ability to sow the strains of sixties sensibilities.

This early music was revolutionary for its time. It was as if the Ramones had suddenly developed a hankering for meeting Gram Parsons around a campfire, as if the Clash had found commonality with Merle Haggard, and the Rolling Stones and Willie Nelson had agreed to preside over it all. At the time it was called cowpunk, and given California's traditional free-spirited symbiosis, it was a natural transition that would eventually lead to a significant strain of Americana. The Byrds, Buffalo Springfield, Poco, and the Flying Burrito Brothers may have bridged the divide between rock and country a decade or two earlier, but the origins were yet to be fully vetted. Still, additional inroads were being made, and the new bands that shared their sounds with the denizens of Southern California—and eventually the rest of the world—were paving the course to a sound and style that would impact the American mainstream over the course of the next thirty years.

This was the landscape in which Yoakam found himself when he opted to explore the ever-shifting environs and opportunities of Los Angeles. Until that time, Yoakam's travels had taken him through the heartland, far afield of more daring circumstance. He was born October 23, 1956, in Pikeville, Kentucky—by all accounts a perfect place to foster the music he'd make later on—but soon moved with his family to Columbus, Ohio, the place where he would be raised. His parents named him Dwight David Yoakam, an all-American name at the time, but he insists it was not chosen in honor of America's current president, Dwight David Eisenhower. "My father's name was David," he recalls. "On the other hand, my uncle would always call me Ike."

Yoakam's first musical ambitions steered him toward rock and roll and making music with garage bands while he was still in high school, although he also expressed some interest in acting. The two pursuits would serve him well later on, all part of a career that would become striking for its diversity. A brief stint at Ohio State University ended when he decided to move to Nashville to seek his fortunes as a singer. At the time, Nashville was basking in the afterglow of the film *Urban Cowboy*, a significant step toward bringing country culture and the artists involved into the musical mainstream via hits that landed on top 40 radio. Nevertheless, Yoakam quickly decided that it wasn't the vibe he was looking for. In an instant, he changed course, headed to California, and suddenly found that he felt at home.

"In 1978, I went to the Whiskey and saw the Blasters and Robert Gordon, and that was all it took to inspire me to play the rock clubs," Yoakam remembers. "Over the next couple of years, when I moved to the San Fernando, I was playing the hillbilly clubs. When (producer/guitarist) Pete Anderson and I got together in 1980, I was playing this bar called the Corral in the Valley. It was this blue collar, classic 'Urban Cowboy' audience. I had the sense that something was about to shift in terms of the paradigm that was going on around this music. Country music—my version and the way I was doing it—allowed me to have all these great players on my early demos. David Mansfield played fiddle and mandolin, Terry McGee was playing guitar, and all these other great musicians were contributing."

With his self-released debut EP, *Guitars, Cadillacs, Etc. Etc.*, Yoakam established a touchstone by which all his future endeavors would be measured. It had a reckless, rock and roll attitude, a swagger and a stance that was decidedly in sync with the newly dubbed "cowpunk" style. Both critics and contemporaries weighed in quickly.

"I grew up listening to the country music my folks would play, but I didn't care for it," recalls Mic Harrison, leader of Knoxville, Tennessee's revered roots rock band the High Score. "In 1986, a couple of country records came out that changed my mind. One of which was *Guitars, Cadillacs, Etc, Etc*. It had great songs, great vocals, and Pete Anderson absolutely blew my mind on guitar. It made me realize I could love AC/DC and someone like Dwight Yoakam at the same time."

Even though Yoakam had struck a nerve, no one knew quite what to call his sound. Americana had yet to be recognized as a genre all its own. "When we finished the sessions, I said to the engineer, 'It's so hillbilly, they're going to call it rock and roll,'" Yoakam remarks. "A couple years later, in the fall of '84, I opened for Nick Lowe at the Hollywood Palace over on Vine Street, and I remember Bonnie Garner, who was running RCA at that time, saying 'I don't know, it's awfully rock and roll.' So my prediction came true. I was able to seize that moment. I said to Pete, 'I think I can book us into these other clubs.' When Pete and I began to play together in '82, he and I would get fired from the country nightclubs. I was kicking off my set with Bill Monroe's 'Hear Me Calling,' but they wanted to hear the current, contemporary hits like Kenny Rogers. I was a man without a country or a radio station."

Fortunately, he wasn't alone. With his preference for low-slung cowboy hats and embroidered denim jackets, people figured him for a contemporary country artist. He aligned himself with the sound of Buck Owens and Bakersfield, but his cool posturing set him apart, much like Elvis Presley had been when he was pegged as a country crooner before breaking from the ranks and establishing a singular style. Like Elvis, Yoakam bridged both worlds.

"I grew up listening to car radio," Yoakam says. "Car radio

exploded when I was growing up. *Guitars, Cadillacs, Etc. Etc.* didn't have any cowpunk on it. It was neo-hillbilly music. But we were in that scene, and it allowed us to present that traditional hillbilly music. They didn't call it 'country' because what we were doing was more raucous. When '83 rolled around, there was a scene that emerged with bands like Lone Justice, Los Lobos, and all these other bands that were made up of punk players who were attempting to interpret country music. We were able to walk in and say, 'Did you mean this?' and then I'd do my version of hillbilly music. There was a sense that we were on the precipice of the moment, and that the door would open and allow me to do this for a large audience. It made me realize I could have the success, which came later. It made me realize how and where it would lead."

The formal christening of Americana was still years away, but Yoakam was clearly on to something. Critics and audiences who had warmed to the Byrds, Burritos, and Bakersfield found something they could easily relate to without having to cede it entirely to the commerciality of country. Consequently, success came quickly. A remake of Johnny Horton's "Honky Tonk Man" became the first country music video to get played on the then fledgling MTV.

Yoakam's signing to Warner Bros. Records had proved to be the turning point in his career, and after returning to the label that helped launch him after his short stint with the more progressive New West Records, Yoakam couldn't contain his enthusiasm. "I am fortunate that I was signed to a label that allowed an artist to maintain their bearing in terms of intuition, no matter what," he remarks. "The first time I met [Warner Bros. president] Lenny Waronker was at the 1986 record release show for *Guitars, Cadillacs, Etc. Etc.*, after we rereleased it on Warners. He called me the next day, after he introduced me to John Fogerty and Emmylou Harris the night before, and said, 'You don't know me other than meeting me last night. I've listened to this record and I saw you in person last night. The only advice I have for you is that if anytime throughout your career, if anyone tells you to do something that's against your instincts or intuition, do not do it.' I think that's a pretty impressive thing for the president of a major record label to tell one of his artists."

Yoakam took that advice to heart, and it paid off quickly. After *Guitars, Cadillacs, Etc. Etc.* was re-released on the record label that subsequently signed him, a steady string of super success-ful LPs followed—*Hillbilly Dance, Buenas Noches from a Lonely Room*, and *If There Was a Way*—all of them released within the span of the next four years.

Yoakam's efforts immediately captivated both country and rock critics alike. As of this writing, he's garnered seventeen Grammy nods, all in the country music category. "Country radio embraced 'Honky Tonk Man,'" he recalls. "They embraced *Guitars, Cadillacs, Etc. Etc.* They embraced the next albums and gave us several hits, including 'Little Sister,' 'Old Ways,' and 'Streets of Bakers-field.' They didn't embrace me as an artist, but they embraced the tracks because they worked for their format, and it allowed them to embrace a disparate audience at times."

"We toured a lot, and Dwight has a strong image on stage," Anderson recounted in that *Dallas Observer* interview. "The girls like him. He was exciting, and the band was hot. It was the same band that played on the records. The band played like they were invested. Most Nashville bands hired folks to go on the road and try to replicate the records. That wasn't us. We were like Buck Owens and the Buckaroos or Merle Haggard and the Strangers. All of the players were great. And since there was not a lot of country music going on in Los Angeles, it wasn't like anyone was busy doing sessions. I made a decent living touring with Dwight, and I was proud of putting on such a strong show. We started off playing with bands like Los Lobos and the Blasters. Playing with bands in the rock scene helped us cement our audience. We were Americana before there was Americana. Warner Bros. got involved, and we got our records played on mainstream country radio, and we found an audience there as well."

With the sudden willingness of country radio to feature art-ists who were slightly askew of the traditional tears in their beers sentiments—newcomers Steve Earle, Lyle Lovett and k.d. lang chief among them, it was quickly becoming clear that a new roots-related movement was taking form. It had a lot to do with attitude and the willingness to revive a sound and style Dylan, Gram Parsons, Emmylou Harris, John Fogerty, and Chris Hillman had successfully done before, albeit in limited measures. Seizing

on those sentiments, Yoakam also managed to bolster his standing with rock audiences, touring with hardcore bands such as X
and Huker Du, covering songs by Queen, the Clash, the Grateful
Dead, and Cheap Trick, and collaborating with artists who might
have initially seemed far afield of his rootsy origins—Beck, Kid
Rock, ZZ Top, and Warren Zevon among them.

"We were doing what Americana became," Yoakam says. "I was
part of this other scene. *Guitars, Cadillacs Etc. Etc.* didn't have
cowpunk on it. It was neo-hillbilly music. But we were part of
that cowpunk scene, and it allowed us to integrate that traditional
hillbilly music. They didn't call it country, because what we were
doing was more raucous. I remember when I was playing a string
of dates in London, and Dave Edmunds and Nick Lowe came out
one night, they got it. They knew what Americana was before we
had a term for it, as evidenced by the music they were making
with Rockpile and Brinsley Schwarz. Then in 1991, I met Mick
Jagger when he came to my show at the Hamersmith Odeon. We
had a rock audience there that night. He brought along Ron Wood,
and again, those guys got it. They realized that it was something
that transcended a genre boundary."

"I'm really fortunate and lucky to be able to continue doing
this and have this much fun doing it," Yoakam responds. "But I
never thought about it too deeply. I might have had more of those
Grammys if I had. I've had success, but it's always relative. I did
This Time in 1993 and then I did *Gone* as the follow-up. I might
have been more successful if I did *This Time, Part Two*. The label
asked me why I named it that. We had four million in sales on
This Time, and while *Gone* was successful, it sold maybe only
half of what its predecessor did. I didn't want to do a remake of
the album that preceded. If I was more concerned, I could have
done that. But the last person I want to bore is me, and that's
a strength, but probably a weakness as well. I don't want to be
bored musically, and I don't think anybody wants to be! I want
to be inspired, especially when it comes to music."

Still, that initial embrace by country radio had its limitations.
Yoakam not only readily recounted the string of successes, but
also his failures. "I had a run of about eighteen top twenty commercial country radio singles," he continues. "The album *Buenas*

Buddy Miller (left) and the author, Cayamo Cruise, Norwegian Cruise Lines
Pearl, February 19, 2011

Scott Miller (left) and the author, Cayamo Cruise, Norwegian Cruise Lines
Pearl, February 19, 2011

Seth Avett (above) and Scott Abbott (left), Orlando Calling Festival, November 12, 2011

Elizabeth Cook, Orlando Calling Festival, November 13, 2011

Chris Isaak, Orlando Calling Festival, November 13, 2011

Dwight Yoakam, Orlando Calling Festival, November 13, 2011

Sara Watkins, Bonnaroo, June 8, 2012

Chris Thile with Punch Brothers, Bonnaroo, June 9, 2012

Jackson Browne, Newport Folk Festival, July 29, 2012

Sara Jarosz, Bonnaroo, June 10, 2012

Chris Isaak, Fillmore Theatre Miami, September 14, 2012

Brandi Carlile performing with John Prine on Cayamo Music Cruise,
February 14, 2011

Emmylou Harris, Telluride Bluegrass Festival, June 20, 2013

Chris Thile, Telluride Bluegrass Festival, June 20, 2013

Jeff Austin (Yonder Mountain String Band), Telluride Bluegrass Festival, June 22, 2013

Sam Bush, Telluride Bluegrass Festival, June 23, 2013

Bela Fleck at Telluride Bluegrass Festival, June 23, 2013

Steep Canyon Rangers, Grand Ole Opry, Nashville, September 19, 2014

Jason Isbell, Lauderdale Live, December 8, 2013

Jason Isbell and Amanda Shires, Lauderdale Live, December 8, 2013

Raul Malo and the Mavericks, Parker Playhouse, Fort Lauderdale, Florida, May 1, 2014

Robert Plant and Patty Griffin with Buddy Miller, Americana Music Awards, Ryman Auditorium, Nashville, September 17, 2014

Lyle Lovett, Sandy Beaches Cruise, Norwegian Cruise Lines *Pearl*, January 11, 2015

Kris Kristofferson, Folk Alliance International, Kansas City, Missouri,
February 15, 2017

Raul Malo (the Mavericks), Americana Music Awards, Ryman Auditorium, Nashville, September 16, 2015

Shawn Colvin and Steve Earle, City Winery, Nashville, September 20, 2016

Infamous Stringdusters, Cannery Ballroom, Nashville, September 22, 2016

Noches from a Lonely Room had two very quick number ones, but other things off that album didn't work for them. The greatest hits album didn't work at all for country radio in 1989. I had two more hits in '88, but nothing in '89 and nothing in 1990. Then *If There Was a Way* came out and we had four top five singles from that album. Then there was a bit of a lull until '93 when 'Ain't That Lonely Yet,' 'A Thousand Miles from Nowhere,' and 'Fast as You' all charted."

Nevertheless, as the nineties progressed, radio's infatuation with Yoakam began to taper off. With his cowboy hat, tight jeans, and penchant for posturing on stage, Yoakam was being seen by some by some as a novelty act. A string of albums in the late nineties and early years of the new millennium—*A Long Way Home*, *dwightyoakamacoustic.net*, *Tomorrow's Sounds Today*, *Population Me*, *Blame the Cain*, and a soundtrack, *South of Heaven*, *West of Hell*—were well received critically but failed to match the success of his earlier outings. Ironically, Americana, the very style he had helped pioneer, was now starting to emerge. Naturally Yoakam was quick to see its potential.

"The whole Americana environment and the whole subgenre that it is, is one of the healthiest things that could have happened to American roots music," he says in retrospect. "Any form of American music that has that singularity about it, that has to do with the larger scope of American culture, the admonition to go west, young man, go west is, in a bigger sense, at the heart of what this country is all about. It's that nineteenth century admonition that our forefathers paid heed to, and that this nation's early settlers were listening to even before that, when they left the comfort of where they were and went seeking what was over the next horizon. That's what Americana is at its best. It's a reckless abandonment and a wonderfully elegant musical journey. The term is rightly applied. It is what America can be. It's about imagination and ambition, and a gaze toward the unknown that takes you right to the edge of disaster at times, but ultimately leads to a brand new world of discovery. The thing about Americana that we have in common is our independence. The irony is what we have in common, as I heard Billy Joe Shaver say a couple of weeks ago, 'What we all have in common is our differences.' What a genius, brilliant kind of comment. That truly is Americana. Whether it's Old Crow Medicine Show or the Black Keys, they all kind of meander through the Americana camp. We all wander out through the wilderness and come back to camp occasionally."

Admittedly, Yoakam has always demonstrated a certain disparity in his style—that of a singing cowboy who somehow found acceptance with the punk rockers and insurgents before scoring points with the country crowds—but also a man who sometimes seems determined to keep the world guessing. That seems to define Yoakam as a man devoid of pretence once he's off stage. An artist determined to connect, regardless of his audience.

"I feel from time to time that I've changed," Yoakam admits, displaying his typically unbridled honesty. "Ignore the man behind the curtain!"

Whatever the reason, it took him awhile to regain prominence and re-establish himself as a contender. Appearing seven years after his last album of original material, *3 Pears* set the stage for a resurgence of sorts. Critics hailed the album as a return to form. It's steeped in the thick twang that's been at the heart of Yoakam's music since the start, but he's attempting more sounds and styles here than at any time since 1993's *This Time*. This is an album where one song in no way predicts what comes next. Yoakam has surprised by digging deeper into every one of his obsessions, creating a record that captures the careening, adventurous spirit of the sixties without ever feeling doggedly retro.

Barnes Newberry, who hosts the popular Americana program *My Back Pages* on mvyradio.com, further expounds on the difficulty of trying to peg Yoakam to any particular style. "Is he country, honky-tonk, or rock? Dwight Yoakam defies specific categorization. In his early days he called his music 'hillbilly,' but he has been almost chameleon-like in that he can cross genres with ease on his many albums and in live concerts. I think a loose tag, such as neo-traditionalist, with a foot in Bakersfield (country) as opposed to Nashville (country) and another in rock, might better describe what he is able to do. His 2012 album *3 Pears* successfully straddles these genres and simultaneously entered the country, rock, and Americana charts. The man has also received multiple Grammys. Well-deserved too."

"If that's the case, it's gratifying," Yoakam responds. "I just keep looking at what I loved to begin with the music. I once wrote a song called 'I Want to Love Again' and it really wasn't about romance. It was about music. It said, 'I want to love again, feel young again, the way I did when it was true.' It wasn't about the business of it. It was about the excitement of it, and the inspiration of it."

For all the retro posturing, however, it was Beck's presence (who helped produce a pair of the album's tracks) that turned the most heads. Yoakam was back, and while his allegiance to classic form was still unwavering, his desire to explore the reinvention that's so crucial to the changing face of the new Americana was propelled forward as well. To Yoakam, it's a stirring and grandiose concept, one that has to do with far more than the music.

"You can have someone like Robert Plant step up and say, 'I've got that in my genes. It's from the Irish, Scottish, Welsh folk traditions,'" Yoakam muses. "There's a great book called *The United States of Appalachia* that discusses how the culture evolution of the United States is pretty much tied in the micro and the macro version of that mountain chain, with the great American ballet, 'Appalachian Spring,' being a touchstone of that spot. Americana is that. It was those people, who against the king's command, came across the ocean, crossed that mountain range, and forged off into the Appalachian mountain chain and said there's land we're going to settle and create our own life and our own music and make our own music. And that's what Americana music is. It's its own music. From Bessie Smith and Nina Simone to the Stanley Brothers who were hard proponents of the Appalachian music and its cultures. Americana is Route 66. It's that road that took us way out west."

"I don't choose the songs," Yoakam insists. "They choose me. That's what it felt like with this record. They kind of call on me. All I know is, knock wood, I need to be grateful. And really, really appreciative to have the opportunity to do the music I want to make."

While the definition of Americana may shift due pending on circumstance, one thing is clear. Yoakam's ability to push at the parameters, to reinterpret the sound of classic country and make it palatable for a rock and roll audience, has contributed to both its growth and its broader definition. Americana might still have prospered if Yoakam never came along, but it's doubtful that it would have embraced such a broad reach. Yoakam remains fully aware of his contribution to the process, but he also looks at a bigger picture.

"The thing about Americana is our common quest for independence," he muses. "The irony is, as Billy Joe Shaver said a couple of weeks ago, 'What we all have in common is our differences.' What a genius, brilliant kind of comment. That truly is Americana. Whether it's Old Crow Medicine Show or the Black Keys, they all kind of meander through the Americana camp. We all wander out through the wilderness and come back to camp occasionally."

Yoakam has reason to be grateful, not only for the fact that he was welcomed back to the camp, but that he was allowed to find his own way in and out. He clearly finds it gratifying.

No matter who it was—my manager, my record company, my fans—they always left me to my own devices, and I had fun doing it. That's all I can ask for."

15

. . . .

Holly Williams

Heir to a Legend

Hank Williams, the greatest songwriter in history, died way too young, the victim of his own excess at the age of twenty-nine. He never had the opportunity to reap the rewards and feel the appreciation of every generation of singers and songwriters that followed in his footsteps. Indeed, if Americana had a godfather, his name would be Hank.

Consequently, in order to retrace that firsthand connection, we turn to those he sired—including his granddaughter, Holly Williams.

Unfortunately, on the day we spoke, Williams was not feeling well. "Would you mind if we postpone our chat?" she asks apologetically, barely able to restrain a coughing fit that's clearly gotten the best of her. "No problem," we reply. Knowing her voice is essential to her stock and trade, sympathy is assured.

Still, it's definitely rare to find Williams to be less than her best. Given her family pedigree—her grandfather, the legendary Hank Williams, and father, Hank Williams Jr., established a country music dynasty, while her brother, cowpunk upstart Hank III, has broken barriers of his own—she could have easily coasted along while reaping the benefits of hereditary. "I never think about it as much," she demurs once we reconvene. "I love most of the music my father and grandfather made. I'm super proud to be in the family."

However, as her album *The Highway* suggests, she's always

been adept at plotting her own path, staking her name and reputation on individual achievement. After racking up three albums, achieving two major label affiliations, owning and operating a renowned high-end Nashville boutique called H. Aubrey, and maintaining a food and lifestyle blog, www.theafternoonoff.com, it's apparent Williams is not only a whiz when it comes to multitasking, but an exceptionally capable entrepreneur as well.

"I try to balance it all, especially with the music," Williams insists. "At the end of the day, my touring and my music life reign over everything. My husband has been complaining lately—rightfully so—that I seem to work from the time I wake up until the time I go to bed."

In recent years, Williams has been more active than ever. Aside from preparing a new album, contributing to 2011's *The Lost Notebooks of Hank Williams* (a compilation of her grandfather's unfinished material produced by Bob Dylan), and participating in *Let 'Em In*, a tribute to Linda McCartney, she also oversees her own label, Georgiana Records. "I like to call it 'exciting stress,'" she says of the latter. "Sometimes I think I'm going to have a crying breakdown. I find all these little things that I never thought about before—photo shoots, album artwork, release dates—but in the bigger picture, I'm glad to have control. I'm so much more involved on a day-to-day basis than I was with a major label because there isn't that disconnect. I love that. It feels like such a natural thing."

Much like her forebears, Williams's trajectory hasn't been easy. In March 2006, following the release of her first album, 2004's *The Ones We Never Knew*, she was involved in a near-fatal car crash that severely injured her arm and forced her sister to undergo a series of twenty-nine surgeries. The follow-up, *Here With Me*, wasn't released until June 2009, but it plunged her into an extensive period of touring and television appearances to promote the new effort.

"After the accident, I didn't really know if I'd ever be able to go out on the road again or whether I'd even be able play. But after having that kind of near death experience, it makes you want to live every day to the fullest. It sounds like a cliché but it's so true. So I took a break for a while, got married (to fellow musician and longtime collaborator Chris Coleman), spent time at the store, and reassessed. I really thought I'd adapt to the family mode, but the highway came calling again. I can never get away from that live performance because I love telling stories through my music and playing new songs for people. Music will always be first for me."

Of course, given her famous surname, the need to make music is practically mandatory. "If anything, it's kind of a challenge," she says of her legacy. "There will always be people who say, 'Oh, of course, you're a singer. Yawn.' With the first record, I got comments like, 'She's just another famous person's daughter.' So you just have to keep proving yourself over and over, letting people know that this is in my blood, this is real. I'm not just doing this because my dad and grandfather did it . . . I'm different. I'm following this kind of folk, Emmylou Harris kind of career path. I'm not wearing a cowboy hat and going to country radio. People might compare me to my grandfather, but no one can really live up to that."

Nevertheless, Williams makes it clear she's perfectly content making her own music and unwilling to dwell in the shadow of her father and grandfather. "It's funny—I've had two albums, I've been touring forever, I've had critical acclaim, but yet I feel like this is my first album in a way. I'm reintroducing myself and telling people that it's real this time. I'm not going to take another four-year hiatus. I have part of the next record written already. This is number one for me . . . being on the road and playing songs. It's about letting people know I'm back. I'm a travelling singer-songwriter, and the music will keep coming."

16

·····························

Sam Bush

From Bluegrass to Nu-Grass, and Stopping in Nashville in Between

Of all the strains of Americana, none attracts as much of a populist following as that permeation of bluegrass and contemporary songwriting popularly known as nu-grass. And no one had as much a hand in developing that tack as the New Grass Revival, and Sam Bush in particular.

He's variously known as the King of Telluride, a sideman to the stars and one of the most versatile and prolific musicians plying his skills today. But to those who have seen him in concert, he's known mainly as an amiable and entertaining showman, one whose ever-present smile, obvious enthusiasm, and good natured personality have made him a crowd favorite in whatever venue he appears.

Variously accomplished as a singer, songwriter, mandolin player, fiddler, and band leader, Bush is remarkably versatile, but the thing that impresses the most, especially in conversation, is that he's as amiable offstage as he is on. Despite a career that dates back more than forty-five years, he clearly remains as enthused as ever, eager to embrace his next project and/or collaboration with the same verve and commitment he's shown since the beginning. From early outfits like the Bluegrass Alliance, which he joined when he was only a teen, through to his trendsetting, attitude-changing efforts with the New Grass Revival, and then onto his nearly thirty-year-long solo career, Bush's energy and exhilaration have never faltered.

Consequently, when I had the opportunity to chat with Mr. Bush just prior to an appearance at the Rockygrass Festival, it was all too easy to get him to open up on a variety of subjects, from his surprise collaboration with Del McCoury to his thoughts about a possible reunion with the New Grass Revival and reflections on the realities of Nashville (the show as well as the city), radio, and the state of contemporary country.

One of the many things that's so consistent about a Sam Bush performance is that you always look like you're having such a great time. That smile never seems to leave your face.

Well, it is fun, and I've said this before . . . what we do is travel for a living. We're paid to travel. Our reward is playing music. Playing a two-hour set is a joyful experience, and of course, getting to play with the guys I get to play with all the time in the Sam Bush Band . . . well, they're wonderful, and I couldn't ask for better players and better people to play with. We're having a good time. It's reached the point where you don't have to even say anything and we can crack up because we're instinctively sharing the same joke. When everything's going right, as you stand there and play, the music overtakes you. It's a joyful thing. I've always been lucky in the fact that if I wasn't feeling good, or something wasn't going well business-wise or whatever, once I start playing, I'm fine.

That's a wonderful way to earn your livelihood.

I feel fortunate.

So what's was it like playing with Del McCoury?

In playing with Del, it's a guitar and mandolin and that's it. So I have to take all the solos. You know me . . . I love to play rhythm even more than I love to play lead, and rhythm playing is not quite as prevalent with Del, even though with Del, what we do is sort of like Monroe Brothers kind of music, singing duets. It is as much of a challenge to me as anything I've ever done because Del is such a force the way he plays rhythm on guitar. It's like a big hammer coming down. It's a thrill, and I'm thrilled to call Del my friend. It's a true joy; it really is.

So we have to ask . . . any chance of recording again with New Grass Revival? You have had opportunity to reunite with the various members onstage at Telluride in particular.

It's been discussed. But honestly, it's just really hard to schedule anything when it's not what you do for a living. In other words, we're all busy in other areas. John (Cowan) is playing with the Doobie Brothers. Bela (Fleck) plays in so many different music configurations, it's amazing. And of course, I have my own band. That's what I want to keep afloat as long as possible . . . just keep the band going. I love playing with this band. I wouldn't say we'll never do it, but it's just hard to get around the time-consuming part of it. We were always very meticulous about rehearsing and practicing, and we always wanted to hit the studio fully prepared because we couldn't afford to experiment. You have to hit it with a plan, so I don't know how we could ever get enough time to actually get it done. The last album we made, *Friday Night in America*, we probably rehearsed four to six months of working on songs. Sometimes we had a song worked up and we would scrap it and decide it wasn't right. So it's a long process. It's hard enough just to agree with myself. [*laughs*]

And yet, it seems like it would be deceptively easy due to the fact that you're constantly jamming with those same individuals.

A jam session is one thing. [*laughs*] I think all the members of the Revival believe, when we listen to our old records, that we did our best and accomplished our goal. I don't think we ever made a stinker. In fact, I think the last one we made was the best one, so we feel pretty good about that, looking back on it.

Considering your vast catalog and all you've done both solo and in the company of others, does it become a challenge not to repeat yourself?

Yeah, you are aware of that. And it's not lost on me that when I'm doing interviews and a new project is about to come out, and I'm talking to people and discussing the new record that's about to come out, one of the first questions that I'm asked is, "What's different about this record?" It's interesting. I'm a huge fan of Little Feat and have gotten to play with them over the years. So when Little Feat put out a new record, I didn't want it to sound like the last one, but I sure wanted it to sound like Little Feat and what I love about the band. I think we're all aware of the fact that when people like the way you play and sing, not that much is going to change. It's still you playing and singing. But you do try to make for a little distant twist. My recent album, *Circles Around Me*, had parts of it that were some of the most bluegrass-style songs I've ever recorded. I didn't use any electric instruments except for electric bass on a few songs, and so that one was a conscious attempt to keep it acoustic. In the past, I've always mixed acoustic and electric sounds. And tried different instruments. On my next one, there are songs that sound like out and out country tunes to me. I'll just play the twin fiddles, sing the song, and get a steel guitar player and a piano player. The guys in my band can play any kind of music, so if we want to do it that way, we might do a couple of songs that way. There might be a little variety in the styles. It certainly won't be as much bluegrass.

Again, with all you've accomplished over your career, do you feel like you have set such a high bar that you are always obliged to achieve? Do you ever find it intimidating?

Yeah. I think that anyone who continues to record is aware of that. Do I like this as well as the last project? Have I succeeded in this way? But really, I think that's more self-driven than the perception of what [feedback might come] from other people. You want to be able to look at it and ask, "Have we progressed since the last one?" As a singer and player, that's always my goal. Whether it's recording or live, I have to ask myself, "Am I getting better? Am I continuing to improve?" which I hope is always the case. Really, I've never been satisfied with my own singing and playing, so if I do get there, I'll let you know.

Maybe someone should nominate you for an Emmy for Best Supporting Actor on *Nashville*. We saw you pop up on stage in one particular episode as part of the band at the Bluebird.

[*Laughs*] All of us in Nashville watch that show to see who got work that week. [*laughs*] That's the great thing about it. They're using Nashville musicians, and I have gotten work behind the scenes cutting songs. Just this month I was working on some songs for the new season. And sometimes that leads to you being on camera looking like you're playing, and sometimes it doesn't. It's all a matter of scheduling. I've been out of town for a couple of weeks, so if they're calling to see if I'll go on camera to look like I'm playing, I can't right now.

It must be a lot of fun.

It's just an interesting process, but the great thing is, it's employing people in Nashville. . . . I mean hundreds of people, not just the people you see on camera, but also set builders, the sound man, the lighting people, hair, makeup. . . . I mean, it's amazing. Especially when you see a scene like the famous Bluebird in Nashville . . . well. We're not really in the Bluebird. They meticulously rebuilt it on a sound stage. It's right down to every promo picture on the walls. It's amazing. Those shots of someone standing in the Bluebird and playing . . . well, that's a twelve hour day, and so you stand around on that set for a few hours and you forget you're not in the real Bluebird. The great part is that all the actors are really doing their own singing.

The songs are good!

I've wondered if those aren't some of the best songs I've heard come out of Nashville on that very TV show. I just played on a song the other day that John Randle, the guitar player from New Grass Revival, wrote. I thought it was a great song, and he said, "Yeah, nobody wanted it for country radio." And so somewhere somebody knew about the song and it tied in with the storyline. But he got it on the show. I'm sure some songs are written spe-

cifically for the show. You've got a storyline, so it gives you something to say, and it's not just about tight-fitting jeans.

**TV can be a great outlet. Radio certainly isn't so reliable
anymore.**

Yeah, and I think it's always been that way. I think that some of
the great jazz players in the sixties must have been wondering,
"What the hell is all this stuff on the radio, and why is that good
music?" There's always been that division in music, where you
have people saying, "I can't believe people listen to that." I've
had people tell me, "Well, you're not playing music like Taylor
Swift." Well, Taylor Swift isn't playing for us. She's playing for a
generation of really young people and they all relate to the subject matter, and the type of music she's doing, and she writes it
all herself, and I think she's damn good. It doesn't appeal to me,
but she's not writing it to sell to me. She has her audience, and it
isn't at all like the one that people like me play for.

17

Kinky Friedman

An Irascible Icon Speaks Out

Kinky Friedman is many things—a singer, a songwriter, an author, a satirist, and even a politician. But he's also irascible and, when he wants to be—which seems more often than not—politically incorrect and pointedly critical of the absurdities around him. Often mislabeled as a misogynist, his most famous songs—"Ride 'Em Jewboy," "They Don't Make Jews Like Jesus Anymore," and "Get Your Biscuits in the Oven and Your Buns in Bed"—have thwarted most attempts to take him and his band the Texas Jewboys seriously, even though his pioneering role in creating country's crossover to rock and roll made him one of the first authentic architects of modern Americana. His friendship with Willie Nelson and Bob Dylan is legendary, and if any individual can compete with their iconic stature, suffice it to say Kinky himself can.

It took Kinky an incredibly long time to release an album in the new millennium—more than three decades, in fact—which made the appearance of his most recent effort, *The Loneliest Man I Ever Met*, a significant milestone of sorts. However, like most things in Friedman's life, it's accompanied by no small degree of irony. Although he made his name by writing songs, the new album found him doing covers—or, as he likes to say, "interpretations . . . of material penned by Dylan, Nelson, Merle Haggard, Warren Zevon, and other notable songsmiths. The arrangements are bare-boned, sung with straight sentiment and even real reverence as well."

Although our interview was supposedly going to focus on the new album, suffice it to say that holding Kinky Friedman to a single subject is practically impossible. Consequently, our conversation frequently veered off into different tangents, mostly having to do with politics and the cynicism of society in general. Kinky kept us laughing, but beneath the sarcasm lurked a man of tremendous wit, wisdom, and conviction.

Your new album is your first new release in thirty-two years. But you haven't exactly been idle, have you? You've spent a great deal of time in politics. And you attracted a decent following as well.

In 2006 my independent race for governor found us winning everywhere but Texas. We had issues that were way ahead of the curve. You can chart them. Supporting gay marriage. I was the only candidate statewide that was supporting gay marriage at a time when Hilary and Obama were decidedly against it. So what the hell.

So how close did you come to winning?

We got 13 percent of the best of Texas. That represented about 600,000 votes.

That put you on the map, however.

Well, yeah. The late Ray Price told me it was a really mistaken thing to do because Jesus would have lost if he had run as an independent against Rick Perry.

On the other hand, Rick Perry just dropped out of the race for the Republican nomination for president for the second time.

He's not a bad guy. He's just been in politics for too long, He was groomed right out of college. Not that I ever worked much. I bummed around, but I was in the peace corps and did some other things. Politics is really the only deal where the more experience you have, the worse you get. That's what America is say-ing. That's why it was going for such polar opposites as Bernie Sanders and Donald Trump.

So who were you leaning toward in 2016?

Bernie Sanders and Donald Trump. One of them. I'm not sure which one I was leaning toward. The two of them would have made a good ticket. They're not corrupt at least. I talked to Jamie Johnson about running on the same ticket. I would run for pres-ident, and he agreed to run for vice president, and it would be the Kinky Johnson ticket.

But when you were running for governor, was it not a seri-ous campaign on your part? It wasn't a joke. Did you ever get the feeling that your name might have been some kind of hindrance?

Well, not in Texas. But if I didn't run as Kinky Friedman, I would have won. It was all garbled up. They really kill ya. Your name isn't even on the same page as the ballot. It's like the Crips and the Bloods. I couldn't believe it. I thought they'd have all the names on the same page. But no. You have to turn a page and then another page until you finally get to the independents, if you haven't already voted a straight ticket. And then all the chick-ens come home to roost, that's all. There was one point where we were winning. We were in the high twenties. The Democrats are very good at demonizing, and the Republicans are very good at having a lot of money and being corrupt. Not that the Democrats aren't corrupt too. One is no better than the other. It's the same guy combing his hair in the mirror.

Still, for all the great music you've made and your forthright stand on the issues, wasn't the name Kinky Friedman and the Texas Jewboys always perceived as some kind of joke?

Yeah, sure. It was a blessing and a curse. No doubt about it. My college roommate gave it to me. But it didn't stop Nelson Mandela from appreciating me. Nelson Mandela had some of my tapes in the cell with him, and he could have listened to "Get Your Biscuits in the Oven and Your Buns in the Bed." But the song he'd listen to all night was "Ride 'Em, Jewboy." That's remarkable. Do you know who his favorite singer was?

No, I don't.

The same guy who turned me on to this Mandela thing, who I met in South Africa, was Tokyo Seuchwhale. Tokyo was Mandela's right-hand man and was in the cell right next to Mandela for the duration, so he could hear what songs Mandela was playing. He says for me not to get a swelled head about this because I was not Mandela's favorite singer. Maybe I was fifth or sixth down the list. He said his favorite was Dolly Parton.

You must have admired Mandela for that reason alone.

That's the kind of candidate that doesn't come along very often. Do you see any little Mandelas rising up?

There doesn't seem to be any JFKs or Roosevelts rising up, either.

Or Abe Lincolns. In Europe you don't see any Churchills, either. That Mark Twain quote is exactly right. "History does not repeat itself but sometimes it rhymes."

So you like Donald Trump?

I think what he's doing by not apologizing for anything is admirable. Our shit's really fucked up, as the title of the Warren Zevon song on my album explains. It's an apt description of the world today, and I don't know that it's fixable. I don't normally admire and respect people who put their names all over the wings of children's hospitals like Trump's does. I prefer Mr. Anonymous. Take the office of president; it ought to be a purely inspirational job. It ought to be occupied by those who do what Harry Truman did, which was to make some really significant big-time calls. Imagine what Obama would do with a Hiroshima situation. He probably wouldn't have done it. Once he got through talking to his lawyers, he'd probably back down. So imagine where we'd be today. . . . We'd have lost millions of Americans and Japanese because there would have been a land war in Japan. So that was the choice. What I said after I lost the governor's race was that the crowd always picks Barabbas. It's really fucking true. They always do the same thing over and over. They say, "Free Barabbas. Not Jesus." That's why Rick Perry was the longest-serving governor in Texas history, and why you have Jerry Brown in California, and why Schwarzenegger was such a good candidate as well. It's because people like that always get elected. To slip a Churchill or a Lincoln in there is almost impossible. The people won't let it happen, and I'm a man of the people.

Were you friendly with Rick Perry or George Bush when he was governor of Texas?

George Bush and I were pals, mostly through his wife Laura, who was a secret Democrat . . . back when the Democrats were good. She's really got it. Of course, she's a librarian. The kind of person Fidel Castro has been arresting for the past forty years. But W. and Bill Clinton are my two guys. In fact, I'm the only guy who's slept under two presidents at the White House.

Umm. You better explain that.

I was an overnight guest during both their administrations.

Wow!

I was close to be both of them. Again, like Churchill said, "History, with its flickering lamp, stumbles down the trail to the past." So we don't get George W. right yet. He's a very decent man. And he got really screwed because, like me, he had a really strong disdain for television. And so he would come across very stiff. In truth, he was very witty and funny. I'm the kind of guy who hangs

around with Don Imus. Bill Clinton who is very witty and spontaneous and leads from the heart—which sometimes gets him
in trouble—is a natural. W., when he's off the air, is very funny
and very quick. And he doesn't come off like he does on TV. And
of course the Democrats spent all their financial capital demonizing him. They're horrible. Mention Benghazi to any Democrat
and they'll go, "You're a bigot! You're a racist!" Benghazi revealed
some things to us about our wonderful Hilary. She turned out to
be an empty pants suit.

**You seem to be especially popular with overseas audi-
ences. Why do you think that is?**

They loosen you up a little bit, and you realize you're represent-
ing something overall. These people are looking to America and
they're looking to Texas . . .

It's a myth they're looking to.

Yeah, there's all that going for it. And those young German audiences that have made me the new David Hasslehoff are remarkable. You look around the room and I'm the oldest person there.
I can't tell you how impressed I am with these young people.
They've read my books, many of them in German, and I'll be out
there signing stuff after the show—I'll sign anything, except bad
legislation. I signed a man's scrotum in Scotland once. They're a
great audience because they're so emotional. They love Native
Americans. They love Gram Parsons. They love Tom Waits. They
love Iggy Pop. They love Van Dyke Parks, and they love Shel
Silverstein and Warren Zevon too. They love the right people.
They're singing along on songs like "Old Man Lucas Had a Lot
of Mucus Coming Out of His Nose," which I wrote when I was
eleven, nearly sixty years ago. So you ask these Germans where
they learned that, and they say, "My parents taught it to me." And
that's true all over Australia and Canada too. Americans are still
going to Celine Dion concerts because we just don't care. I was
arguing with Willie about this in Nashville last year. I was talking about how Nashville just doesn't have it anymore. Its win-

dow is closed. It's a corporate town. Everything's coming out with click tracks. Every song is written by a goddamn committee, and it all sounds like background music for a frat party. And Willie says, "Well, you're being too harsh. It's still the place, it's still the dream where a kid in a pickup truck with a guitar and a suitcase full of songs still goes." That's how Willie sees it. I have nothing against Toby Keith. I never met him. I have nothing against Garth Brooks, who I refer to as the Empty Hank. . . . He truly is. They're all nice guys, but each of them has made more money than Willie Nelson or Hank Williams or Bob Dylan or Waylon Jennings or Kris Kristofferson or Merle Haggard ever made put together.

Bob Dylan's made a lot of money.

He's made a lot of money, but please—nothing like what Toby Keith or Garth have made. Toby Keith is coming up on a billion dollars. The only guy that can touch that is Barry Manilow. And Barry Manilow writes songs that make you feel good for a short period of time. These guys I admire write songs that might stay with you a lifetime, and they might make you think, and that's the purpose of this record I've made, *The Loneliest Man I Ever Met*, which wasn't recorded in Nashville by the way . . .

Good segue!

Yes it is! I've become rather facile at this. But I'm a struggling songwriter. I've always been one and I hope I always will be one.

You represent yourself well, however.

Unfortunately, it's quite an index of an empty life. I'll tell ya, it's a privilege to get this many gigs easily after all this time and not really having a hit . . . and to make it a financial pleasure to go out and do this. It's a joy. It's absolutely great. A pleasure. It really is.

Your legend becomes you, sir.

Well, thank you very much. I don't want to make this all about quoting Willie, but I love that quote of his: "If you fail at something long enough, you become a legend."

But how does that apply to you? You haven't failed. You've established a singular identity in an iconic sort of way.

Maybe so, but I prefer to be with that little fraternity of men that thought they were failures. It's incredible to believe that, but I know it's true. I've read about Lennon. He always thought McCartney was the genius, which was totally not correct. McCartney was the lightweight who did write a couple of great songs, but so did a lot of other people. Churchill thought he was a failure too. He architected the whole war, and then they pulled the rug out from under him. The crowd picked Barabbas.

You're right, Kinky.

I'm always right. I was living with Miss Texas 1987, and I let her slip through my fingers. I feel that the ones you let slip through your fingers are the only ones you ever keep.

So you miss Miss Texas?

Yeah, I miss Miss Texas.

I sure hope we don't miss you and have to wait another thirty-two years before a new record arrives.

No, that won't happen. I'd much rather be a musician than a politician, I guarantee ya.

No more runs for us then? Politics is behind you?

I hope so. It's an addiction, like when I walk into a restaurant in Austin and there's applause all round. You do miss that after awhile. [*chuckles*] Now they just say, "Hey Kinky, how are ya doin'?"

18

....

Guy Clark's Melancholy Musings

For a man whose music was so expressive and whose words convey such intimate feelings of vulnerability and despair, the late Guy Clark seemed remarkably reserved. Not that he wasn't willing to share; far from it, in fact. It's just that he preferred to come quickly to the point, answering questions directly in a no-nonsense matter that often made the responses almost seem a given. Or perhaps it's the fact that after nearly two dozen albums recorded over a career spanning nearly four decades, his songs speak for themselves.

It's no wonder, really. As the man responsible for such classics as "Desperados Waiting for a Train," "LA Freeway," and countless more, he saw his songs recorded by a veritable who's who of Americana elite—Johnny Cash, Emmylou Harris, Brad Paisley, Rodney Crowell, Ricky Skaggs, Vince Gill, John Denver, and Kenny Chesney among them. He also mentored any number of up and coming artists, people like Steve Earle and his pal Townes Van Zandt, artists whose no-nonsense style made their debt to Clark all too obvious.

Over the course of a phone conversation from his home in Nashville, Clark was both amiable and unassuming, speaking on a variety of subjects that spanned his entire career, from humble beginnings through his last new album—his first in four years—the austere but revealing *My Favorite Picture of You*. Speaking slowly, with prolonged pauses between thoughts and an unmistakable rasp, he sounded like a true survivor, a man who, at age seventy-two, had come to grips with his mortality while still struggling to cope with his recent loss to cancer of his beloved wife of forty years and writing partner, Susanna. Though hardly revelatory, the discussion was revealing nonetheless.

Who were some of your influences early on?

I started playing guitar in '58 or something like that. I was into traditional folk music. There was Woody Guthrie and Pete Seeger. Bob Dylan. He was making his name. Living in Houston, you could go see Lightning Hopkins or Mance Lipscomb just about any night you wanted to. So there was a songwriter right there, ya know? Mance wasn't doing other people's blues. He was doing his own. I didn't want to be a white boy singing the blues, but those guys were songwriters. And that's what I gleaned from them . . . just write your own songs. I mean, that's what they were doing.

When did you know that you could do this for a living? Because here you were, writing songs for other people. . . . Was there a definitive moment when you knew you wouldn't have to take a day job?

I decided, I guess, when I was about thirty to move out to LA, and I just started doing it. Doing whatever it took. And I wound up with a publishing deal out there, and then I moved to Nashville and proceeded on—whatever I could do to further that approach to music.

Many people credit you with being among the forerunners of the so-called outlaw country genre. Did you find it tough going in Nashville due to the route you were taking?

Of course I did. I was never a hit songwriter in country music in that sense. I was trying to do it my way, whatever it took. I don't know about being an outlaw. . . .

That's the standard cliché.

I know. I just did what I could until I was able to do what I wanted.

What made you decide to transition in the mid seventies into being a performer and singing your own songs?

I had always been a performer. I was always planning on that. I wrote songs for other people, and they were obviously out there to be done, but I had no reason to be writing songs unless I was going to play them for the folks, and no reason to go play them for the folks unless I had new songs. That was always in the mix to do that. Nobody could do those songs like I could.

It would seem your songs are inspired by real-life circumstance that you've actually experienced.

Yeah. They are. If I didn't see it happen, I know somebody that did. [*chuckles*]

That's a contrast from some songwriters that divorce themselves from their material and create a storyline from their imagination.

Well, I do that sometimes. Not so much on this record. I mean, it's not brain surgery. They're just songs.

Ah, you're being modest. You're such a great storyteller. Have you ever thought about writing a book?

That's a whole other discipline. It takes years and years to where you can do that. You don't just write a book because you can.

It was four years between the release of your last album, *Songs and Stories*, and this new one, *My Favorite Picture of You*. Were you writing the entire time?

Yes. Sure.

How did you narrow down the material that you eventually decided to include?

Well, they weren't all good. [*chuckles*]

Knowing your track record, that's hard to believe.

Well, that's true. When I make a record, I just pick the ten or eleven best songs I've got, and that's when I make a record.

Do you ever go back and tap into some songs that might not have made the cut the first time around.?

No, not really. I pretty much made that decision as they came up. I did all the good ones. [*chuckles*]

But have you ever thought of putting out an album of rarities, maybe as part of an anthology?

Not really. If I've got one good enough to record, I'm going to do it. It goes to the top of the list.

You've also been credited with nurturing so many great singer-songwriters who have come along in your wake.

Well, that's true. Whenever I hear someone who I think is really good, I make sure they get heard. They should be heard.

What's remarkable is that you were able to recognize these gifted individuals, like Townes and Steve Earle. They became legendary in their own right, and you were the one that helped them on their way.

Yeah. Steve Earle for sure. But Townes, he had it going on, on his own, ya know? [*coughs*] Sorry.

But how is it you're able to spot this talent and know it's worth recognizing?

Because I like it. [*chuckles*] I like what it sounds like. I think they're doing good work.

You have an amazing track record.

Well . . . I have really good taste. [*chuckles*]

At the same time, the list of people who have recorded your songs is also quite impressive. Johnny Cash, Emmylou Harris, Rodney Crowell . . . and yet given that your songs are so personal, how do you like those other versions when you hear them?

I'm happy about it. I'm flattered that someone else would do one of my songs. I don't always particularly care for their version of it—it's not always the way I would do it—but for the most part, that's what I set out to do, to be a songwriter and have other people do the songs.

When you write a song, are you ever thinking of how another person would do it?

No, I'm thinking of me doing it, but if someone else wants to do it, that's just wonderful.

If they happen to pick up on it . . .

Yeah, right.

There's that common thread that runs through your music, that raw vulnerability, that poignancy. When you're writing and recording these songs, are you in a state of mind where your sensitivity is given free reign?

Well, I'm just like that sometimes.

Maybe when you're writing, it saves a trip to the psychiatrist's office, we're guessing.

That's what I'm getting out of it. [*chuckles*]

So are you going to tour behind this new album?

I have a few health problems right now. I've had both knees replaced, and I'm trying to get through rehab and get my body in shape to do that. It's hard to do that. It's hard work, you know? I've got to get a handle on getting my legs to work and remember some songs and remember how to play the guitar. I'm just starting from scratch, ya know?

But you build guitars, don't you?

Yeah I do.

So it seems it would be an easy thing, if you build guitars, to know how to play them.

[*Chuckles*] I don't know if it's easy.

What do you think of your tribute album, *This One's for Him*, **that came out a couple of years ago? Did you have any part in the making of that album? Any oversight?**

No. I knew it was being made, but I purposely stayed out of it. I didn't want to color it in any way. The other artists that were covering those songs didn't need my help, or they wouldn't have been asked to do it. The production was in good hands with Tamara Saviano and Shawn Camp, and they did a marvelous job. It was just better if I stayed out of it.

Were you pleased with the results?

Oh sure, man. It was great. It's great to have other people do those songs.

Speaking of Shawn Camp . . . he's been a steady collaborator with you for some time now. When did you first start working with him?

Oh God, I can't even remember. It must be fifteen or twenty years ago. He is a wonderful player. Very talented guy all round, Songwriter, musician . . . he's one of my favorite people.

How do the two of you collaborate, particularly as far as the songs are concerned? Does one person have a germ of an idea and then the other finishes what the other one starts?

Well, sometimes, but you got together so you have to make an appointment. "Come over tomorrow at two and we'll try to write something." Sometimes somebody has an idea—as you put it, a germ of an idea—and sometimes you have nothing, but you just start from scratch. Sometimes you have a song and you have it half written and you need help finishing it. The scenarios are endless.

Do you have a studio in your house?

No, not anymore. I used to have one, but I just found out I don't like punching buttons. [*chuckles*] I couldn't keep up with everything. I have just a little tape recorder for vocal and guitar.

That seems pretty old school.

Yeah, very simple, but I don't really like studios I found out. I tried to have one and figure out how it worked and everything, and all it did was piss me off.

You seem like a very straightforward kind of guy, no nonsense.

Well, I try.

Have you mellowed as you've gotten older?

Yeah, sure. I think so. I'm not as crazy as I used to be.

And yet, on the new album, there are songs that are very topical and outspoken.

Well, if you got something to say, say it.

That sounds like the perfect quote to end this interview.

[*Chuckles*] Well good. Thank you. I appreciate your calling and your interest.

19

....

Billy Joe Shaver

A Rebel with a Cause

Billy Joe Shaver is, in a word, a legend. One of the prime movers of the so-called Outlaw Country Movement, he, along with Willie Nelson, Johnny Cash, Kris Kristofferson, and Waylon Jennings, helped establish a standard for Americana that was once considered on the fringe, but which is now solidly part of the mainstream.

It's little wonder then that his weathered Texas accent is ever as world weary as one might expect from a man who was, at the time, in his late seventies and who, in fact, accomplished so much. It also indicates he's not inclined to hold anything back, that no aspect of that life is off-limits. Then again, as an esteemed songwriter whose songs have been covered by several leading lights—Elvis Presley, Willie Nelson, Patty Loveless, and Waylon Jennings among them—those frank observations are what have set his songs apart for the better part of forty years.

"I found out a long time ago that if you're going to be honest, you have to write about things you know and what's going on with you," Shaver insists. "So I decided to just be honest, and that made it necessary to write about things that happened to me, as well as the way I felt about this and that. It worked out good and it's stayed that way. I enjoy writing. It's the cheapest psychiatrist there is . . . and I still need one, of course."

Shaver's album, the adroitly titled *Long in the Tooth* bears that out. With songs that cover his usual array of vices—alcohol, his insurgent attitude, his decided difficulty in dealing with the Nashville establishment—it adds another sterling chapter to Shaver's superb songbook. His first studio album in six years, it also features a host of like-minded musicians, among them producer Ray Kennedy, old pal Willie Nelson, Tony Joe White, and Leon Russell.

"I love it. I'm real satisfied with it," Shaver says. "I wanted this album to be special. I wanted the material to be fresh right out of the cooker. I wrote a bunch of songs in the studio and I just aimed to get the best ones I could. My album's going to shake a few trees I think. I'm thankful I was able to pull it off."

Shaver deserves to be pleased, considering his share of hard knocks. Raised by a single mother, he left school after eighth grade and picked cotton. He joined the Navy at seventeen before taking a series of low-wage jobs. It was while working at a lumber mill he lost two fingers on his right hand in an industrial accident. Yet when it came to his songwriting, he remained undeterred.

"I knew I was good," Shaver reflects. "I've been writing since I was eight years old. When I cut my fingers off, I fell back on music. I said, 'God, if you help me get through this, I'll do what I'm supposed to do.' I knew I could make it in music."

Clearly confident, Shaver decided to hitchhike to California to seek his fortune, only to end up in Nashville. "I tried to go to LA, but I couldn't get a ride because I guess I was on the wrong side of the road," he laughs. "The first guy that came along picked me up and he took me all the way to the other side of Memphis and set me down on the road to Nashville. It was just luck, that's all. Or maybe it was the will of God."

In Nashville he quickly found a job when Bobby Bare hired him as a songwriter for the princely sum of $50 a week. He subsequently came to the attention of Waylon Jennings, who used several of his songs for Jennings's breakthrough album *Honky Tonk Heroes*, a record that's still revered as one of the first examples of the new and emerging outlaw country genre. "Waylon was great, but it was kind of a double edged sword," Shaver recalls. "He covered all those songs, and he was the only one who would do them. But right after that, he told *Rolling Stone* that he would never cut another one of my songs again because I was getting all the credit."

Indeed, it did open doors, eventually leading Shaver to record an album of his own. His landmark debut, 1973's *Old Five and Dimers Like Me* was produced and financed by Kris Kristofferson, a budding singer-songwriter himself at the time. "I'm real proud of that one," Shaver beams. "Kris had to borrow money to get it done. He heard a bunch of my songs and felt like he had to help me. And he did."

The album received immediate notice and solidified Shaver's standing in the outlaw country circles. "I still don't know if it shook the world," Shaver admits. "But it's solid. I know that."

Still, despite those early triumphs, Shaver's challenges continued. He married his wife Brenda three different times and divorced her twice, only to have her die of cancer within months of losing his mother in 1999. On New Year's Eve 2000, his son and guitarist Eddy Shaver succumbed to a heroin overdose. The year after that, he suffered a heart attack on stage and was forced to undergo heart surgery.

"That was tough," Shaver says now. "I've had my moments, but all in all I've taken it well. I'm real proud of myself that I was able to stand up and carry on. There's always someone that has it worse than you. I don't feel like I was picked on or kicked down. That's just the luck of the draw. You play the hand you're dealt with."

That hand includes his rowdy reputation. In April 2007, he was accused of shooting a man after a confrontation in a Texas bar. After fleeing the scene, he eventually turned himself in and was later acquitted. It led him to write "Wacko from Waco," a song that recounts that confrontation. Bob Dylan's name-dropped him in song, singer Kinky Friedman made him his spiritual advisor during his Texas gubernatorial campaign, and his friend Robert Duval cast him in several of his films, recognizing that as a cantankerous character he was a perfect fit for those roughshod roles.

"Way back when it started, Waylon and me were like outcasts," Shaver reflects. "The people in power didn't really want us in there. It was quite a drastic change. It went from suits to blue jeans. But it was time for a change, and I think a lot of other artists were happy to see it come. It seems like it just suddenly turned over. And now it's still turning over. God's in his heaven, and all's right with the world."

20

··

Ray Wylie Hubbard's Past Perfect

"As you get older, you kind of think about your own mortality. I've had a bunch of friends who have passed away and so I've started to think about that. I'm at that point where I kind of hope God grades on a curve. I'm not a saint and I'm not Attila the Hun, but maybe somewhere in between."

His thoughts on longevity aside, Ray Wylie Hubbard was the perennial late bloomer. Although his recording career dates back nearly forty years, to his 1976 debut album *Ray Wylie Hubbard and the Cowboy Twinkies*, he's quick to insist that he really didn't start to flourish until he was in his midforties. By that time he'd already transitioned several times, from folk enthusiast to alt-country pioneer to honky-tonk hero. However, it wasn't until his string of nineties recordings, beginning with *Loco Gringo's Lament* in 1994, that Hubbard, newly sober for the first time, hit his stride and began making records on which he could stake a reputation.

"I never really had a music career in my twenties and thirties," Hubbard explains. "I was just kind of floundering around. I was writing, but I never was recording. So *Loco Gringo's Lament* was the first record I did where it didn't come with excuses taped to it. It had mandolins and fiddles and accordions, and it was a real folk rock thing. I was forty-five years old and I didn't know if I would ever get another record deal."

In a very real sense, Hubbard was starting over. "I don't know if I reinvented myself, but I kind of got into being a real song-writer in my forties," Hubbard recalls. "I learned to play guitar all over again, took lessons and learned finger-picking. I got into country blues—Lightning Hopkins, Mance Lipscomb, Doc Watson, and that sort of thing. Lyrics are very important in folk music, so it was kind of a good foundation to start out in folk and then build in that finger-picking technique with that deep groove. So like I said, I don't know if I reinvented myself, but I'm in a comfortable place now."

Hubbard's album, slyly titled *The Ruffian's Misfortune*, deliberately retraced an archival sound that effectively emulates those who initially established the template. "We went into the studio trying to capture the vibe that was prevalent on the Beatles' first record, the first Rolling Stones record, the first Buffalo Springfield record," he explains. "They didn't have a lot of pedals. They didn't have a lot of time. They'd go in there and plug directly into the amp. They didn't change their drum heads. They didn't even change their strings. And so what you hear is real guys and real playing. We didn't use a lot of gadgets either. We used old amps and even left the hum on. [*laughs*] When you listen to those old sixties records, you could hear the amps buzz. You could hear the string noises. It added to the reality of it and added to the beauty of it."

Hubbard's recording methods were honed while revamping his career in the nineties, thanks in large part to the oversight of producer Gurf Morlix, who remained behind the boards on many of those seminal efforts. It's a dusty, dirty sound—gruff for the most part and uncompromising to say the least. While the intention might have been deliberate, in practice, their methods all but ensured the results.

It also helps that he records for his own independent label—run by his wife, no less—and that he's not under any pressure to attain a certain sales quota. As a result, his criteria is narrowed considerably.

"I just try to write some good songs and make the best record I can," Hubbard insists. "I can't recommend this for everybody, but sleeping with the president of the record company helps. She tells me, 'You write your songs and I'll try to sell them.' So I have that freedom to write whatever I want. That's a great place to be, to be able to tap that freedom so some publishing company doesn't have to get their cut. I don't have to write a love song for Kenny Chesney or somebody else to record. It doesn't really matter to me if people understand what it's all about it or not, as long as it sounds good."

In a sense, Hubbard's attitude parallels a view that's prevalent in Americana realms these days. Make the music for the sake of the music, not for any purpose other than to share it and reinforce the communal bond. It's a populist notion that Hubbard has been quick to embrace.

"It's really good that roots music is getting recognized and gaining traction," Hubbard observes. "You talk about bluegrass, and suddenly a guy named Sam Bush is getting known outside that genre, and they know him in LA and they know him in the rock clubs. Same thing with a lot of these guys. It has to do with the emergence of the whole Americana thing. It's a combination of bluegrass, blues, folk, and roots rock, and yet it also has to have something about it that makes it good. There's a certain integrity about it. The types of people who are making it are artists, not necessarily celebrities. They're not doing it because they want to be rock stars. They're doing it because there's something they want to share, something they want to express."

To hear Hubbard talk about it, it becomes clear that music is more important to him than ever, and that at age seventy, he considers himself a part of a tradition passed down over the decades. "I think the music we're discussing here is the kind that touches all of us in a way," he suggests. "It touches our humanity. Once people become aware of the Americana genre, then all of a sudden they're going to seek it out. Of course, the whole *O Brother, Where Art Thou?* phenomenon brought a lot of that music to the mainstream. Once people hear it, they can't go back. [*laughs*] Once you hear someone like Lucinda Williams and Nanci Griffith and Doc Watson, it's hard to listen to the stuff that's coming out of the Nashville corporate record labels. This is the real deal. This music is significant.

"Here's a little story for you," Hubbard offers. "When I was recording one of my early records with Gurf [Morlix], I was playing some slide guitar. My slide hit the neck and made this kind of plunk sound. So I stopped, and Gurf asked me what I stopped for. So I said, 'The slide hit the wood.' And he said, 'Lightning Hopkins wouldn't have stopped. But the Eagles would have!' It wasn't a putdown of the Eagles. It was more like 'What kind of record do you want to make?' The point is, the performance is just as important as perfection. Some of those albums, they may not have been perfect, but the performance worked. So we went in with the idea to make a record where people might not like the singer or the song, but hopefully they'll like the sound."

21

David Bromberg

Sideman as Superstar

On first impression, David Bromberg doesn't come across exactly like the storied musician whose forty-something year career found him mingling with the likes of Bob Dylan, George Harrison, Jerry Garcia, Ringo Starr, Phoebe Snow, Gordon Lightfoot, Kris Kristofferson, Carly Simon, Willie Nelson, and the scores of others who have availed themselves of his guitar skills. In fact, with his graying bushy beard and amiable way with a conversation, he could easily be mistaken for wizened rabbi, a man whose age and outlook belies his storied past. Replying to a compliment about his latest album, he confirms that unassuming impression. "Oh thank you," he says humbly. "I'm real proud of it. I like the thing."

Given that his early efforts first took flight on the folk circuit while backing such venerable singer-songwriters as Jerry Jeff Walker and Tom Paxton, that humility seems to come naturally, although the series of critically acclaimed solo albums he recorded throughout the seventies made him a candidate for stardom all on his own. Nevertheless, he abruptly retreated from the spotlight in the early nineties, changing his tack and becoming a full-time violin maker.

"I stopped performing for twenty-two years," he explains. "I got burnt out and I was too dumb to realize I was burnt out. At one point I was on the road for two years without being home for two weeks. Then later, after I was home for awhile, I realized that I hadn't written anything, I hadn't practiced, I hadn't played with anyone. I hadn't touched a guitar. I interpreted that as meaning I was no longer a musician. I didn't want to be one of these guys who drags himself onstage and does a bitter imitation of something he used to love. There are enough of those guys around. They're no fun. So I decided I needed to find something else to do with my life that I would enjoy. The only place I found any intellectual stimulation was in a violin shop. I was fascinated with how some people can look at a violin and tell you where or when it was made. So my first step was to go to violin-making school, so I did that and I broke up the band. It was a sharp left turn. My career was going upward, but one of the reasons was because I was working too hard."

His return to live performing was precipitated by a series of acoustic jam sessions he organized in his newly adopted home of Wilmington, Delaware, urged on by the city's mayor, who asked his help in resuscitating the local arts scene. "Nowadays, my ideal is to go out for three or four days at a time on the weekend and that's it," he insists. "I don't do any gigs I don't think I'll enjoy, and I don't go back to any place I didn't like. I don't do any late-night club gigs, and to my surprise, I don't need to."

In 2007, Bromberg returned to recording after an absence of twenty years with *Try Me One More Time*, setting the stage for the equally entreating *Use Me*, a brash, oftentimes bombastic set of authentic traditional Blues-based songs featuring a variety of big name guests — among them, Dr. John, Levon Helm, John Hiatt, and Widespread Panic. "First off, it's not that they're not guesting with me," he points out. "The fact they're performing on the tracks is the least of what they did. I asked each of them to write a song for me and then produce me doing that song. Use me! It's really extraordinary that each of these people said yes. I asked all these guys to use me, and they all knew how to do it."

In fact, Bromberg was frequently used early on in any number of sessions with a veritable who's who of notable musicians. "I was a pretty good guitar player," he explains with typically wry understatement. "Somebody would hear me with somebody else, and they would tell somebody else to book me and I did a lot of dates. Some of them went well; some of them not so well. But the ones that I did well got me more gigs."

One of his more famous employers was none other than Bob Dylan, who recruited him for the albums *Self Portrait* and *New Morning*. "He called me," Bromberg recalls. "I think I was a little intimidated. But only a little, and I knew enough to put it aside as much as I could. You can't perform effectively if you're shaking in your boots. I sometimes think that nervously is an excuse for failure."

So what was the Bobster really like? "He was a guy," he replies matter-of-factly. "He was very cooperative and inventive. Every now and then we'd just step out on the stoop and talk things over, and it was a very friendly, cordial thing. He was very forthright and direct, a real mensch."

Bromberg can also claim a songwriting credit with George Harrison, an unlikely collaboration that ended up on Bromberg's eponymous debut called "The Holdup." "I met him in Columbia Studios . . . and he sang me one of my tunes, a song called 'Danger Man,'" Bromberg reminisces. "He told me he learned it from Bob. I was flabbergasted. . . . Nobody had an idea we'd write a song together. We just did. We were both at a quiet family Thanksgiving dinner. It was my manager's house in New Jersey, and it was just his family, me and George. His daughter had a gut string guitar, and George and I, both being guitar junkies, passed it back and forth and we realized after a little while we were writing a song, and so we finished it. Some of the very best lines are definitely his. I came up with stuff, he came up with stuff, but for the life of me I couldn't tell you who came up with what."

He pauses, reflecting on a trajectory that now finds him moving comfortably at his own pace. "I've been a very lucky man in many, many ways."

22

Delbert McClinton Peruses the Past,
While Contemplating the Present

"I have great memories of things," Delbert McClinton insists. "I was there at the birth of rock and roll, when all these incredible things were going on. I remember going to a midnight movie—which at that time was the most far out thing you could do in West Texas, because nothing happens after midnight that's good for young people—and the movie I saw was *Rock around the Clock*. When that thing started, the place was just packed and everybody suddenly started screaming [*sings*] 'One two three o'clock, four o'clock rock' and it was magic! It was as magic as I could imagine, because it affected us all so deeply. There was this music that was ours. And after that, so much happened at once. Chuck Berry and Fats Domino, Little Richard, and on and on and on. Nothing like it has happened since."

McClinton has reason to reminisce. After all, he played a small but memorable role in the music's emergence in the late fifties and early sixties. His first bar band, the Straitjackets, backed up blues champions like Sonny Boy Williamson, Howlin' Wolf, Jimmy Reed, and Lightnin' Hopkins, venerable musicians from whom many a seminal British band would take its cue. He achieved regional success in his native Fort Worth, and then made an indelible imprint when he added his harmonica to Bruce Channel's hit "Hey! Baby" in 1962. The subsequent success of that single took Channel, with McClinton in tow, to England, where a nascent band named the Beatles supported a couple of their dates and a budding rock and roller named John Lennon insisted McClinton teach him the finer points of playing a harp.

"When 'Hey! Baby' was number one in England in 1962, and Bruce got booked for a six-week tour of the British Isles, the promoter said, 'Well, we have to have a harp player because that's a big part of the song.'" McClinton explains. "So I got to go, and the Beatles were the opening act on some of the shows we did. Every day, somebody would show up in our dressing room with a harmonica and say 'Show me what you're doing,' because at that particular time—you have to put this into perspective—nobody was playing a harmonica except in blues music. It wasn't a popular instrument in rock and roll. Of course, it's hard to show anybody anything on a harmonica. But later, John Lennon told someone I showed him everything he knew. Just like anything, it gets romanticized."

Nevertheless, McClinton has fond memories of his first trip abroad and of those budding Beatles in particular. "I was just this kid from Texas, and I hadn't really been out of the state before. And I loved it. I couldn't get enough. I remember on one particular occasion when we were playing the Cavern Club in Liverpool, this young girl comes up to our dressing room and says, 'You've got to come down and hear this group. They're the hottest group in the north of England.' She was talking about the Beatles. They had just gotten back from Hamburg. We saw them and it was obvious they were amazing. I can't say I had any idea what they would be or what they would become. I didn't know that they would change the world. But that was what was so cool about it. We were all on common ground. No preconceived ideas or anything. We were just a bunch of young guys out to change the world musically, and we were convinced we were going to do it. So it was wonderful. You can't stop somebody with that kind of feeling."

McClinton would pave his own path to success in the years and decades that followed that fateful encounter, first with a band called the Rondells (their 1965 single "If You Really Want Me to I'll Go" became a regional hit in Texas), and later with his group Delbert and Glen, a duo he formed with fellow Texan Glen Clark. After the band split, McClinton went solo, scoring more hits as a songwriter ("Two More Bottles of Wine" for Emmylou Harris and "B Movie Boxcar Blues" for the Blues Brothers, among them) than he managed to accomplish on his own. Nevertheless, he became a staple of modern blues, recording dozens of albums for different labels, scoring a top ten hit of his own (1980's "Givin' Up for

Your Love") and garnering a Grammy for his 1991 duet with Bonnie Raitt, "Good Man, Good Woman." He won another Grammy in
2006, this time for Best Contemporary Blues Album for *The Cost
of Living*, one of the most critically acclaimed efforts of his career.
Another pairing, this time with Tanya Tucker on the song "Tell Me
about It," boosted him to the highest tiers of the country charts.

Still, even by his own admission, McClinton's never hit the
heights of stardom attained by some of his peers. Even having a
hit single as significant as "Givin' Up for Your Love" didn't necessarily get him there, one reason perhaps why McClinton tends to
downplay its importance. "Even at that time, I was pretty old," he
recalls. "I don't care how good the music is, do you want to watch
this old guy or this pretty little thing here? The latter is going to
win every time, man. The radio exposure certainly made it better, but it didn't turn me into a superstar by any means."

Asked if that's what he wished for, McClinton denies it emphat-
ically. "I never wanted to be a superstar," he insists. "That's the
biggest bunch of shit in the world. I know too many people
whose lives are a mess because they can't even go out in public
anymore. Some people don't have any more sense than to think
these people have the secret to life, and so they stalk them. You
get to the point where you can't be who you are, or you end up
spending so much time pretending that is who you are. Then you
spend those late nights when nobody's around wondering what
the fuck you're doing. 'What have I done to myself? I'm here, but
I don't know where else to go.' I think you have to have passion,
true passion, to take you through life. If you don't have it, you're
going to come to a place where you can't put up with your own
jive bullshit anymore, and then you end up doing so many really
sad things. I've seen so much of it."

Nevertheless, at age seventy-six, McClinton continues to tour
on a limited basis, while devoting much of his time to his Sandy
Beaches Cruise, an excursion that laid the foundation for what's
become a burgeoning industry, that of the ocean-going music
festival.

"It's so important to me to keep good music alive," McClinton
maintains. "A lot of the stuff that's dished out nowadays is for lit-

tle kids—specifically little girls. It breaks my heart to see people spend so much time on something that's nothing more than a primitive beat, something that's hypnotic, something that's like a drug where all you hear is this [*taps his fingers on the table*] for twenty hours. I don't understand the principle of how it works. If you're going to play music and do it good, it's got to be a life-long passion. And if you don't have the honesty and intention to get better at it—if all you have is a click track and some little jive ditty, a few words you can say over and over—then why bother? I don't understand it. What the hell is that about? Where's the emotional commitment in making something that's not even very good? It's crazy."

Ultimately it's clear McClinton is grateful for the gift he's been given. "I feel so very lucky, because I've been able to spend my life doing what I wanted to do, and I think, to get better at it," he says. "That keeps me standing pretty tall, because I didn't cheat and I didn't lie, I did the best I could, and it paid off."

The Transition
Is Complete

Americana Today

It's those inroads provided by those predecessors that turned the tide and transformed country rock, roots rock, blues, and bluegrass into the universal umbrella now universally referred to as Americana. As festivals like Bonnaroo, Telluride, the Americana Music Festival, Folk Alliance, and Merlefest have become magnets for devotees, the enthusiasm has spread and given the spotlight for artists to gather and share their skills with the faithful.

In addition, the late eighties and early nineties ushered in another major milestone in Americana's ongoing transition, a singular development that would lay the template for what was soon to follow. It was originally identified as the No Depression Movement, birthed by the band Uncle Tupelo and named for their influential debut album. The term would later be adapted by the magazine of the same name, which championed the cause and bands spun off from Uncle Tupelo's initial incarnation—Wilco and Son Volt, not to mention the countless bands that followed in their footsteps.

In Part 3, we continue the journey from past to present and into the future by spotlighting those artists who picked up the baton and made music that looks both back and forward all at the same time.

Indeed, it's a diverse amalgam of sounds and styles that makes a precise definition of Americana sometimes still seem elusive, but it's that reverence for the roots that creates a common bond. In the following chapters we'll hear from several current artists who consistently carry Americana forward.

23

....

John Oates Takes a Rural Route
off the Mainstream Mile

Every artist strives for success, but the sad fact is that commercial credence doesn't always guarantee creative satisfaction. It's the rare musician who can claim super stardom without being bound to repeating the same formula over and over simply to win continued favor with fans.

It's even rarer for a musician to be able to proceed in dual directions—one that allows him or her to reap the financial rewards that come with selling out stadiums, and another that provides for artistic exploration without regard for commercial considerations.

Credit John Oates for managing to do both. While he's been known for more than forty or so years as the "and Oates" portion of the Hall and Oates banner that graces many a marquee, he's also maintained a career as a successful solo singer, songwriter, and sometime producer, courtesy of a string of solo albums that have brought him back to his first love—authentic down home country, folk, gospel, and soul. Indeed, those are the sounds that inspired him well before he connected with his longtime musical partner Darryl Hall in the early seventies. Although he was raised in a suburb of Philadelphia, it was this fascination with the music of the rural south that he eventually reconnected with when he veered out on his own in 2003, as he detailed in his 2017 memoir *Change of Seasons*. It's also addressed on his new album *Arkansas*, an adroit blend of the aforementioned musical styles that encompasses both original compositions and classic covers.

Indeed, it's mined with authenticity and an ageless sound that brings to mind the kindred spirits of Doc Watson, Mississippi John Hurt, and Bill Monroe, arcane arrangements played with reverence and refinement.

"The album was recorded quickly," Oates explains. "We went into the studio, I played the band the songs, and then the musicians picked up on the arrangements immediately. There were no rehearsals per se. It took us about two weeks, recording around two songs a day. Then we took off a month and went back in for another two weeks to tweak and tie it all up."

Oates did do some research before the sessions began, focusing on the songs' sources and eventually choosing a few vintage selections for inclusion—Emmet Miller's jaunty "Anytime," the romantic murder saga "Stagger Lee," and Jimmie Roger's nostalgic "Miss the Mississippi and You." "I knew I could never best the originals," he admits. "My idea was to see what they'd sound like performed by a band."

The album title was chosen to underscore the southern origins of the sound. "Other places are given credit for birthing the blues and Arkansas often gets short thrift," he suggests. "However, you can follow the route the music took from Memphis to New Orleans, all the way through to the Deep South, and find that Arkansas was the place where it all ended up."

Oates will take the band that played on the album on the road in the next few months, allowing him an opportunity to share the songs live. He's particularly pleased that some of the shows will include famed fiddler and mandolin player Sam Bush, who figured prominently in the proceedings.

Oates himself doesn't seem to mind playing the role of a journeyman musician. In fact, he's quite used to it. "It's what I do," he says succinctly. "I've accepted the fact that it's part of my life. When people ask me where I call home, I usually say it's in a hotel somewhere."

Of course he's well aware that making music as part of Hall and Oates allows him to pursue his own career as well. He's happy to reap the rewards that come from hit records and sell-out concerts, all of which have made them one of the most successful musical duos in music history. In fact, he still feels genuine pride in performing with his longtime partner and a band he says is great in every regard.

"We don't phone it in," Oates says of their shows. "We put everything into it. At times it seems like it's another life, but I still love feeling the appreciation that comes from the audience and the joy it brings to the fans when I see them singing along."

Although he accepts the fact that his work with Hall and Oates is what he's mostly recognized for as far as mainstream music is concerned, he's also appreciative for the growing acceptance he's getting from the Americana community, particularly in Nashville, where he spends much of his time when he's not out on the road or at his home in Colorado.

"There are some people who aren't aware of the music I make on my own," he concedes when asked if it's been easy to break with the branding bestowed on him by Hall and Oates. "However, those that are really knowledgeable about the Americana music scene are recognizing my solo work as well."

Of course, he has no reason to complain. His co-writing credits include some of the pair's biggest hits—"Sara Smile," "She's Gone," "Out of Touch," "You Make My Dreams," "I Can't Go for That (No Can Do)," and "Maneater" among them. An inductee into both the Songwriters Hall of Fame and the Rock and Roll Hall of Fame, his success as a musician has long since been established.

"I realize I'm blessed to have this dual career," he says humbly. "How many other artists can have the kind of success that allows them to do whatever else they want to do?"

24

....

Steve Forbert and the Art of Compromise

Steve Forbert's backstory could easily pass for the great American novel. An aspiring young singer-songwriter, he left his home in Meridian, Mississippi, to seek his fortune in the big city. After trying his luck at busking in New York's Grand Central Station, he eventually got his big break in Manhattan's teeming club scene, playing such venerable venues as Max's Kansas City, CBGB's, and other nightspots that were more akin to hosting the punk posers of the day as opposed to travelling troubadours. Bands like the Ramones, Blondie, and Talking Heads dominated the scene, making it not exactly conducive to a folk-oriented minstrel like Forbert. Regardless, his winsome melodies and amiable approach allowed him to work his way up the ladder of success, scoring both a record contract and a hit single in "Romeo's Tune," while making him a singular sensation all at the same time.

Forbert's early string of albums further affirmed his abilities, but even after he parted ways with the major labels, he continued to release records on his own. His audience is more specific now, and his flirtation with the airwaves seems to have ceased, but the quality of his craft continues to flourish.

Whether it's due to his rural upbringing or simply his unabashed admiration for tradition, Forbert's music forms a direct link to the joys and glories of the American heartland. His 2004 tribute to one of the first stars of country music, Jimmie Rodgers, an album entitled *Any Old Time*, not only reaffirmed his debt to early Americana precepts, but also garnered him a nomination for a Grammy in 2004 in the best traditional folk category.

I caught up with Forbert while he was in Wales as part of a tour through the British Isles. Age sixty at the time, he still retained the soft-spoken, small-town cadence of his youth. If one was unaware that he was a veteran artist of considerable distinction, it would be easy to imagine that the voice on the other end of the phone belonged to a simple southern boy whose greatest joy might be sitting on a back porch entertaining the neighbors with a quiet voice and a supple strum.

It's pretty amazing that after all these years you still have a knack for writing great original songs. How do you keep your music so fresh?

If that is true, then I have to say I just love this art form or idea or concept or what have you called the song. Fortunately I've had the inspiration I've had for all these years.

Is it ever a challenge though? How do you avoid repeating yourself?

I don't ever go, "I've written this one," but when I do decide to work on a song, and I make the commitment to myself with the subject and a melody and what I think is the so-called groove, it is a commitment. If it takes a week or it takes a month, it is still a commitment, and I have to take that amount of time to get something that I'm happy with. It's not like it was when I was in my twenties and I could write a song in 45 minutes without even thinking about it. These days I know it may take considerably longer. So I'm making a commitment to the song and the idea.

Do ideas come to you naturally, as if they're floating through the ether, or do you purposely sit down and set aside the time to write in order to focus on an idea?

It's the former. I don't purposely sit down and say I'm going to make an album. I make an album when I'm able to, when I have fifteen or so songs and I know there's an album there. Sometimes I'll go back and re-record something that's older too, or one from the past that's remained unrecorded. But there's usually ten or eleven songs that I have written. But no, I don't sit down with a schedule. I habitually work on songs in my mind. When I can stop running, I usually sit down to work on a song.

Have you ever thought about trying your hand at literature, in the form of either a novel or a biography?

Well, I'm just about finished writing a memoir. Everyone else has done it. I got started on one a couple of years ago, but I'm just about finished with it now. A lot of it centers on my early days in New York City, because that period has kind of turned into Rock 101 or 107 or whatever it is. So I have been taking a crack at that, and it veers into songs, and my thoughts on songs and things like that. But I've never thought about writing short stories about any of these rock-related scenarios of mine. They just turn into songs. It sure is fun to get up and sing them in real time, and I happen to love that live part of it.

What do you recall of your early days in New York City? Does it bring back fond memories?

Oh yes. I basically loved all of it. I was able to do everything I wanted to accomplish within a year and a half, and fortunately it moved along well enough so that it was always forward motion. I went to New York because I knew if I had to sing in the streets I could do it there, which isn't true of LA or many other cities. It turned out that I couldn't just audition and get into clubs. It took awhile to get the lay of the land and to get any kind of recognition just to get a paying gig. So I wound up singing in the streets. Fortunately, things moved along quick enough so that I didn't feel like I was stranded or not making any progress.

Still, it must have been quite a culture shock for a kid in his early twenties from Mississippi. Was it intimidating or scary at all for you?

The "folk scene" was not intimidating. It was exactly what someone like me was looking for. There were kids there from all over the country trying to see if they could get started as performers or songwriters. That was just fun. It wasn't intimidating. But when I tried to move into more aggressive areas like Max's Kansas City or CBGB's, that was a little more intimidating. I was the odd man out just by having an acoustic guitar as my means of performing. It was weird. David Byrne played acoustic guitar back then too, but he was clearly in a rock band.

Yours is the perennial all-American success story. A small town kid goes to the big city and makes it all on his own. That's the dream. So how were you discovered?

Danny Fields heard me at CBGB's when I managed to get some shows there. He and Linda Stein were managing the Ramones, and when they said they were interested, I said, "Sure." So they became my managers. John Rockwell saw me at Kenny's Castaways and wrote a very favorable review in the *New York Times* before I had any kind of record deal. So those two things helped cut through the jungle and get me a major label contract.

Your second album propelled you into the stratosphere it seemed, and "Romeo's Tune" more or less clinched that success for you. Did those first two albums, *Alive on Arrival* **and** *Jackrabbit Slim*, **set such a high bar that all of a sudden you felt like you had some kind of expectations you then had to meet?**

Clearly I never did follow up that kind of success. I only had one bona fide hit. I did my best, but I didn't match the right song with the right recording after that. But I've been able to keep playing because I'm doing the kind of music that's developed into Americana. You could call it folk music if you like. I can play solo with this sort of thing. I don't think the Ramones could have ever considered simplifying their show, but I could in the field I'm in. I have been playing solo for most of these years. I'm occasionally with a band, but I'm usually solo and I happen to love it.

People were throwing the "New Dylan" label at you, and in fact, there were a lot of parallels between you and Dylan. What did that feel like?

I tried to make it clear whenever the subject came up that I sort of bristled at it and thought it was silly. I also knew it was kind of a working cliché by then. They said that about John Prine, and they said it about Bruce Springsteen and maybe Elliott Murphy too. It wasn't a joke, but it was a cliché. It was a nice working thing in print to say something that implied an emphasis on the lyrics. But I always wanted to make it clear that I didn't take that sort of tag literally.

Still, it must be nice to be compared to the all-time gold standard. That's quite a compliment.

That's the Sally Fields syndrome. I did my best to make the best records I could, and I always try to stick with a song until I'm really happy with it. I'm not trying to be evasive, but that's what I set out to do coming up in rock and roll bands in Mississippi, trying to write and contribute some really good songs and maybe convey an idea or two in there lyrically.

Your album *Compromise* found you reunited with John Simon, the man who produced your early albums. How did that come about?

I wanted to work with John again and to get him to come out to California to work on *Over with You* in 2012, but at that time, he couldn't make it. So I kept on about it, and when I saw that I was going to start recording that record, I tried again. And as you can see, we were able to make it happen.

Was there any kind of readjustment period? Or did it just flow like in the past?

There was some getting reacquainted. I went to stay with him and his wife Caroline for about three days in the Catskills, and it was fantastic. So he and I were able to get reacquainted, We went over songs one after another, and we really worked out what the production values were going to be, checking out tempos and that kind of thing. So we had a great time doing that. It might have been the most fun part of making this record. And then we recorded with a band I was touring with at the time, which included [bassist] Joey Spampinato and friends, so I brought them to Woodstock and that's where we did a whole lot of work on the record. And John goes to Florida for a certain amount of time every winter, so he went on to Florida and I finished the record in Cape Cod with a fantastic co-producer who is also a studio owner and musician, Jon Evans. So that's the way it happened.

What prompted you to do a cover of "Send in the Clowns?" You really do a different take on that song.

There's about six or seven or ten songs that I'd like to do along those lines. I've never done an entire record of well-known songs, giving them my interpretation. But I didn't want to wait anymore on that one. I've wanted to do "Send in the Clowns" for about five years. I ran it by Joey in some band rehearsals, and he was very encouraging, so we ran ahead and did it. There wasn't really any thought to it other than I thought I had that groove for the song, and that it didn't necessarily have to be a "ballad." The lyrics could be a little more jabbing. They're kind of sarcastic.

Why was this so different than your previous albums in that regard?

Well, I always work them until I get them where I'm pleased with them. But this was just a long process. John Simon couldn't finish it, so I had to go elsewhere, and one thing led to another. And I was just kind of angry too. I was approaching sixty and I wanted to make a rocking record, and I wanted to make it competitive. Which is a little bit of a joke. I certainly don't see this record on top 40 radio or competing with anything out there now. But I did want to make it good and energetic.

Why were you angry? Were you frustrated? Acting out in a rebellious rock and roll sort of way?

I felt a lot of responsibility for getting what I wanted. I don't know. The previous records hadn't done anything and I really wanted to . . . whatever you just said. I'm sorry . . .

You said you were angry, and I'm curious why you felt that way. Were you angry because the previous records had not performed the way you hoped, or were you simply trying to emulate the insurgent rock and roller?

Well, I think all of that. Like I said, I wouldn't want to make another record like this because it took so much work, just trying to get so many details. Fortunately, I don't think it sounds completely labored over, but it took a long time, and I was touring at the same time, etcetera, etcetera. I put some of my own funds into making this record. So I was hell-bent and angry . . . to get some kind of aggressive result. This isn't going to strike anybody who listens to Metallica as aggressive, but for me, it's not just a complacent folk record.

25

A Lot to Lovett

The great state of Texas is known for many things—great football, great barbecue, big oil, women with big hair, men with big hats, and the fact that, um, everything is supposedly bigger there. The latter assertion may be cause for debate, but one thing is beyond question—the fact that among its other accomplishments, Texas has birthed some singular singer-songwriters, Jerry Jeff Walker, Townes Van Zandt, Guy Clark, and Robert Earl Keen among them.

In a career that spans more than thirty years, Lyle Lovett can claim inclusion in that distinguished legacy. With thirteen albums, four Grammys, an honorary Doctor of Humane Letters degree from the University of Houston, and the rarefied distinction of being cited as the Texas State Artist Musician for 2011 by the Texas Commission on the Arts, he's gained fame as a tireless troubadour whose modesty and humility belies his considerable prowess.

"I really do appreciate the notice I've gotten and the recognition I've received," Lovett replies. "I value those honors highly. I remember each and every experience—getting the Grammys, being part of the show, getting to be a presenter and being able to be around people I admire and that I'm a fan of. That's exciting. I got to go to the state capitol and receive the official Texas musician honors. That's great recognition. But ultimately, I really try to do my best work for myself. I think I'm a tougher critic than other people are. So if I write songs that I like enough and that I'm confident enough to play for people, I feel like I'm in good shape. The songs have to get past me first, and that's the toughest part."

We chatted with Lovett during a rare week off, back home in the rural south Texas community called Klein, which his ancestors first settled in the mid-1800s. It's where he was raised, and he's resided there ever since. Mostly though, he's out touring with either his large band or his acoustic group, two outfits that largely overlap and vary only in their numbers.

You seem to spend a lot of time on the road.

We average about a hundred dates a year. It's my job. That's how I make a living. I just try to keep it all going. Playing is a real pleasure, especially when you get to play with some of the best musicians in the world.

So what distinguishes the large band from the acoustic group these days?

With the acoustic group there are six of us instead of the fourteen we have when we play as the large band. But everybody in the smaller group gets to play more than they get to in the large band. When we're with the large band, we have to respect the arrangements and stay within the lines.

It's been a few years since your last album Release Me. **Do you have anything new on the horizon?**

I continue to play, write new songs, and try to figure out what I'm going to do next. I would like to put out a new album sometime soon.

You recently left your long time label, Curb. Have you decided who you're going to sign with, or whether you'll opt to go indie?

I don't know yet. I've been talking to some labels but haven't decided what to do. I've first got to decide what kind of album it's going to be, but I haven't made the final decision as to what direction I'm going to go in, or who I'm going to do it with. I'll do something for sure, but I'm not ready to sign on the dotted line.

One of the hallmarks of your career is the fact that you've never been afraid to dabble in different genres. You've gone from country to swing to big band to gospel and touched on practically everything in between. So what inspires that eclectic muse of yours?

I've been really lucky to have been associated with business people who allow me to follow my natural inclinations. That's a wonderful thing. I've never felt as if I had to restrict myself to one particular genre. I've actually been encouraged to do the kind of stuff I want to do, and to look into different types of styles, and then combine them to make them all come out in a unified way. I've always just liked different kinds of music. I feel like it's a natural tendency not to be locked into one particular thing and to be able to appreciate a variety of styles.

Do you ever find your fans are a bit baffled by your stylistic shifts back and forth? Is there ever any pushback on that front?

No, fortunately I really don't feel pushback from my fans. They've been so supportive over the years. Then again, I don't engage in any kind of ongoing dialogue on the subject either. I think it's really important as an artist—or in any kind of business at all—to lead. You have to do what you think is best, and hope that people will appreciate what you do. You can't just guess what some perceived audience might want. You just have to do what you think is right. And if you do that, and do a good job at it, the people who do support you will be happy. I've gotten to make records and tour around, but I haven't had the kind of huge mainstream success that tends to lock you into something. So being a little under the radar might be liberating. When you have a certain amount of success, there's pressure to repeat that. I've been lucky enough to make money for the folks that I'm in business with, but not so much that they come at me and say, "You've got to do that again." In a way, being a little bit under the radar is a good thing.

You come from a hallowed tradition, one you share with a host of legendary Texas singer-songwriters—Jerry Jeff Walker, Townes Van Zandt, Guy Clark, and Robert Earl Keen among them. Do you feel a kinship to those musicians?

I'm such a fan of Guy Clark and Townes Van Zandt and Steven Fromholtz and Ray Wylie Hubbard, all those guys that were playing out when I was first learning how to play guitar, and I was sort of dreaming of how to play myself. I'm more an admirer of all that from a fan's standpoint. I feel grateful that I got to know Guy Clark, and that I knew Townes and I've gotten to be friends with Steven Fromholtz over the years. I'm grateful for those relationships, but I have trouble trying to rise myself up to that Texas tradition. I hold those writers in such high esteem, so just to be mentioned in the same breath is quite a compliment.

I guess getting killed off can be a little harsher than your average, everyday pink slip.

[*Laughs*] It's a pretty violent show, but it's still a lot of fun really. And it's gotten good notices.

26

No Baggage for Bela

Bela Fleck is something of an anomaly when it comes to today's Americana mind-set. He completely defies the notion of what a banjo-toting player has come to represent—a musician who's unafraid to venture into realms far afield of bluegrass or the traditional turf that's always provided the banjo with a comfortable fit. Both on his own and in collaboration with his various star-studded associations—the New Grass Revival, Strength in Numbers, and Bela Fleck and the Flecktones—he's consistently pushed the parameters and fearlessly experimented with jazz, folk, pop, Americana, classical, and avant-garde. The fact that he's been nominated for Grammys in more categories than any other musician on record is testimony in itself to his striking diversity and ability to bend the boundaries. Even so, Fleck eschews any attempt to categorize him as a technocrat. He's a regular attraction at most major music festivals both here and abroad, and even with all his critical acclaim, he's managed to maintain a populist perspective. His recordings are as inviting as they are intriguing, and regardless of genre, his music offers broad appeal for the masses.

I caught up with Mr. Fleck between gigs, and asked him to share a bit of background and also offer some insight into the things that motivate him as a musician.

When you first started playing the banjo, was it always your intention to stretch the possibilities of the instrument in such non traditional ways?

I just loved the sound of the banjo, and when I finally got one in my sweaty little hands, I couldn't put it down. I think I evolved into my particular playing style from growing up in New York City in the sixties, and everything that that entailed.

Given the way you expand the boundaries and use the banjo in such nontraditional settings, do you ever have your doubts as to how its going to work out? What inspires you to go into these uncharted realms?

I don't ever imagine it not working, so I just do it. You must believe! As far as inspiration, all my favorite musicians were, and are, individualists who push into new territory. I figured it was just what you were supposed to do.

Given your incredible scope, and the diverse categories that have garnered you your many Grammy nods, which genre do you feel is really your comfort zone? Is bluegrass home base and your launching point?

Bluegrass is a touchstone for me, although sadly, I play it remarkably rarely. That being said, some of it is in everything that I do. The Flecktones are a home base as well, whatever we call that music. It comes back to life regularly, and I know what to do instinctively in those situations.

Did you play guitar prior to picking up the banjo? How did you acquire your banjo skills so quickly?

I started on guitar, which taught me how to press my fingers down on a neck. But I never caught fire until I got my first banjo. Then I put in the time that was needed to make fast progress.

Did you ever get any pushback from the country/bluegrass establishment when you began venturing into your other arenas?

You know, a lot of people had already taken a lot of heat by the time I came onto the scene. Tony Trischka, who was my teacher, really took a whipping for being so progressive. I was just more of the same, and people had cooled off somewhat by then. New Grass Revival also took some amazing crap, but they got their due, and ended up at the top of the scene before it was all over. I played with them from 1981 to 1990.

There seems to be a lot of improvisation in what you do, especially with the Flecktones. Is that really the case, or is it all mapped out beforehand?

There is a lot of improv, but it doesn't tend to be the form that is improvised. We do know what's coming next and the basic thrust of each section. People get to fill in the details freely and spontaneously each night.

How much of your playing is improvised in concert?

Quite a lot of it is improvised, except when I play my banjo concerto, which is 99% set.

You do a lot of session work in addition to your own projects. When you play sessions for other people, do you still have a chance to improvise and veer away from the template?

When you are learning new music and recording, you have to do a lot of experimentation to create the template. And since the music is new to you, you can't fall back on anything, and so you have to improvise. Some great things happen at those sessions, and quite often it becomes difficult to improve on what you played the first time.

After all the accolades and critical kudos you've received—especially your many Grammy nods—do you still relish the recognition after all these years?

I am always a little surprised to get the attention. I keep expecting people to get tired of me and stop being so nice! That's not what I do this for, but I can't say it isn't fun . . . at least until I've been on tour too long that is, and then it can be an ordeal. The trick is to keep the trips from getting too long, so that you can put your best energy out to the people that appreciate what you do.

There are a lot of artists pushing the parameters of Bluegrass these days. Are there any musicians of that ilk that you follow and consider yourself a fan of? And why do you think that bluegrass music as a whole lends itself to such different treatments?

I love all the offshoots, and I love the guys that do it the old fashioned way. It's all good. Bluegrass is a relatively simple form, and I've learned from classical music that simple music is easiest to develop. Think of all the great themes and variations Beethoven and Mozart did!

When you formed the Flecktones, did you have a specific concept in mind? What was your vision for the band and how did you go about recruiting the musicians that became part of the group?

I wanted to surround myself with weirdos like me. I wanted the nerds to run the show! The right people turned up when I was ready, and no sooner.

Is there any genre you've yet to tackle that you haven't had a chance to do yet? If you had a bucket list as far as your musical goals are concerned, what would be on it that hasn't yet been scratched off?

The big focus these days is composing for banjo and classical musicians. I wrote my first stand-alone banjo concerto last year, and followed it with a piece for banjo and string quartet. I love composing, and it's fun to sink my teeth into a complex and lengthy piece that great musicians will be able to play on sight.

27

....

Jay Farrar Talks about a Prodigal Son Volt

If Uncle Tupelo sired the second coming of Americana, then its off-spring, Wilco and Son Volt, allowed it to thrive. Yes, there were other bands that blazed the trail before—the Byrds, Flying Burrito Brothers, and Poco chief among them—but when it came to stamping a niche in the burgeoning modern rock arena of the midnineties, no one did more than these three bands to bring Americana into the mainstream, where it's been welcomed ever since.

Jay Farrar had been a prime mover in Uncle Tupelo, the band that gave a name to what became known as the No Depression movement, a handle borrowed from one of the group's more prominent LPs. However when the band split, he and Jeff Tweedy, Uncle Tupelo's other chief mainstay, parted company and set off in their individual directions. For awhile they were following parallel courses, and while Wilco continued to evolve and still remains a vital force today—albeit with a different musical calling—Son Volt splintered, reformed, and shared its own influence, especially in a more traditional way. The band's extended hiatus in the late nineties, accompanied by Farrar's pursuit of a solo career, suggested that Son Volt had perhaps run out of momentum, but their rebound, marked by a further string of successful albums, suggested their initial inspiration was in fact intact and would remain so for the foreseeable future.

Still, their progress was anything but steady. It had been more than three years since 2013's *Honky Tonk*, Son Volt's last album, and it was nearly three years before that when its predecessor, 1998's *Wide Swing Tremelo*, appeared. Nevertheless, *Notes of Blue*, released in 2017, marked a return to form, and I took the opportunity to talk to Jay Farrar about the group's current effort and to bring up some old business as well.

Trace of Blue contains all the classic qualities Son Volt is known for—the weary ballads and the edgier elements as well. Yet there seems to be an added element added to the mix.

I've always wanted to do a recording that focused on the blues, one that had a blues element to it. This album gave me a chance to expand on that concept. In particular, I wanted to explore the guitar tunings of Skip James and Mississippi Fred McDowell. At the same time, I was going for a folk-oriented project based on the music of Nick Drake. The two projects kind of merged, and ultimately there seemed like there was a kind of commonality of purpose. The blues formed the roots of country music from the start—Jimmie Rogers and Hank Williams were prime examples of that—and so I was aiming for the point where blues, folk, and country music converged, and then Nick Drake inserted himself into the process.

The fact that the new album goes back to the roots might offer a reminder for those who tend to forget that the lessons of the past can affect the future.

I think so. There's one song in particular that makes some observation. It's the song "Cherokee St.," where I write about the high rate of incarceration in this country. But overall, I don't have a lot to do with politics. It's named for a street in St. Louis where there's real diverse group of people, a lot of Mexican Americans in particular. It's a very vibrant place. You can grab a taco and then go to some good bars and restaurants. I've also written some new songs that focus on current events.

There's certainly no shortage of things to write about. Will they be released as Son Volt or under your own aegis?

I'm getting ready to tour with the band, so it will most likely be part of another album with Son Volt.

There have also been some recent Son Volt reissues and retrospectives. Were you actively involved in those projects?

I did dig up the demos that were included on the Trace reissue, so I guess you can say I was involved. At least in terms of digging up material . . .

You've certainly been busy on your own. Aside from your solo projects, you ventured into soundtracks. What about that attracted your interest?

With my first one, *The Slaughter Rule*, the guys that did that movie contacted me and said they wanted me to do the music score. So I said, "Sure." I looked at the script and came up with some music that seemed to suit it. It was my first foray into pick-style guitar, so that was a good experience.

Then you did the soundtrack for the film about Jack Kerouac, *One Fast Move or I'm Gone***.**

I was working with a guy that was actually related to Kerouac's family, and he was doing a documentary, working from one of his books.

Do you find inspiration when you read someone like Kerouac and get a kind of aural idea that ties into the imagery?

I did, for sure. Kerouac's style of writing really resonated with me and a lot of other people. That stream of consciousness really lent itself to writing songs, and that was the basis of it. So Kerouac was definitely an influence. His stream of consciousness style was definitely influential for a lot of folks.

You worked with Ben Gibbard of Death Cab for Cutie on that project. Any chance the two of you might work together again?

I've thought about it. We haven't really crossed paths in awhile, but it could happen again.

Then there was Gob Iron, your duo with Anders Parker. How did that come about?

Anders and I have been friends for years, so we got together and spent some time in the studio. We've talked about doing another Gob Iron record, but so far we haven't done it yet. But we will be touring together some, so there is a likelihood it could happen.

28

·····························

Chris Isaak Aims for Arcane Americana

Some artists happily embrace Americana. Others are all too eager to emulate it. In the case of Chris Isaak, there's no need to even think twice. It's not a secondary issue, or one that lurks in the background. Indeed, Isaak is the personification of enduring Americana as it exists in the present day. He does so effortlessly, as if the lessons learned are part of his DNA.

On the day we spoke, Isaak was enjoying some rare downtime when reached at home in San Francisco prior to a tour in support of his latest album, a collection of rock and roll standards dubbed *Beyond the Sun*. Not that he was taking it easy; with a new offering to promote, he was engaged in a string of telephone interviews with enquiring journalists like yours truly. At that moment, however, he was a bit distracted. His manager's playful Maltese had him in stitches, sprinting and sliding deliriously across the floor, as if mimicking the surfers that were braving the waves just outside his window. "You wouldn't believe how hilarious he is," Isaak effused. "He's really having some fun."

Isaak should know. After all, celebration has always been inherent in his MO, especially when it comes to emulating the sounds that moved him early on. That made *Beyond the Sun* especially significant. For starters, it was his initial offering for his new record company, the revered folk label Vanguard. For another, it was a long-planned ode to his earliest influences, specifically producer Sam Phillips's Sun Studios and its remarkable crop of rock and roll pioneers—Elvis Presley, Johnny Cash, Jerry Lee Lewis, and Roy Orbison chief among them. Given that Isaak's had more or less emulated that music for nearly three decades, the album became an obvious by-product of his reverence and admiration.

"I tried to go for a balance," Isaak said of the selection. "I wanted to pick material the average listener would know. But I also wanted to use my expertise to say, 'There are a few things you might not know, but might really like.'"

Granted, a number of the songs ("Ring of Fire," "Great Balls of Fire," "Can't Help Falling in Love," "It's Now or Never") are quite well-known, especially to oldies enthusiasts. Wisely, then, Isaak chose to toss a few obscurities and a handful of originals into the mix.

"I hope that people go back and listen to those originals," Isaak mused. "Hopefully someone will say, 'I didn't know this body of music was out there . . . but now I do.'"

In keeping with its vintage style, Isaak did his best to ensure an authentic ambiance. He took his longtime band—bassist Rowland Salley, drummer Kenney Dale Johnson, guitarist Hershel Yatovitz, pianist Scott Plunkett, and percussionist Rafael Padilla—to Sun Studios to do the recording.

"When we recorded it, we did it like they did it in the fifties," Isaak recalled. "We cut it all at one time, everybody in the room, listening to each other. No overdubbing, because that's cheating. Everybody got excited, and that made a big difference. I told the guys, 'This is the way it's going to be: If I'm singing good, you better be playing good, because if that's my best vocal take, guess which one we're gonna use?'"

Over the course of his fifteen critically acclaimed albums, Isaak's smooth croon and unassuming attitude have positioned him midway between Roy Orbison's brooding melancholia and Rick Nelson's squeaky clean sincerity. Indeed, it's his everyman image that makes him so accessible, an assumption borne out in conversation. Along with his hits—"Baby Did a Bad, Bad Thing," "Wicked Game," "Somebody's Crying" and so on—his cool good looks have also fostered a budding acting career, beginning with cameos in such films as *Married to the Mob, Wild at Heart, The Silence of the Lambs*, and *A Dirty Shame*, and leading to the title role in his own Showtime sitcom and an interview show on the

Biography Channel. While he hints that acting is still a possibility, Isaak insists that his new album is his main interest now.

"This was the definition of a labor of love," he noted. "When my manager asked how many songs we cut, I informed her we were up to thirty-eight!' And she sighed and asked, 'Do you know how much it's going to cost to mix that many?'"

29

Shawn Colvin

Covers Girl

Shawn Colvin is another of those artists whose own career has paralleled the evolution of Americana, simply by looking back as she propels herself forward. Consequently it's no surprise that she's inspired by songs that have a history all their own. Her album, *Uncovered*, found her once again covering material by some storied songwriters and giving it a fresh interpretation. With the help of producer/guitarist Steuart Smith and occasional cameos by David Crosby and Marc Cohn, she effectively redefines such well-ingrained standards as Gerry Rafferty's hit "Bakers Street," Bruce Springsteen's "Tougher Than the Rest," Graham Nash's "I Used To Be a King," and Creedence Clearwater Revival's "Lodi," taking them down to their emotional essence without sacrificing the melodies that made them so memorable to begin with.

Released more than twenty years after *Cover Girl*, her first album consisting of other people's songs, *Uncovered* could be considered a belated sequel of sorts. "I would have liked it to be the twentieth anniversary—that would have made more sense, but I didn't get it together then," Colvin explains. "I had amassed a bunch of cover songs between *Cover Girl* and now. I'd been doing 'American Tune,' 'Acadian Driftwood,' and 'Hold On' for a long time. I also keep a running list of things I want to explore, and 'Bakers Street' was one of those. I gravitate toward songs when I think if I can pull them off, and I think it will be a new way for people to hear them."

Despite nine albums and an ample catalog of original songs, Colvin's interpretive skills date back to her earliest phase of her professional career. It began with her initial move to Austin, where she got her start as part of a western swing band. She then made a foray into folk music, relocating to New York City, performing Off-Broadway and eventually playing a role in the so-called fast folk movement that sprung up in Greenwich Village in the early eighties.

"I consider myself good at interpretation," she says. "I didn't write my own material for a long time, and when I played solo in New York City, I was just doing gigs to make ends meet. Three or four hours a night, all by myself in rooms where not a lot of people were listening. So rather than cover the obvious things I did in my early twenties like Joni and James Taylor or Bonnie Raitt, I decided I needed to expand and do some unexpected things. That's where most of the songs on *Cover Girl* came from. It's really not a difficult formula for me. It's bringing a personal touch to a song maybe one hasn't heard pared down and more intimate."

These days, Colvin's choices have more to do with simply finding the right tune. "They all mean something to me," she insists. "I can't make it work or be inspired otherwise. They mean something in different ways. With some of them, the music caught me first. With others, the lyrics caught me first. Some of them just seemed to ask for reinterpretation. With 'Tougher Than the Rest,' I thought a woman ought to sing this song and draw out the vulnerability in it. It was a song with a guy emanating a bit of swagger, and I don't think Bruce meant that entirely. I think it has some humility to it."

Colvin's first big break came when she was hired to sing backup vocals on the song "Luka" by Suzanne Vega, gaining her a recording contract with Columbia Records, an opportunity which led, in turn, to her well-received debut album *Steady On*, which brought her a Grammy for Best Contemporary Folk Album. Her sophomore effort, *Fat City*, also received a Grammy nomination, while the featured song from that album, "I Don't Know Why," garnered a Grammy nomination for Best Female Pop Vocal category. Her return to Austin in the midnineties marked another key move in her trajectory, spawning several significant recordings, including a best-selling album (*A Few Small Repairs*), reaping her Grammys for both Song and Record of the Year and a number one single on the Adult Contemporary charts for "Sunny Came Home."

Colvin, fifty-nine, has worked with a number of high profile producers throughout her career, including her longtime friend Buddy Miller, a present day Americana icon that she met the first time she moved to Austin in 1976. Her debut album *Steady On* was produced by John Leventhal, who also shared co-writing credits for "Sunny Came Home." With *Uncovered*, she reunited with Steuart Smith, touring guitarist with the Eagles and the man who sat behind the boards for her early albums *Fat City*, *A Few Small Repairs*, and *Cover Girl*.

"I really wanted to work with Steuart again," she recalls. "We have a kind of shorthand, which is always good when you work with a producer. He's very direct. I like his taste. A good producer will push you and be supportive at the same time. I need that. I don't need anyone being a stern taskmaster, but I do appreciate someone saying we can do it better. He's a great guitar player and a really good keyboard player as well. So we just had a lot of fun making the record. Nothing was overdubbed, and that kept it simple. Sometimes we didn't use the band at all because we thought the songs came off better with nothing on it, or very little. We both believed that was the way to do it."

Despite her early success, Colvin's also had her personal challenges. She's battled depression and substance abuse throughout her career, resulting in her 2012 book *Diamond in the Rough*, which detailed her ongoing struggles with those afflictions and the impact they've had on her life and her work. According to Colvin, they even had a bearing on her direction, leading her from covers to her own original songs, and in the case of *Uncovered*, back to covers again.

"Getting to the place where I am now was so circuitous and silly really because I cut my teeth on writers and solo acoustic styles and like Joni Mitchell, Jackson Browne, Paul Simon, James Taylor, and Judee Sill," she recalls. "I always thought I could be an interpreter like Bonnie Raitt, but that was never enough for me. If you're a solo acoustic performer, you have to be a writer, but I wasn't doing that. But I can sing anything. I'm a good copy-cat. Just give me a job. So I tried several things and enjoyed all of them. I became a lyricist, but not a very good one. Then I cleaned up my act. I got sober and it just came to me almost in an imme-diate way that what I did best was play guitar and sing. I began to write differently, and the first song that I completed that I felt I found my voice on was 'Diamond in the Rough.' And that set the stage for everything past that. I had that epiphany that that's what I did best."

30

....

The Mavericks

Renegade Rockers

In 1989, the year the Mavericks first convened, the divide between pop and country was still relatively wide, and Americana was a term that hadn't quite entered the popular lexicon just yet, and Nashville was still off-limits by and large to any artist who arrived sans a cowboy hat and a good ole boy attitude to boot.

Not surprisingly, then, the cultural expanse was larger still, making any attempt by a group from Miami of all places—boasting a lead singer of Hispanic heritage no less—seem all but certain to face indifference at best, and outright rejection at worst. Nevertheless, singer-songwriter/guitarist Raul Malo's obvious obsession with American icons like Roy Orbison, Hank Williams, Gram Parsons, Johnny Cash, George Jones, and Elvis Presley eventually prevailed, and within six months after the release of their eponymous debut on the small South Florida independent label Y&T, they landed a contract with MCA Records and the respect and admiration of the industry as a whole. Between 1991 and 2003, they landed no less than fourteen singles on the Billboard country charts and produced a string of successful albums, among them *From Hell to Paradise*, *What a Crying Shame*, *Music for All Occasions*, and *Trampoline*, each a showcase for their unlikely blend of country, pop, Latin music and big ballads. They took the country music world by storm, and left an increasingly diverse musical landscape in their wake.

In the liner notes that accompanied that self-titled debut, yours truly wrote: "The Mavericks deliver a rich blend of pure Americana. Here's a band that mixes country comfort with rock and roll attitude, a group that also proves that soul music can reach beyond the streets of Detroit or Philadelphia." Looking back, the choice of verbiage seems to suffer from overreach, but happily, the Mavericks' music never did.

In 2004, the band underwent a bitter breakup, frayed at the seams from internal strife and pent-up animosity. Each of the members went their separate ways, indulging in side projects and sessions that allowed at least momentary fulfillment. Malo himself was the most prolific, issuing six solo albums that gleaned everything from his love of traditional Latin melodies to his admiration for classic American standards. In an interview in 2010, he told me that a reunion with his former colleagues was clearly out of the question, and anyone that still hoped that it might someday transpire would best to buck up and move on.

It was somewhat surprising then that in 2012 the band opted to reconvene, original members Malo, Paul Deakin on drums, and Robert Reynolds on bass, joined by longtime keyboard player Jerry Dale McFadden and the group's most recent recruit, Eddie Perez, on lead guitar. An EP, *Suited Up and Ready*, preceded the release of their comeback album *In Time*, an effort that was lavishly praised and given an apt title, especially considering the decade of inactivity that preceded it.

We caught up with Malo at his home in Nashville and asked him about the current state of the group and what led to the reunion. Seemingly relaxed during a rare respite from a touring schedule that had them on the road the better part of a year, he was casual, candid, and overtly optimistic about the Mavericks' future fortunes.

Last time we spoke, you completely dismissed the idea that there would ever be a Mavericks reunion. So what happened?

It's just life, ya know. It was really like a perfect storm scenario. What happened, at least musically, was that these songs were starting to come out that really sounded like they needed to be on a new Mavericks record. If ever there was a chance to do a Mavericks record again, these songs would be perfect . . . at least in my mind. Fast-forward, my manager at the time said we had this offer for the Mavericks to play a couple of festivals. And I thought, "Really? That sounds interesting." And the reason I thought it was interesting is because I know this business doesn't operate on nostalgia or feelings. So when money gets put on the table, there's a reason for it. So I started thinking, if a promoter is willing to do this, maybe there is money for real somewhere—not enough money for us to retire on or anything—but that maybe a record label would be willing to put up some money for us to make a record. So I asked my friends over at Big Machine Records if they would be interested in a Mavericks album, and they were like, 'Hell yeah!' So that changed everything, because what my manager wanted was just to go out and do some summer festivals and then call it a day. But that's not what we were thinking, or at least what I was thinking.

So it wasn't just about the money?

In all honesty, I figured if the Mavericks came back it wouldn't be for a paycheck and then to call it a day. I'd rather have left it alone at that point. I respect other bands that would do that, but the Mavericks were always about a lot more than a paycheck. If we're going to bring it back, then we're going to make some music, and hopefully we'll make some important music and some relevant music as it pertains to our career and what we've done. It was the music that steered the thing, and once Big Machine said yes to the project, then everyone was up for it. And that was it. That's pretty much it in a nutshell. We made the record and, boom, here we are now.

So was there an elephant in the room once you guys reconvened. Was it awkward in any way? What was the vibe like?

It's like anything. I think time heals all wounds. So you throw that stuff out, forget about it and kind of put it aside, learn from it, and then move forward if you want to do it. And we all really wanted to do it. We really wanted to make the record, and we knew that the record was going to be a special record. We didn't know why, but we knew there was a lot of energy around it. There were high expectations of course, but everybody's energy was there. And we knew we had to have a special energy for this thing to work. We tried to make the best record we could, and lo and behold— without trying to sound like I'm bragging here—I think it's one of the best records we've ever done.

It really sounds like no time has passed at all. It sounds like you guys were right back in the proverbial groove.

That's pretty much how it went.

So was it just like old times? Did everyone just transition into their roles?

Yeah. In the past, we'd always do a whole bunch of demos and do a lot of preproduction and all that kind of stuff. But this time around I told the guys that I didn't have time to make a bunch of demos. I just wanted to go into the studio. Initially we were going to go in for just four or five days and do a couple of songs to get the group going, but by the second day we had recorded five songs. So there was definitely a lot of positive energy and thinking that, yeah, we're back. That's kinda how it was.

Was there any lingering resentment?

When we initially got together, everyone said their peace. We made sure that the miscommunication and the lack of communication and the lack of openness that had happened before within the band didn't happen again. There had been a lot of third parties communicating for us, and that's never good. It's never good in any communications, because then you'll end up with a stalemate. Part of the problem was that we were younger, and back then, honestly, I was burned out. I didn't want to hear from anybody; I didn't want to hear from anything. I was just as burned out and fried as I could possibly be. As was everybody. We didn't really take care of our business. We let others do it, and that was a big mistake. It was a big learning curve in that we realized that no one can take care of your business as well as you can. So there was all this stuff going on back then that really led to the breakup. I think this time around, everybody is more aware. Everybody wants this to work, and we're having so much more fun than ever before. That's really the big difference now.

What are the audiences like?

The fans are going nuts, and not only that, we're seeing a younger audience too. They're discovering the band through their parents. We're getting into that echelon of elder statesmen [*laughs*] and it's cool because we're seeing those different demographics in our audience.

The music business is a fickle business, and when you're away ten years, it can seem like a lifetime. But from what you're saying, it sounds like people didn't forget and they hooked into it right away. Was that the case?

It's unbelievable. Certainly during those years in-between, I was still out there doing my part to keep the Mavericks name alive. As I told the guys, no matter where I went, no matter who I was making music with, no matter what groovy little project I was doing, the conversation always turned to 'When are the Mavericks getting back together? What about the Mavericks?' At first, I was like, 'Aw geez. Give it up already. It's over.' But I think that after a while, it was maybe because they were such relentless pains in the ass, it just eventually influenced my sentiments. It was like, 'OK, what about the Mavericks? Why aren't we doing stuff?' Looking back on it now, I think that had a lot to do with it. I'm just being honest. How could it not when everywhere you go, people are asking about it? It's not that they didn't like my solo stuff, or they didn't like what I was doing. I don't think that was it at all. It's just that the Mavericks meant something to them. They meant something to a lot of people. That's nice to finally realize.

So how has this affected your present mind-set?

All those things, all the emotions, all the bad blood, all the mistakes, the apathy or whatever you want to call it, makes you stronger and a better musician. At this point, we don't have to play the game. We don't have to cater to radio or adhere to trends or whatever. We can do whatever we want, and our fans kind of expect that. We can be a little more carefree.

In a sense, it seems the time was right to reconvene. When you started out, you were ahead of the game. You guys broke the barriers. Yes, there was the underlying country flavor in your music, but you broadened the scope, and these days that seems to be the norm in general.

Absolutely. And not only that—sociologically, things have changed. The industry is more open now than we were, say, twenty years ago, when we first arrived. Imagine a Hispanic lead singer named Raul. They couldn't even pronounce my name. [*chuckles*] I think that plays into it as well. We're seeing so many young Latin people coming to our shows. It's amazing, because I've always considered this band a truly American band. It's a blend of all these things and a blend of all these cultures. We embody that in many ways, and nowadays our audience is so vast. It's fun to watch and it's fun to see that. We love it. Everybody's welcome at our shows, and it just runs the gamut. We're loving that part of it too, and we want to make a statement. We want this band to be a band for everybody, as it should it be. That's the way we see ourselves and we're enjoying it, because it's proven that we were on the right course all these years. After all these years and all the hard work, it's very gratifying.

How long have you been on the road since reuniting?

It's been about two years. When you think about that first festival which instigated this whole thing, that was about two years ago. That first gig was the Stagecoach Festival in 2011, and since then it's pretty much been nonstop. We haven't been on the road continuously since then, but almost. The band is a well-oiled machine.

It sounds like the Mavericks are now an ongoing concern, at least for the near future. You're back, and this is now business as usual.

Well, at least for another record for sure. We'll see where it goes from there. The thing about it now is that everybody realizes we can do the Mavericks, we can do the solo stuff, we can do all the little things we want to do. The main thing for me is that I like to do a lot of different things, and if I get stuck on one thing for too long, I'm going to get bored and I'm going to want out. So if I can try different things, and everybody does their things every now and then—as we all will—there's still no reason why we can't do those side projects and do the Mavericks as well. So that's the goal.

So what is the status of your solo career? Do you have future plans in that regard?

Not right now, because I'm so involved with the Maverick thing right now. But at some point, that will be part of the equation.

At that point, will it be a challenge in determining which material goes to the Mavericks and which songs are reserved for your solo outings?

Right now the Mavericks are so at the top of their game. I don't think that will be an issue. You just know. As the writer, you know which songs will work best for the Mavericks and which songs will work best for a Raul Malo solo project. I think that becomes apparent. But honestly, some of the songs from my solo career that we play live find the Mavericks just killing it. When the Mavericks play something, there's something special about the Mavericks. Those guys are just amazing. So we'll deal with it when the time comes, but again, right now I have no plans for a solo record. The Mavericks are pretty much occupying all my time.

You reissued your first independent album, the one that you made before you guys signed with MCA.

Yes, and we're thrilled about that. That record started it all off for us. Perhaps things would have still happened, but they wouldn't have happened the way they happened without that record. We released it and six months later we were signed to a major label, so whatever that record did, it was kind of a little portal that allowed us to skip a step or two and get our music to the right people at the right time.

I personally think that it was a great album. But regardless, it's time the public was reintroduced to that album.

It is what it is. We were young, we were kids. I'm not ashamed of that record at all. I listen to it and think, 'All right. Not bad.' Of course as a songwriter, there are things I wish we had done a little differently. But I still do that now. We're proud of that album.

31

The Steep Canyon Rangers

Bluegrass Boosters on a Steady Ascent

It's interesting to find today's music lovers tapping an age-old tradition once nourished by Bill Monroe, Lester Flatt, Earl Scruggs, Jim and Jesse, the Stanley Brothers, the Osborne Brothers, and scores of other artists who brought bluegrass its initial popularity in the 1940s and 1950s.

Sixty years later, bands like Mumford and Sons, although not traditional bluegrass bands, use bluegrass instruments and have helped spread the popularity of bluegrass. But Mumford and Sons aren't the only band to have ridden this wave of revived traditionalism. The Steep Canyon Rangers have carried that bluegrass banner to the point where they now stand at the highest peak of the musical vanguard—bluegrass and otherwise—thanks not only to their creative and compositional prowess, but also to their much-ballyhooed tours with Steve Martin, several Grammy nods, and most of all, their exemplary 2013 album, *Tell the Ones I Love*, which still sets a standard for today's bluegrass resurgence. Nevertheless, given the emerging world of modern bluegrass, nugrass, and all things Americana, the field of competition appears to have increased exponentially with every passing day. This is the realm of new populism, after all, and where once this music was confined to back porches and intimate gatherings, it's now played for crowds numbering in the tens of thousands via festivals and prestigious stages worldwide. It clearly opens the door for a band like the Steep Canyon Rangers, a group whose music stays true to the traditional trappings while also opening up expansive possibilities for commercial success.

Despite some unassuming origins, Steep Canyon Rangers' success came relatively quickly. Founded in 2000 by core members Woody Platt (guitar), Graham Sharp (banjo), and Charles R. Humphrey III (upright bass), all students at the University of North Carolina in Chapel Hill, they were soon joined by mandolin player Mike Guggino, a childhood pal of Platt's. Original fiddler Lizzie Hamilton was added to the fold soon after, helping Steep Canyon Rangers become festival favorites from North Carolina to Colorado. Two early albums, *Old Dreams and New Dreams* (2001) and *Mr. Taylor's New Home* (2002), helped extend that popularity and, among other things, helped garner them a first prize award at the prestigious Rockygrass Festival band competition in 2001. Despite Hamilton's departure in 2003, the band continued to pursue its heavy road regimen and recorded an eponymous third album, released on Rebel Records in 2004. That same year, the group recruited Nicky Sanders to fill the fiddle role in the lineup and subsequently set about recording their next effort, *One Dime at a Time* (2005). The recording won the band several awards from the International Bluegrass Music Association, thereby boosting their profile considerably.

Still, that doesn't account for the band's ability to cross over into other realms as well. In many ways, the Steep Canyon Rangers have picked up where bands like the Nitty Gritty Dirt Band, the latter-day Byrds, the Flying Burrito Brothers, Poco, the Band, New Grass Revival, and the Grateful Dead left off in the early to midseventies. When those groups initiated the first crossover from rock to country, they began by taking their cues from bluegrass innovators—the Dillards, David Grisman, John Hartford, the Kentucky Colonels, and Del McCoury among them—and then combined that sound with an irreverent attitude and edgier material that appealed to a contemporary crowd. While Steep Canyon Rangers have taken pains to purvey a more wholesome image— they're rarely seen on stage without sporting their matching suits and ties—their young, fresh approach conveys a verve and vitality that audiences find instantly endearing.

The Steeps' big break—at least in terms of greater awareness—

came in 2009 when Steve Martin tapped them as his backing band after opting to take his banjo playing acumen on the road. The tour brought them from Carnegie Hall to Bonnaroo, Austin City Limits, the Telluride, Bluegrass Festival, the Royal Festival Hall in London, and even the West Lawn of the US Capitol for the nation's annual Fourth of July celebration in 2011.

Steep Canyon Rangers' prominence was clearly on an upward ascent. The band has collaborated with Martin on three albums thus far: the Grammy-nominated *Rare Bird Alert* in 2011, which remarkably features a cameo appearance from Paul McCartney as well as the Dixie Chicks; 2013's *Love Has Come for You*, ostensively credited to Martin and Edie Brickell, but featuring the Steep Canyon Rangers as the primary backing band; and 2017's aptly named *The Long-Awaited Album*. The former garnered them Entertainers of the Year honors from the IBMA, which they shared with Martin in 2011. That same year, they signed with Rounder Records, one more sign of the recognition they were reaping. Indeed, their first album for the label, *Nobody Knows You*, struck pay dirt almost immediately, winning them a Grammy for Best Bluegrass Album.

"I like to get to know the people that support us," Woody Platt comments. "I don't feel like we're too big or too special not to do that. It's a real organic kind of lifestyle that we live, so it's natural to kind of get to know our fans. I want to stay with that philosophy."

32

....

The Punch Brothers Get Punchy

These days, any number of bands have pushed the envelope forward by making themselves festival favorites, picking up on the populist connection that typified Deadheads, Phish Heads, and other groups of core fans who followed their heroes from show to show and developed that feeling of community around a common bond.

Over the course of the past decade or so, the Punch Brothers—Chris Thile, Gabe Witcher, Paul Kowert, Chris Eldridge, and Noam Pikelny—have nurtured that devotion among their fans and followers, while at the same time establishing themselves as one of the most innovative acoustic outfits of the modern era. That's thanks in no small part to its members' ability to improvise and interact with such remarkable finesse. Ostensively a bluegrass band, their sound and style generally defies any attempt at typecasting, making them a crowd favorite in concert and a reliable commodity on record as well.

Bassist Paul Kowert affirmed that feeling when we spoke prior to their performance at the Springfest Festival in northern Florida.

Bluegrass music certainly seems to have evolved in recent years, especially in terms of how people once perceived it. Bands like yours have certainly stretched the perimeters and shattered the stereotypes. Is that a statement you'd agree with?

You're likely referring to acoustic music and the kind of acoustic instruments that we use. There are theories that suggest this kind of music ebbs and flows in popularity. Every fifteen years or so there'll be a resurgence, and something happens where people will get into it again. I think people are drawn to music that can happen just around a campfire, something that kind of has an organic feeling and brings people back to the basics. We use acoustic instruments because that's what we do. We all grew up playing acoustic instruments and that's how we express ourselves. It's something that we all love and have studied, but we're not trying to just to capture that. We're just trying to make our music.

Even the fact that you play a standup bass says something about that adherence to tradition. Now it's fairly common, but at one point it was really associated with an old-time kind of sound, like with rockabilly or traditional music of some sort. It was very old school.

If you can hear it acoustically or it's amplified really well, that's a sound that you can't get another way. You can't get it with electric bass. I tell myself that every day that I lug that damn thing around.

When did you first begin playing?

I started playing when I was nine, but you don't think about those things then.

Have you always played standup as opposed to electric?

I've played electric periodically. I started both at the same time. When I was nine I got a friend's electric bass as well as an upright, but I kind of stuck with the upright. I started playing violin originally when I was three, so I was drawn to the bow and an acoustic instrument, as well as the music. I grew up in a household that embraced classical music, so that's another reason why I stuck with the upright.

Are you classically trained?

Yes. I went to the Curtis Institute of Music in Philly, a classical conservatory.

Did your former professors express any disappointment that you didn't join a symphony?

Not at all. They're open-minded fellows. I owe a lot to them. Hal Robinson and Edgar Meyer were my teachers at Curtis, so I was very lucky.

The Punch Brothers seem to indulge in nonstop touring. You're on the road constantly it seems.

We had a good stretch of staying out on the road for a good portion of the year, but in February of 2013, that was the beginning of a break from touring. Before that, the biggest record of our career was *Antifogmatic*, and we wanted to get out there and share it all the time. But when it came time to make a new record, we needed to take some time at home, to get healthy and experience some things to write about and come up with some new ideas. We came off the road and decided to spend our time writing together in one place. But we still played some festivals here and there.

Indeed. Here you are at Springfest, and then tonight you're heading to Savannah.

Well, yes. This is our first tour since February. We're all together in the bus again.

And how is life being back in the bus?

It takes me right back to 2012.

One of the most amazing things about your band is the way you guys manage to multitask. You each have your own individual projects and side trips, and yet you also manage to find time to do the Punch Brothers full-time. How do

you coordinate the schedules to accommodate everything you want to do both as a band and as individuals?

The thing that makes it work is our unanimous devotion to the Punch Brothers. While we all have our individual projects going on, we all make it work with the idea we came up with democratically for the Punch Brothers. We talk to each other on the phone, we get together and we make it all work for the Punch Brothers.

It just seems like an incredible amount of multitasking.

Every once in awhile you get a double booking and you have to figure out what to do. You try to avoid it of course, but it's a matter of staying organized, and management helps out with that.

What particular project are you involved with outside the band?

I have a trio called Haas Kowart Tyce, because it's Britany Howard on fiddle and I play bass and it's Howard Tyce on guitar, and we just made a record. That's one thing I've been doing, and I've also had some gigs with Dave Rawlings Machine and various musical projects here and there.

Again, you're proving my point. You guys have so much going on. It's just dazzling the way you make it all work.

It's all about the calendar. We spend a lot of time looking at the calendar.

That must be a fascinating way to spend your time . . . just staring at the calendar.

Oh yes, utterly fascinating. Such fun. [*chuckles*]

When did you join the band, Paul? Have you been with the group since the beginning?

I'm the only one who was not in the band at its inception.

So you're still the new guy?

That's right. I've been in the band for six years. The other guys had been playing together since a couple of years before that.

So how did you come to hook up with the other four?

It was a bunch of reasons. The old bassist Greg Garrison was a fantastic bass player, but he had some kids and the Punch Brothers were amping up their tour schedule, and people's goals started to diverge. So they called me.

It seems like your audience following has really grown in the past couple of years, and now you have this really devoted fan base now.

It's extraordinary to have that support and to be able to continue to grow. Hearing the audience singing a song that I helped write is really neat. It feels good. We're just liking the fact that the audiences like what we do. It feels really good.

Where did the name Punch Brothers come from?

Mark Twain. Mark Twain wrote a short story called "Punch Brothers Punch" that's about a poem of questionable quality that the narrator can't seem to get out of his mind. It's kind of a funny analogy about what we do.

It's always good to have a literary connection of some sort. That's very impressive actually.

Well, Mark Twain is a good guy to align with.

Definitely. Getting back to your touring regimen . . . you also do a few of these music cruises. I saw you on "Mountain Song at Sea," in fact. How do you like doing these special events as opposed to the smaller, one-off venues?

Having the variety is cool. The variety is great. Ending up here at Springfest is really amazing, just stepping outside the bus and being surrounded by Spanish Moss and wonderful weather. But it's also wonderful to play for an audience that came out specifically to see you in an environment that's a little more controlled, where the sound is more controlled. But both scenarios are good. It's fun to reach people that maybe haven't seen you before, which often happens at a festival.

How did you enjoy the cruise experience?

I loved the cruise. It was fun for me because it allows me to work at my ability to vacation. The fact that we were technically working also allowed me to kick back when I wasn't playing, which is kind of a ridiculous thing—just being on a boat with people I really like musically, as well as with a bunch of friends. The bluegrass cruises are a really good time.

Where do your songs come from? Do you guys work collectively to come up with the material?

It's not the same for every song. Sometimes you have Thile coming in with a song that's not fully formed and has to be arranged for the instrumentation. Sometimes he comes in with an idea and we develop it together. And sometimes it's someone's else's idea, a little cell from which you can build an entire song. Oftentimes it's something that sounds really good on the instruments, so it kind of remains intact and we build from there. There's a bunch of different ways it happens, and much of the stuff we write doesn't happen on paper at all, but sometimes we have counterpoint sections where the most effective way to create it is on a computer program like Sibelius, something that you can fiddle with a note at a time and hear how it affects everything. And then we'll take it from the music on the paper. But still, that's rare for us. By far, the majority of it doesn't happen with any paper.

Does it come out of jams?

The stuff that sounds that way usually came about that way. Most of our music comes by ear, sitting around in a circle, and some of it comes from jamming. Some of our music has come from the nonsense that we play when the show is over as we're walking down to the green room. There's all this energy that we have bottled up. The show is over, the lights are off, and as we're walking off we just start playing some nonsense or whatever we're thinking. Sometimes it sounds really cool. We've had a couple of things come out of that.

Isn't it a bit awkward to walk and jam with a stand-up bass?

It's awkward.

Still, you guys have this very spontaneous aura about you, as if a lot of your music is strictly improvised. How do you pull that off night after night? Is it in fact well rehearsed?

Yeah, that's an insightful thing to say. I think that spontaneity is something we hold dear. That's something we want in the music and we build it in. We create a framework in which spontaneity can be recurring every night. Sometimes one person's part isn't completely figured out in a way, so they can change it every night. Sometimes it's sectioned where we can all figure out where we're going. It's the opportunity for spontaneity has been built into our music and that's really what we love, that improvising.

What's different about an upcoming album that gets you so psyched?

Our success and mistakes combine every day to give a new perspective. One thing we're trying to do is to get back to playing more instead of singing all the time. It's a place we had largely arrived at. We always prefer live performances because we're good at it, but we want that to be represented on the record and represent that aspect of what we do.

33

Yonder Mountain String Band

A Testament to Telluride

Call it the mountain muse. The happiness of the heights. Or maybe it's simply the mix of altitude with attitude. Whatever the case, Yonder Mountain Band consistently captures that spirit, a connection that has more to do with their sensibilities than with their name alone. Notoriously independent, they blend the frenzy of Bluegrass with jam band instincts and populist sentiments, a combination that's helped them become both festival favorites and indie entrepreneurs. For more than a decade, this Colorado-based quartet—now departed mandolin player Jeff Austin, guitarist Adam Aijala, bassist Ben Kaufman, and banjo player Dave Johnston—entertained audiences with their savvy and synchronicity, earning them legions of devotees both in their home state and throughout the nation. After initially developing their frenetic stage shows in clubs and other intimate environs, they quickly graduated to bigger venues, with a featured performance at the 2008 Democratic Convention in Denver helping to elevate their profile and affirm their intents.

I caught up with the foursome backstage at the Telluride Bluegrass Festival, an annual gig of which they're justifiably proud, and I took the opportunity to ask them about their affinity for the festival and the audience interaction that helps spur them on.

So how many times have you guys played Telluride?

Jeff Austin: Fourteen. Really fifteen since we made our first appearance. We stayed in a house in Telluride right behind Elk's

Park. It's really nice now, but it wasn't as nice when we stayed there. A show would let out and we'd be picking on the porch, and people would kind of gather and listen. Vince Herman (of Leftover Salmon) lived in the same neighborhood, and he was really adamant that we should expand our boundaries. "You guys got something to play and you need to get people to hear you," he said. "It doesn't matter if it's on a street corner or on a bus at six in the morning. Just do it. Be passionate about it. Why hold back?"

So was that the seed that started you on your way?

Adam Aijala: We actually got an invite to play the festival that first year. It was '99, I think. We played the stage in Elk's Park. We had been doing a few other gigs around Colorado, but this gig was our most far afield. I remember we got a good response, although I don't remember how we sounded or anything. So that year that we played here, and we also played Rockygrass for the first time, which helped develop our relationship with [festival promoters] Planet Bluegrass, and we've been playing here ever since. They told us, "We don't really know what you're doing, but we really love the energy." They seemed to see something special. As you know, this isn't just a Bluegrass festival. They always bring in eclectic stuff. And having the endorsement of a group like Leftover Salmon didn't hurt either. To have people like that speaking up for you—"Oh, you've got to give them a shot"—was really cool. That's mileage in years. You can gut it out and do these cool little gigs, or if you have someone who believes in you, who's a cornerstone of an event that's a staple, find yourself in a position that's wildly helpful. So suddenly here we are on the main stage, and it's like, "What the hell are we doing here?"

Have you noticed any changes in the festival over the years? In the time you've been here, how have you seen Telluride evolve?

Ben Kaufman: There seem to be more dogfights in town. People bring their dogs and they seem to get in more fights. Actually, I think the vibe has kind of mellowed. It used to be hardcore hippie and now it's a bit more respectful. But the fundamental feeling hasn't changed too much.

You guys play a lot of festivals. That's part of the basic MO, right? How does Telluride distinguish itself from some of the other big gatherings you play, like say Bonnaroo?

Adam: Obviously, aesthetically, there's nothing like this place that I've ever seen. For me, that's the main thing. When you're on that stage and you have that killer view in front of you, that's one reason to like the place in itself. I love it for that alone. And over the years, we've met more and more locals and made so many cool friends. There are so many things to do around here. You can play golf and go fishing. You can hike up to the waterfalls and see all kinds of cool stuff.

Jeff: For me, it's the historical aspect of this thing. It gives us a boost, not only for our Colorado audience, but suddenly when we're playing in San Francisco, and we're having drinks at a bar, someone will say, "I saw you at Telluride Bluegrass." That's another aspect of this festival. This isn't twelve thousand Coloradans. There are people from England, from Japan, from Connecticut, from all over the world. Festivals do that. Every year—and this might sound morbid—I think if this was my last Telluride, this is the one I'd miss the most. Our roots are here. I'd say I've slept a total of nine hours in all the years we've done this festival, either due to just hanging out, or to playing with friends, or to not wanting to miss a moment. Feeling that if I left something out, I'd miss something. When you come out the other side of it, those experiences are what I cherish the most. Every year, the first time I see the falls and the canyon, it's that moment that really gets me. We see people here that we don't get to see except maybe once a year. So you get to have some quality time while spending some time with friends and musical friends.

Adam: Even though it's chaotic like every other festival, it's pretty organized. Everything is pretty easy. Not only for us, because we're artists, but I don't hear fans complaining about it either. There are moments that happen here that don't happen anywhere else.
Jeff: The fact that there's only one stage and not a need to run around to pick and choose means there's a lot of focused energy. It's not

a scattered thing. "Oh, I have to cut out so I can get over to see Primus." All of a sudden, when a place suddenly becomes the second biggest city in the state, things do tend to get somewhat crazy.

Your recorded output seems fairly evenly divided between your live recordings and your studio efforts. In fact, your live albums seem more predominant than your studio endeavors. There's a reason for that obviously. . . .

Ben: You're right. We're not on Columbia Records. We don't have anyone looking over our shoulder. . . .

I suspect that it's an attempt to capture the energy and essence of your live performances, which is, after all, what you're all about. So the question is, do you find it difficult to make the transition from the concert stage to the recording studio without sacrificing that spontaneity in the process?

Jeff: It is a challenge. But the most recent experience we had, where we recorded four songs for an EP, was so easy and fun. And wouldn't you know it, the minute we stopped obsessing over it so much was the minute we get the recordings where I said, "Yup, it sounds like us. We finally did it." This is absolutely what we sound like. I'm so happy.

But it can be a challenge, no?

Adam: One of the things we found out is that you can record as long as you want and go over it and over it, and get it to where you want it to go, but when you don't have a stage and you don't have a crowd, you know it's going to be different. Still, we generally record all our tracks live. We may overdub our solos and vocals, but we record those live too. At least that's the way we've done it in the past. So we do try to capture that live energy so it approximates what we do onstage. And we can't ask for more than that. We can't raise our expectations higher than our ability to make it happen. We can't expect it to sound live when it's not. But when we record it live, it's still approximating the same sound.

How do your songs evolve? Does someone come in with the basics of a song and then the rest of you improvise or add your individual contributions to refine it into a finished product? Does it then further evolve through the live performance?

Dave Johnston: Everyone writes and each of us develops certain sounds and ideas on our own, so it's not like we say, "Here's a song, and here's the solo part," and all that. But oftentimes it will be something like one of us will present a song and someone will say, "What if we do this instead?" And then someone else will say, "Oh, that sounds great." So it's a pretty cool thing in that regard. And then sometimes we write together. Or sometimes it takes a Phil Lesh to say, "Oh you guys totally jammed that outro! It's such a great part—why would you cut it short?" And sometimes we'll take an old tune, and somebody will say, "Why don't we do this with it?"

Ben: We can take an old song that we've been doing for fifteen years and make it a jam vehicle or an improvisational vehicle. We'll try to have some space in there so that may be the guys—or myself if I'm lucky—can always come up with something new. Plus, there's always this sort of new generation of material that always keeps you thinking. Dave's got a new one that almost sounds like Motown, which means I get to come up with the best James Jamerson–sounding bass line that I can possibly do. I've never had that opportunity!

Jeff: It's also the undeniable, energetic impact of a live crowd. I may write a song where I'll imagine these reaction points, like "Here is where the crowd will react," and then you bring it to the stage, and the crowd reacts in a totally different place. Therefore what it does is become an instinct composition. All of a sudden, you're instantly composing it anew. The reaction happens in a totally different spot and it sends you in this totally different direction where instantaneously you're recomposing your own thought process of what you thought you had. Which just shows you that you can really screw it up, because in truth, you can go with your best intentions and the audience will give you something totally different. Which is great, because then it becomes that communal thing where they're helping you write that stuff. It's like, if they're reacting to this thing, why don't we hold it for another eight bars or another eight count, or maybe stop it here. There are times when we'll do something almost unintentional and the crowd reacts in a very positive way and you go, "Oh!" What do we know?

Adam: It's a case where the audience is the fifth member of the band. Their contribution is essential to what we do. You feel it. The importance of the audience in terms of their energy is hard to talk about in words, but it's essential. And when you feel it, it makes you go bigger and bigger and bigger, and you want to be better and better and better.

I think the audience senses that. . . .

Jeff: I gotta believe the audience we play to are so savvy they would smell bullshit a mile away.

Dave: We always do different shows anyway, so we can't have a polished set. That's not the way we work. On any given night, we might do a song we've been playing for ten years, and it might be ten more beats, or a faster pace or a slower pace, or a different jam section. Even our onstage patter is different. We never say the same thing between songs from one night to another.

Jeff: That wall between the band and the crowd goes down. We may have a set list, but their input to us is so important. We're not depending on it, but it's really great when it happens. This festival is a prime example. Songs have changed here that have stayed that way. You pick up on that vibe that's been given to you, and oftentimes it's wholly unexpected.

That must be very gratifying.

Adam: I remember once when we were playing this song, and all of a sudden the crowd went "Yaaaaayyyyy!" They all went nuts, and we thought, "Hey, we're really nailing it!" And all of a sudden, the security guys are dying laughing. Because there's some dude that's climbed a tree behind the stage and he's tripping his balls off, and that's what they're reacting to! So we hired that guy, and he's been with us ever since!

34

Greensky Bluegrass

Breaking Down Barriers

Formed in 2000, the five-piece Michigan-based band that goes by the unlikely handle of Greensky Bluegrass also owes much of its success to its tenure at Telluride Bluegrass. In 2006 the band—lap steel player Anders Beck, banjo player Michael Arlen Bont, guitarist Dave Bruzza, bassist Michael Devol, and mandolin and ukulele player Paul Hoffman—garnered their first major accolade by winning the festival's coveted band competition. A prime example of a band that borrows from bluegrass but adds their own contemporary trappings, they're still winning kudos from the Telluride troops and others as well. After their fourth album, 2011's *Handguns*, debuted on Billboard's Bluegrass Charts at number three, it capped its acclaim by spending nine weeks on the chart, eventually garnering number thirty-three on the magazine's year-end list. I met up with them backstage at Telluride in 2013, and took the opportunity to ask Paul Hoffman about the challenges and triumphs of their trajectory thus far.

So how does Telluride differ from the other festivals you've played?

This festival is perfect for us. I feel like we thrive here . . . and we love it.

But what is it about Telluride that makes the vibe so good?

What they've done throughout their entire forty years is to integrate other music into the mix, as opposed to presenting a single style of music all day long. And that's exactly where we fall in. We're a bluegrass band that can do other things too. An indie band that also plays bluegrass. The audience that comes here really appreciates bluegrass, but they can also be into seeing someone like David Byrne here as well. And that's perfect for us, because the audience is really attentive. They really are listening. A lot of festivals we do are more like a party—which I'm into—but here they're really listening. It's hard work to be at a festival for four days . . . it's hot, you've got to stake out a vantage point every morning . . . it can be a bit distracting.

Are you guys still based in Michigan?

Yeah.

That doesn't seem like the most likely place for a bluegrass band. How were you accepted there?

It's a really cool scene up there, but we haven't spent a lot of time up there lately. We've been out on tour quite a bit.

How was it initially, though? Was that kind of a difficult place to hone your craft?

I'm tempted to say kind of, but it was also great to have the challenge of developing and creating our sound. It started out pretty informally. I remember when we were doing shows on the west coast of Michigan—we used to do a few shows every weekend, and we would just tour up and down the state on a regular basis— I felt like we were really converting people to bluegrass. There are people in Michigan that are into bluegrass, but they don't go to bars and clubs. I was the one that was booking the band back then, and I'd be making a lot of phone calls and I'd always be telling the club owners, "Don't worry, they're going to like it." We weren't their normal kind of band, so I'd really have to convince them. But after the show, people would come up to us and say,

"I really like bluegrass. You guys are really cool!" So we started having a little more fun with the music and playing Prince covers and stuff like that.

What kind of covers were you doing?

"When Doves Cry" is the oldest, most off-the-wall cover we've done. . . . We've been playing that since 2001. That was the real converter. When you're playing a bar gig, and maybe there's a five dollar cover, or no cover, they're just there. They didn't come to see us. They don't care. So we're playing all these bluegrass songs and then suddenly we start playing "When Doves Cry." And the crowd is like, "We know this song," and then they not only know it, but they like it, and you launch into a ripping banjo solo over the song, and they decide they like that too. And a couple of weeks later you might be talking to someone, and it's "I started listening to Earl Scruggs because of you guys."

That sounds like a pretty good strategy.

The earliest advice that a band usually gets is that when you start out, you have to play familiar songs first. That's kind of the typical bar band axiom. So a lot of what we and other bluegrass bands do is play these old songs and arrange them in a different way. So we might all play this song or that song or an old blues song Bill Monroe might have played, but it's all about the arranging. And the better we got at that, the more we wanted to challenge ourselves by reaching out. The day Michael Jackson died, we started playing "Beat It." We learned it both ways. The original way and then a bluegrassy way. It's all about how to serve the song in the best way with the instruments. It's a really cool thing we do in the band. So those covers for us are a really important exercise. It teaches us how to make best use of our instruments, and in many cases, it's a challenge because we don't use drums or percussion. So we have to figure it out. It's like, "If we do this . . . "

Is it a challenge to take what you do in the studio and try to capture that live sound and translate and harness it accordingly?

Yeah, but I really enjoy the studio a lot. It's different to be in this jam band community where people come to the shows and support the music, but it doesn't necessarily translate into album sales. But still, I value making records in the studio. It's so much fun. It's hard to capture that live vibe without an audience, because when you're in front of a crowd, songs get longer. With certain passages, you start to take your time. But the studio's just not the place for that I don't think. On our album *Handguns*, there's a song called "All Four" that we were playing live for two years before we recorded it for the record. It's a fifteen-minute song when we do it live. It's got a really long improvised section, and we really struggled to figure out how to record it for a studio record after two years of playing it live with people's expectations here or there. We kind of toned it down a little bit, but it's still twelve minutes on the record. We take a lot of time in the studio to think about songs and how we want them to be perceived. We're always trying to do new things. Sometimes we think, "Should we do this two times or four times?" We don't really know. In the studio, you do it, then listen to it, then listen to it again. Then you talk about it and listen to it again, and talk about it again. It's so hyperfocused. I love it.

Do you work with a producer most of the time?

We produced our last record, and we're producing the new one we're working on now. Tim Carbone produced two records of our records, although we didn't even know at first what a producer does. Tim really gets it. He knows the band, he likes the songs, and it taught us a lot. It was nice to have a set of outside ears. The engineer we worked with, Glenn Brown, kind of fills that role. We'll spend two weeks trying to work out different endings to a song, and sometimes you need someone to kind of tell you what's working the best.

Is it difficult to not repeat yourselves? Does that become a challenge at times?

With the new record we're working on now, we're recording it in the same studio, in much the same way as before, but we're also giving ourselves more time. So we can mess around a little bit and try different techniques. We're trying to make art, but when you end up working on the same song for four hours, you have to decide when to wrap it up and move on. On this record there were times when we asked ourselves, "Are we just making another *Handguns*?" I don't know the answer to that, really. Maybe we did. There's a victory and defeat in whichever way you look at it. When you listen to your favorite band and you hear a new record that's totally different, you can be proud and interested in this evolution they undertook, but a lot of times you feel betrayed. So if it's more of the same and it gets better, I don't know if it's too much or what.

Then again, you could use the example of the Beatles and *The White Album*. **Every song seemed to break the mold, and people thought that was wildly intriguing.**

That's kind of like the approach we're taking on our new album. It's kind of like a mixtape. We're trying all these different things. One song is really bluegrassy, and then there's one song which is kind of like my homage to U2 basically. [*chuckles*] Then there's some bluegrassy-esque fusion kind of songs. So it's really all over the place. I love that though, even though I sometimes worry that the album's not cohesive enough. I think that's kind of the charm of our band, and a signature of what we do. Sometimes we're playing a song like "Mountain Girls," and sometimes we're doing something totally dark and scary.

....

The Avett Brothers Redefine the Template

Seth Avett is just about the nicest guy you'd ever want to know. A thirty-minute phone chat brings an instant bond, a sharing of sincere sentiment, a hearty laugh, and a folksy, unaffected down-home demeanor that's every bit as honest and embracing as the seemingly spontaneous, off-the-cuff, and emotionally vulnerable melodies that he and his brother Scott deliver under the moniker of the Avett Brothers. Over the course of the past fifteen years, the band's evolved from their own homegrown devices to a major label success, gaining them a rabid following that's made them festival staples while affirming their populist appeal. Boasting a rustic sound that emphasizes the basics—acoustic guitars, a kick drum, bass, cello, and occasional keyboards—the quartet, which also includes longtime bassist Bob Crawford and their newest recruit, Joe Kwon, is by turns both effusive and heartbreaking, detailing personal declarations of remorse and reflection.

After years of making their name in their native North Carolina environs and a dozen albums and EPs on the local Ramseur Records label, the Avetts graduated to the big time with the release of 2009's *I and Love and You*, which brought them into the America's top twenty. The follow-up, *The Carpenter*, was released soon after and climbed even higher, charting at number four on the Billboard album charts. Produced by legendary wunderkind Rick Rubin, the two albums found the Avetts graduating from home boy heroes to mainstays of late night TV. The charm of their wistful, no-frills approach is amplified by the irresistible urgency of cascading choruses that seep into the consciousness and linger long after the last notes finally fade away. An ideal example of old school, homespun finding a mainstream audience, the Avetts combine old and new in the most imaginative ways.

Seth eagerly talked about transition.

Has your sudden success taken you by surprise?

I can tell you that it gets sort of overwhelming to get on the scale of what it's gotten to. If I look at it with my twenty-one-year-old eyes, then yes. It's unbelievable in a way. You do something gradual every day, year in and year out, and you gain perspective for yourself as well as you can, but you lose the perspective you had when you stepped into the room, and as you're walking through it you lose the perspective that you had when you were walking through the door. I think so much in terms of what's happening right now. We've stayed so busy, I take precious little time to reminisce, precious little time to process, precious little time to bask in anything. I'm talking literally. I'm talking about stepping onstage with Willie Nelson and singing "On the Road Again" in Texas and being in the bus a few hours later and heading to wherever we were heading to next and talking about the set list for the next day and whatever, and not sitting there drinking a beer and thinking, "Man, I just sang with Willie Nelson!" I've tried to appreciate that, but you keep moving so you don't get bogged down. We've had more fortunate and exciting experiences than we deserve. [*laughs*] I'm excited about the lifestyle we've led and the opportunities we've had, and some of them do surprise me. But then again, we're just hardworking guys and we don't take a lot of time to think it through. We're just on to the next thing and the next thing and the next thing.

In a way, your laidback, unpretentious sound has kind of paved the way for a new generation of acts with the same no-nonsense style. I'm thinking of Mumford and Sons and the Lumineers in particular.

I agree. That's something that I like to keep in check. I certainly don't want to take credit for something that's not mine and ours to take. Both of those bands are friends and colleagues. Both are, on average, ten years younger than us, and they have been vocal about our influence on them. So I'm trying to be OK with that and be in the position of gratitude and to accept that gratefully. I appreciate very much that those bands have expressed that and have done good things and received attention for that. Commercially speaking, both of those bands are at a higher level than we've ever been, but they're doing it their way. They're doing their thing and it's being responded to. It's exciting in the landscape of music to see the music each of those bands are making, and the music we're making, and being rewarded with some kind of popularity and some kind of buzz. Yeah, I think that we were part of the building for them, and there are bands that were very much a part of the building for us and never saw a lot of attention. For example, there was a band called the Blue Rags, which was a fantastic ragtime / rock and roll band that I saw when I was sixteen or seventeen years old at the Brewery in Raleigh. God knows that if they hit the scene fifteen years later, maybe they would have seen a lot of commercial success. Bill Reynolds, who was the bass player in that band, actually plays with Band of Horses now. But bands with banjos were never seen on TV back then. That was not a possibility when we started.

You guys defy categorization. You might have a banjo, but your sound can hardly be called bluegrass. You really bend the parameters. That said, being that your last two albums were recorded for major labels, was there any pressure to sew up the loose ends and give it more of a polished sheen?

Not the first iota. It's a weird thing. I can't speak for other folks that have worked with major labels, but for us, our story has been told a thousand times. The label knew we did everything completely ourselves for the first eight or nine years of this thing. That really gave us some leverage. So we thought about the scenario of being on a major label; we had a fan base and we weren't like eighteen-year-old kids who were begging the label to make a career for us. We're well on our way. We're going to have a career, and whether we're going to sell a lot of records or not is completely up in the air and quite arbitrary in our mind. And we wanted to take that step, because it was the right step, and it was with folks that we wanted to work with. Right now, we love working with them, and that pretty much dissolves the negative stigma of the big, bad major label. There have been a lot of horror stories about people working with major labels, but really it's just a group of people who got into music because they love it.

So what was the evolution that came with being on a major label? How did that affect your MO?

The last two albums are more a comment on our development as a band. The reality is, we're just on our path and we're changing. A band that's going to be together for awhile is going to listen to their muse and their inspiration, and they're going to change. And between these two records, you're looking at maybe five hundred or six hundred shows that we've played. So we're not going to sound the same from one record to another, because we're getting better. And we're proud of that. I love the charm of the early records. I was singing with flats and sharps all over the place, but I don't really want to do that anymore. I want to sing well. I want to sing like Sam Cooke, ya know? [*laughs*]

What did Rick Rubin bring into the mix?

Well, he helped break things down. He helped us slow down and see what was working and what sort of needed reworking and to examine it. Again, we did everything on our own, and there's plenty that's good about that, but there's also some shortcomings. And one of the shortcomings is that me and Scott and Bob don't really have great rhythm. We have a rhythm that changes a lot within the songs—sometimes that's OK, sometimes that's great—and we did that for eight years without a drummer. I was the drummer—I'd play drums on the records, I'd play piano on the records, whatever—and I can play drums to my own inconsistent tempo because I was the one that's inconsistent. But when we looked at it, we realized that it was really detracting from the song and making it harder to figure out what we were singing about because we were so distracted by the sway, being slow and fast, slow and fast and so forth. That's just a technical detail, but

Rick helped bring calm to the studio, helped bring a real spirit of experimentation and a real spirit of exploration. Instead of saying, "Hey, that sounds like a real bad idea, let's not do it," Rick would say, "I got an idea and maybe it's horrible," and that's how he is. He doesn't think that everything he does is golden. Not by a long shot. He thinks that if somebody has an idea, let's find out if it's good or not. Let's not just assume we know without hearing it.

So many of your songs are really plaintive and sobering—heartbreaking in fact. Where does that emotion come from? It sounds like your hearts are broken. Are you venting your own feelings through these songs?

Well, the truthful and sad answer to that is . . . yes. The fact is that it is real because we are genuinely sensitive men. [*laughs*] I have a debilitating sensitivity. I am a man that can think myself into absolute heartbreak. I take myself there daily. It's not something that I necessarily need treatment for, but I really grab onto things. And I'm not just talking about heartbreak. I mean joy, and I can be on top of the mountain. And when I am, you'll probably hear it in a song and probably present it in the most terrifying, exciting fashion. This is love, this is compassion, unadulterated, unfiltered . . . and then you're going to get the same thing when I feel hopeless or I feel scared or whatever. I think that's a pretty common trait for a songwriter. If you look at Elliot Smith . . . you cannot separate his status from him as an artist. And that's because that man had an unusual sensitivity for sadness and for beating himself up in a way. We like music that shows vulnerability, music that's honest for good or bad. So we like to present songs that are honest for good or for bad. Scott and I are both aware of each other as people, folks that lock onto emotion and we champion it, and sometimes that's good for our lives, and sometimes it's really, really bad for our lives. Generally speaking, it's always good for art, but not always so good for day-to-day life.

The way you express that emotion is so brilliant to begin with. When you're up there on stage, whooping and hollering and carrying on, is that genuine feeling we're seeing you express?

With the whole hollering and screaming and dancing and shimmering, getting down and having fun . . . the reason we're like that onstage is that it's genuine. Because of the people in the audience, it's something we've developed over the years, over this decade plus, almost a dozen years of creating this relationship with an audience that is highly genuine and highly infectious. It's a beautiful thing to be a part of, but we are not creators of it. There's a beautiful interaction that happens between us and an audience that makes it feel much less like us and them, but more like just us. These shows have become like celebrations and people expect that, so they make it happen. So we just jump in there with them, and we came all the way out here to Arizona, or Tennessee or California or Japan or wherever, not to sit around and brood but to celebrate. So let's celebrate in a healthy way, and let's make it happen. We really are aware that there are only so many times in our lives that we're going to get to do this. It's not going to last forever. It sounds pretty fatalistic, but it's just the truth, so let's celebrate that. I am more on the page now of just connecting with folks than I am with showing off. When I was younger, I was like, "I want to show them my talent, I want to prove that I can do something and I can do it well," which is ironic because at the time, I really couldn't do it very well. So I'm more aware now that the great value in these shows is the celebratory factor and is the opportunity to connect with folks that use our music as a tool. I'll be talking to someone and they'll say, "Oh man, I listened to your music all doing my chemo treatments." That's where it's at. That reminds me how much of a waste of time it is to show off. When you're lucky enough to have that interaction like that with somebody, it tells you that you are being put to use, and what an honor that is. So that's why the shows are like they are. I'm speaking for all of us when I say that—band and crew. We all feel very honored to be a part of it.

When you sit down to write a song, given that naked emotion that comes through, do you have to search it out and grab it, or are you channeling it from somewhere inside?

They do come out of nowhere. It's a very mysterious thing sometimes, but it is something that can be studied and can be nurtured.
For the most part I do make myself available for the songs just by
sitting down with a guitar and my recorder and my notebook and
my sketchbook, and if the melody comes, I try to see what words
fall down in it, and what may seem appropriate or imperative at
the moment. It's not something I can force necessarily, but I can
make myself available by having some discipline.

**You guys play lots festivals these days. How do you bring
the intimacy of your music to these larger stages and still
achieve that personal connection with your audience?**

I think that we try to put our attention on the fact that this show
is the only one that matters. This one right here. If we play as well
as we can, not only do we get inside the songs, but we also get
inside the physical environment, and that will translate. And that
can translate for a hundred people, it can translate for a thousand
people, or ten thousand people. And that comes from being in a
genuine place and being very much in the moment. When most
quality things happen, you have to be present for it. Some of that
is just practice, like learning where to be and how to be, how to
find something that works. It's just like studying how to be a performer. There are certain things that work in a club that don't work
when the person in the last row is a football field or two football
fields away from you. That doesn't necessarily mean more flailing
around or becoming more animated, but it does mean you have to
consider that person even though they're so far away. They paid
their money to be here, and they may be the biggest fan in the
place, so you want to pay attention to them. Also, we went and saw
Bruce Springsteen, so we know how to do it because we saw him.
[*laughs*] He's sort of a major template for us, so we looked at him
and thought, "OK, here's a guy that knows how to do three hours."
He knows how to engage a large audience, he knows how to do it
for the long run, and he knows how to make dynamic records that
span decades. So he's the guy we've got to look at. We have to look
at the Dead. We have to look at Pearl Jam. We have to look at those
bands in terms of the way we want to do things.

You clearly learned your lessons well.

Thank you. Thank you.

You've created such a high bar yourselves, however. Is it intimidating knowing you have to meet your own high standard each and every time?

It's not intimidating in terms of us thinking we made something great. After we made *I and Love and You*, Rick said, "Listen, I don't care what the next record is, but it's got to be better than *I and Love and You*." It wasn't like he was downplaying that album. He thought we had done well and made a record we should be really proud of, but it was all about perspective. *I and Love and You* might be a great record to one person, or a terrible record for another person. It's all in your own perspective, but for us, we knew that whatever ended up to be the record was after *I and Love and You*, it needed to make us excited in a way that *I and Love and You* did not. And that's what artistry is all about. That's what looking forward as an artist is all about. So we're saying, be proud of what you did, but look at how you might do things differently now and see what happens. Just because you did something five years ago, it doesn't mean that it has to dominate what you do now. We want to learn from the things we've done well and the things we've not done well.

36

Amanda Shires Emerges on Her Own

Sometime it's the sentiment that draws an artist to the past and then carries them forward. Amanda Shires is a perfect case in point. She found that out quickly when she and husband Jason Isbell gave birth to their first child two years ago.

Both are highly acclaimed musicians of course. Isbell helms his band the 400 Unit, with whom Shires is a sometime side partner, playing fiddle and guitar. A recent winner of Best Emerging Artist at the Americana Awards festivities in 2017, she also has a successful career, which began at the age of fifteen alongside the kings of classic western swing, the Texas Playboys, and continued through to a later band, the Thrift Store Cowboys. In the time since, she's released five solo albums—*Being Brave*, *West Coast Timbers*, *Carrying Lightning*, *Down Fell the Doves*, and *My Piece of Land*—as well as a duet set with former boyfriend Rod Picott, entitled *Sew Your Heart with Wires*. Now, on the eve of release of a new individual effort, she finds herself musing about home and, as the child of divorced parents, a stability she never had.

Shires spoke to me from the home she shares with her husband and child in Nashville on one of the couple's rare days off.

When you became pregnant, you had to leave the road and spend a lot of time by yourself, we would imagine. How did that affect your work?

I had a lot of time to think and a lot of things to think about. I did things differently. I used Dave Cobb to produce my album for the first time, who I had never worked with on my own, but who I had worked with on Jason's projects before. I already had a dialogue with him, so he was very easy to communicate with. I didn't learn any of the songs ahead of time. I just put them away, and then I went in to play them for Dave, and then we'd start recording. I thought that was a really good way to do it because then you're not already married to arrangements and things, and then you also forget you're recording, so you just think about the song and it takes away the self-consciousness that you can get when you're in the studio.

The album with Dave was your fourth solo album.

I tell everybody that it is, but it's open for debate. My very first record was a fiddle instrumental album that I recorded when I was a side person a long, long time ago. So that one to me doesn't qualify, because it was before I became a writer. I was in Texas and I didn't decide to pursue that until I met Billy Joe Shaver and decided to work with him. So when I moved up here, I recorded *West Cross Timbers*, *Carrying Lightning*, and *Down Fell the Doves*.

One of the predominant themes on that album seemed to revolve around relationships and a place you can call home.

Yes. Sitting around at home, being by myself, I was thinking about that a lot, what we had inherited from home in childhood and in the past . . . the places that we come from. The song "Mineral Wells" I wrote in 2009, but for some reason, I kept coming back to it. That was my initial thinking about the idea of home in song, and I was thinking a lot about Texas—Lubbock and Mineral Wells—and missing it, but also thinking about it as the product of a divorce and such. And then I thought about what home is now, with my husband. I never thought I'd be married with a child, but here I am. Then I was thinking about all the places we go that I love so much, and I was thinking we could live anywhere. Home for me is not a physical location. It's really being around the people that I love.

As a child, you went back and forth between Lubbock and Mineral Wells because your parents had divorced. You were always in transit, it seemed.

I was born in Mineral Wells and my dad's family was from there. My mom went to Lubbock because it was pretty much as far as her car would drive her. It was six hours away. The two land-scapes are completely different, but if I don't claim both those places as home, somebody's going to talk to me on my voicemail about it. [*laughs*]

That must have impacted your thoughts, that sense of instability you must have felt as a child when you had to go back and forth.

The thing that was most constant and stable was when I found the fiddle and learned to play music. That was kind of my stabil-ity. I wasn't one to be whining about my situation. I'd rather my parents be happy when they're not speaking to each other [than have them stay] together.

Having Jason away a lot must have been difficult, too. There's a song on this album called "When You're Away."

I still have many of his things to stare at.

When you have two people in the family who are both accomplished—who are both extremely talented—do you ever feel like you're bringing your work home with you? Is it hard to separate work from play?

I've been in relationships before with people who weren't involved in music, and they didn't work out. Yes, we bring the work home with us, but I think it works out best that way. It gives us more things to talk about, more things to debate—chord usage, lyrics, and things like that. We bounce ideas off each other and try to help each other edit the best we can. It's kind of nice, and I feel really lucky. We don't get exhausted talking about it, because it's both of our passions. To have somebody that can criticize your work, having no intentions other than just wanting the best for you and your work is really nice. If I didn't have that, I don't know. It's better to have someone who can tell you that you have a weak line or something, because you always want to do your best work.

Is it ever intimidating because you're both so accomplished? Do you ever feel like you have to sneak away and write in private so you don't feel overwhelmed?

It works in a couple of ways. A couple of the songs on the new album we wrote together, which was a different experience because we only tried that one other time. The songs "My Love (The Storm)" and "Pale Fire" were the ones we wrote together. It was new territory for us, and I was surprised we could do that together, because we write very differently. But we know each other really well, and what we're trying to say and the meanings we're trying to express. It's not intimidating, because when you're writing a song and it's really personal, we don't show it to each other until it's completely done, especially if it's about the other person. I didn't show Jason "You Are My Home" until we were actually in the studio, because that wasn't open for discussion. He showed me his song "Cover Me Up" after he wrote it because he felt he had done it. But there are other songs he shows me as he's writing them, because he's just interested in knowing if the idea's worth pursuing. We both do that for each other. He went to school for an English degree, so we both feel like we can back up our arguments pretty well. It's not always easy to admit things that are of a personal nature, but I think that in the spirit of writing, it's not a good way to point things out in a way that's passive/aggressive. It's just something you feel, and those feelings are valid, so we don't get on each other's case about that. Writing and music is so cathartic. It can be difficult. If there's a problem and it shows up in a song before you've talked about it, it's like "Oh shit, maybe we should have talked about it before." [*laughs*]

If you've had a hard day at the studio and something didn't go well, does it seep over at home? Is it hard to separate?

Not really when you have the right producer. I started as a side person, so I was paid to do something and a lot of times I did what I was told to do. So that was fine. But once we were together a lot, dating and now married, when something didn't go right and one person has an idea and the other disagrees, we usually just defer to the producer, and so that one person doesn't feel like they need to win. We also pick our battles, and we usually trust each other generally. We don't nitpick every little thing. When things do go home with us, we play the track next week and see if we still feel the same way about it. Ultimately, it comes down to whose name is on the record because that person is ultimately in charge of it.

Do you write for the 400 Unit?

We each write our individual parts, but as far as songs, no. Only when Jason needs help, or has a question, then I'll help him and I'll tell him what I think. He doesn't have to take my opinion. It's just my opinion in the end. But I do like it when he does that for me, when he tells me something is weak or I can do better than that . . . or that maybe I used the wrong preposition. But mainly his name and his brand are his, and what I do is mine. We both write very differently. I have my woman's perspective and he has his white guy perspective. [*chuckles*] In the end, whatever the argument is isn't really an argument. If it's my work, then thank you very much, I'm going to do it my way. If you have advice, I'll take it as I please.

We're not trying to serve up domestic discord.

Oh no, you're not. We talk about all kinds of things all the time. The things we argue about most of the time are about stupid words. Our other argument is about Steely Dan. I can't stand them, and Jason likes them a lot. I had to hide those records.

It's nice that you can each pursue your individual careers without each getting in the way of the other.

It's difficult logistically sometimes. Now there's a little baby in the mix, which makes it even more complicated.

How did you meet Jason?

I was playing in the Thrift Store Cowboys, and we were playing in Athens, Georgia, and Jason was recording a couple of blocks away. So Jason just happened in there, and I met him there. We had about six people in there to see us, and Jason pulled up a folding chair to the center. So I met him, and we started talking about music and became friends. Then he started getting interested in me, but I wasn't having it. [*laughs*] In 2011, we started exploring our love interest in each other. I don't know how that happens but it does.

When you go out to tour, how does that work? Is Jason with you?

No, no. I'm not in a place where I can afford a bus and he is, so the baby goes out with Jason. It's not safe in a van for grown-ups, and it's definitely not safe for a baby. She's only ten months old, and the idea of her having to ride in the van for eight to ten hours . . . that's why I can't have her riding with me. They drive in a bus during the night so she can sleep and then get up and play when they get there. That kind of touring life wouldn't be good for her in a van.

Presumably she has a nanny.

Oh yes. We had tried handing her off to strangers, but that got weird. Roadies don't know much about taking care of babies. [*laughs*] We have a girl named Trish who takes care of her. Her safety and comfort is the primary concern. Also, I don't want her to grow up thinking she has to give up her career when she becomes a mother. It's fine if people want to do that, but I'm trying to lead by example. On the other hand, I don't know what it's going to be like going twenty-one days without seeing her.

Do you tour simultaneously?

Yes. Jason can do all the same things I can do. He can give her a bath, and he knows how to feed her. He's awesome. He's the one that changes all the diapers. He's with the baby right now.

With your solo career, do you still intend to keep your role in the 400 Unit?

The 400 Unit was the band, and they were around before I was around. That's the core. I'm not satisfied just playing other people's music, even if it's Jason's. It's a wonderful experience to play with people I admire, and I will sit in with people like that. But they have to be people I admire. I'll sit in with John Prine. I'll sit in with Todd Snider. I'll go out with Jason, but it's more fulfilling for me to do my own work, too. It would be easier if I gave it all up, but I can't do that. I really like what I do, even if there's only fifty other people that like it. My goal for success was that when I went to a new town, I'd have fifty people listening to me. You have to start small.

Do you play solo, or are you touring with backup musicians?

Both. The Ryan Adams dates are solo—just me opening with my tenor guitar—which is strange because the fiddle is my primary instrument. But it's good to get out of your comfort zone. The rest of them are with a band—a drummer, a bassist, and a guitar player, and myself.

Your early efforts were with the Texas Playboys and then a band called the Thrift Store Cowboys. Tell us a little about those experiences.

I recorded with Thrift Store back in the day. They're not together anymore. The Texas Playboys haven't recorded anything in awhile, but I did record with [guitarist] Tommy Alsop in the past, and I recorded with individuals from the Texas Playboys, but never the whole band together. The Playboys had over four hundred people in the band throughout their career. They were a big band, and then they were a small band and they liked to fire people for things like not having the right shirt on.

Was that intimidating to join such a storied ensemble?

I was very young. I was fifteen when I started with them so my frontal lobe wasn't developed enough to know what I was a part of. It would intimidate me now, but back then I was a kid, and I did what I was told. All my gear worked, and I was easy to get along with, and they kept me around. It was like having seven granddads. I tasted whiskey for the first time and learned a lot of fiddle stuff at the same time. The fiddle player would pull a bottle out of his shirt where he had it hidden. I didn't like it then, but I appreciate it now.

What a credit to your talent that you were asked to join that band when you were only fifteen!

The first time I sang onstage, someone had to hold my hand because I was so nervous.

But how did that even come about that they would ask you to join at age fifteen?

I was taking classical violin lessons at the time. The person I was learning from noticed I was getting a bit distracted and kind of bored and showed me this song "Spanish Two Step." That was my first fiddle song, and I told my mom I wanted to be a fiddle player. She said, "No, you're going to be in an orchestra," and I said, "No, I'm going to be a fiddle player." So she said if I did my orchestra classes, she'd also let me be a fiddle player. And that was fine with me. So that kept me doing what I was supposed to do, and I got to learn both worlds. It's kind of cool the way that happened.

So how did you come to the band's attention?

We had started this little swing band that was made up of all these kids around my age, three part things on fiddles, ranch swing kind of stuff. I met Tommy Alsop around that time, and we became good friends and I learned a lot of things from him. For the older guys, keeping the tradition alive was very important, and they would take time for anybody that asked about the music and the history. So as a way to keep it going they taught me stuff, and I kept going back for more. Soon they couldn't get rid of me, this little kid always showing up at the front door wanting to learn fiddle tunes. So Tommy brought me into the fold.

What did your mom think about all this? Were you out touring with them?

Oh yes. Anywhere Tommy would go, I'd go with him. And she would go with me too. Once I turned seventeen, I got to play in the local bar scene in Lubbock. They let me in, but they put the X's on my hand so I could sit in with whoever was playing. You have to practice improvising somewhere.

What made you want to play fiddle to begin with?

It goes back to that stability thing. I was with my dad and we were at a pawnshop, and I saw a fiddle hanging on the wall and I told him I had to have it. We weren't a family of any means. I don't even know how he had $60 to buy it. But he did. He took a chance. I immediately broke the strings—proof that I'm not a prodigy [laughs]—and so I took it back to Lubbock with me. So here my dad's bought me this present and now my mom has to buy me lessons, but for me it became a constant thing, something that was never changing. While their lives and their relationships were always different, I still had this one thing that was always around.

37

Donna the Buffalo
and the Populist Stampede

"Excuse me, but I have to eat while we talk. Do you mind?"

Tara Nevins is at home doing what most people do as part of their morning routine—scrambling eggs (sorry, "fluffing them," as she points out) while also attempting to answer the questions posed by an inquiring journalist. I caught up to her during one of those rare intervals when she and her band Donna the Buffalo aren't on the road and playing one of the 120 gigs this hardworking ensemble find themselves involved with annually.

Clearly Nevins is adept at multitasking, but then again, as the band's primary singer—not to mention its designated fiddler, guitarist, and accordion player—she has to be. After all, the band is known for its eclectic musical mix—one that incorporates rock, bluegrass, zydeco, folk, and anything else that happens to strike their fancy at any given time.

"We so fly by the seat of our pants," Nevins admits. "It's not even funny."

Formed in 1989 by Nevins and guitarist Jeb Puryear, Donna the Buffalo base themselves in New York State, but their following—a devoted group of fans that refer to themselves as "the Herd"—has made them favorites at festivals throughout the country. Indeed, they're a populist outfit by every definition of the word, drawing the faithful with the same steadfast devotion that characterizes Deadheads, Phish followers, and fans of other groups with a similar sense of purpose.

"It's the music, but its also about the vibe and the message," Nevins insists. "Something about us encourages a sense of community, and people are drawn to that. Community is a great thing. I don't know what it is about that. Is it our songs? The way we play them? It's hard to say what that ingredient is, or what we're trying to put our hands on here."

Accordingly, that fan following seems to have grown organically, a phenomenon spurred by the audience itself and not as a result of any deliberate effort by the band. "In the beginning we were not the greatest band technically, but even then we began drawing people," Nevins reflects. "Our songs, our vibes. . . . The Herd is so self-organized. It started when somebody came to a gig and started talking to someone else. They both liked the music and decided to meet up at another gig, making the soundboard their meeting place. Then other people began joining them there, and it grew from there. The fans kind of developed it themselves. It's really kind of fantastic. I'm not sure why they all stick around, but I guess everybody needs love of some kind. [*chuckles*]"

That rabid fan following evolved despite the negative notices heaped on them by their peers, the critics, and many of the industry insiders. Nevins concedes that at least some of that criticism was warranted.

"Some groups are automatically darlings of the press," she muses. "They come out and the press automatically embraces them. But we've never been darlings of the press. We spent many years undoing a reputation that wasn't very good. When we first started out, we weren't very good, at least technically. We were a bunch of funky gypsies who'd usually roll up to a gig late and come tumbling out all barefoot. But at the same time, the Herd was loving us, loving the vibe we were putting out. Behind the scenes, there was this disparaging attitude in the industry about Donna the Buffalo. We may have deserved some of that. So now we've matured and gotten extremely professional and outgrown all that. This is the best band we've ever had. But you know what they say—it takes forever to establish a reputation, but only a minute to destroy it. Some people were getting where we were coming from, and getting a lot out of it, and building that feeling of community. Everyone else was kind of mad at us, which, in a way, was really funny.

Originally dubbed "Dawn of the Buffalo," the band adopted its present handle after being misidentified as "Donna the Buffalo." More than thirty years later, they're still going strong, headlining four annual festivals in upstate New York and playing numerous others—including the Grassroots Festival in Key Biscayne and the Magnolia Festival in upstate Florida—year after year.

"Jeb and I are the two founding members, and we've seen some personnel changes over the years, but now we have a great crew that we really love, and it seems like everyone's having a great time," Nevins maintains. "It's funny, but we never really questioned how we've evolved. We've never had a lot of money. For our first few gigs, we travelled in two rented station wagons. After that we got an old-school bus, and though we've had several buses over the years, we've always done it like that. We started out from the ground up. A friend of ours did our booking and another friend of ours became our manager. It was all word of mouth and very grassroots from the very beginning. So now we're very self-sufficient, and that's a good thing in this day and age, when its so hard to get backing from the record companies. We're very fortunate, and to have that loyal following is very gratifying. And we've made so many great friends along the way."

And now?

"I think we've made a lot of headway and created a lot of love," Nevins surmises. "Some people's minds may have been changed, for sure. I would sure hope so."

38

A Rose by Any Other Name

A Canadian expatriate who resettled in Austin, Whitney Rose found her footing in the music clubs and performing venues that litter that hallowed destination. Rose is an ideal example of a younger artist who has clearly learned the lessons of the past and still cherishes them immensely. She makes music that was once found in the barrooms and honkytonks of the heartland, and she carries on that tradition with the same exceptional skill and savvy.

Rose's EP, *South Texas Suite*, released in early 2017, marked an important continuum in her trajectory. A self-described love letter to her adopted state of Texas, it found her asserting her affection and enthusiasm for the place she's so happy to call home. It also connected her with Raul Malo of the Mavericks, who, along with Niko Bolas, reprised his role of producer on her second set of 2017, Rule 62, while also contributing to a backing band that includes Mavs drummer Paul Deakin, the Jayhawks' Jen Gunderman on keys, and ace guitarist Kenny Vaughn.

Indeed, it's no small mark of distinction when you can enlist the Mavericks to participate on your album. But it's even more impressive when the sound you produce sounds so confident and assured. Rose's music emulates a vintage template so authentically it could be easily mistaken for a crop of seasoned standards written by Hank Williams, Kitty Wells, or any other classic country crooner.

Suffice it to say, stardom is in her sights.

**With your second album and current EP, you formed
a great working relationship with Raul Malo of the
Mavericks. How did that come about?**

Shortly after I released my debut album, I got a really great booking agent, and he put me on a gig in Toronto to open the show
for the Mavericks. I had always been a fan of the band, but I had
never seen them live. I was completely blown away. There aren't
many bands that can hold a candle to what they do. I was very
smitten with the band, and thankfully they liked me too, because
they invited me on a couple of tours. By the second tour, I had
gathered up enough material to make a record, so I asked Raul
if he would be interested in producing it. It was pretty straightforward how it came about, but I'm so grateful I was put on that
bill with them. Not only have I learned so much in musical terms,
but they've also become some of my best friends in the world.

**When you cover someone else's songs, is it ever intimidat-
ing? Do you think about the writer's reaction to your version and hope that they feel you've done it justice?**

Absolutely. It's scary. When you write a song, it's like giving birth
to a baby. You're creating this thing, and of course it's scary to
take someone else's baby and say, "I think the baby should be
raised like this!" But it's also really exciting to give new life to
someone else's work.

**You've been highly lauded with all kinds of praise for your
initial albums. Does that set the bar higher? Do you now
think that you have to reach the same level you did before
in order to keep the critics happy?**

Not even a little bit. I only have only one goal, and that's to hopefully keep getting better. I like to be constantly learning and creating. Maybe I should be nervous. It's probably healthy. But I just
want to keep moving forward and improving. That's what I keep
in mind.

If you were to think about outside opinion, it would probably hinder you.

Yes. Absolutely. [*laughs*]

So how would you describe your trajectory, from the first album up through the one you just completed?

I'm actually very happy with my trajectory. Obviously I'm not a super star by any stretch of the imagination, but while it's been a very slow move forward, I do feel like I am moving forward all the same, and I'm very grateful for that. Even the fact I got to make my third album assures me that I'm doing something right. Being in the music industry and having experienced a few music scenes, it's very hard to keep putting out new music. I know incredible musicians who have great songs, but they don't have the means to put out records. I'm very grateful for the position I'm in. I'm also very grateful that it has been a slow trajectory, because it gives me so much opportunity to learn, and to learn at my own pace with some great people beside me. It gives me more of an opportunity to build a solid foundation, where if I had a really successful song off my first album, I wouldn't have any touring experience. But now I have a lot of touring experience. I feel very prepared. You have to be grateful for what you have, right?

Exactly, and you've done quite well. Did you grow up in a musical family?

My mother and my grandparents were very much country folk, and they actually ran a bar when I was little. There was country music playing in there constantly. And sometimes they would take the party home after the bar closed. So there would always be a guitar going around. There was a lot of Hank Williams and Johnny Cash. They were huge fans. So I learned that stuff even before I was really conscious of it.

Where did you grow up?

Prince Edward Island. It's a tiny little island off the east coast of Canada. It's a beautiful, beautiful spot. There are a couple of towns, but even the capital is located in a small town. It's pretty gorgeous—a lot of farmland and some beautiful beaches. There are a lot of Celtic influences, but for whatever reasons, that's not what my grandparents were drawn to.

When did you make the decision to become a professional musician?

I kind of always knew I wanted to be a performer when I was little. I did a lot of theater, and when I went to high school, we moved around a lot. I lived in a lot of different places and tried my hand at a number of different things. But music was always around. I played guitar, but it had never really crossed my mind to play my own songs. I was very content to play other people's songs. So I taught myself three chords and just started writing. I have no regrets, but I do kind of wish that I had started earlier, if for no other reason than to be better at playing guitar. I had a pretty late start.

So how did you land your first recording contract?

I was living on a farm in the middle of nowhere, and I was in a relationship that ended kind of badly. So I packed up everything and moved to Toronto. One of the first places I went to was this bar called the Cameron House. It had just come under new management, and they had just started a record label. They hadn't put out a record yet, but they were talking to artists. I ended up playing there, and it became like a second home to me. It's a really beautiful close-knit community. Cameron House has put out a bunch of records, including my debut and Heartbreaker of the Year. We're still really good friends, and I'm really grateful for everything the label did for me. And there was a natural connection when I signed with Six Shooter Records. Six Shooter is so supportive and amazing and really committed to what they do. They're really good people. I'm really proud to be with them.

Why do you think it is that so many wonderful Canadian artists don't get the kind of credit and recognition in the States like they do back home?

I think it's all about where you focus your touring and where you focus your marketing. When I put out Heartbreaker, that's what prompted my move. Now, after moving here, I'm so happy with how much touring I can do in the States and how much support I get when I do. It's just about where you focus.

Was it scary making the move to Austin?

Not really. I had moved around so much in my life. It just felt like the natural next step. It felt right from the beginning. Originally it was supposed to be a two-month residency at the Continental Club, but after the first couple of weeks there, I had just as much of an audience that had taken me years to build up in Canada. It told me that this was the place I was supposed to be. It should have been scary, but it really wasn't scary wasn't at all. Plus, my manager is also my partner, so that made it a lot easier. We made a lot of friends very quickly. Steve, the owner of the Continental Club, has been very helpful to me as well. He put me in touch with a lot of musicians. We rolled into Austin at two in the morning after having never been in Texas before, went to bed, and the next morning I met my new band. We rehearsed and then that evening we played our first show at the Continental Club. Fortunately, it all worked out.

Clearly it has. With her career on a steady ascent, this Rose continues to bloom.

39

Derek Trucks Talks Multitasking, Working with His Wife, and Lessons Learned from the Past

If exceptional accomplishment alone were enough to inspire widespread recognition, then Derek Trucks would likely have several government buildings and national monuments bearing his name. An heir to the Southern Rock tradition and the early Americana origins of the Allman Brothers Band, Lynyrd Skynyrd, and Muscle Shoals, Trucks can claim a remarkable lineage. His uncle, percussionist Butch Trucks, was an original member of the Allman Brothers, and the younger Trucks was named for the Eric Clapton album credited to Derek and the Dominoes. Naturally, then, Trucks's musical career appeared preordained. To his credit, however, Trucks wasn't content to simply rely on birthright alone. While still in his midteens, he was playing with the Allmans, and by the time he was in his twenties, he was also leading his own band and playing a key role in Eric Clapton's touring band.

Trucks's current day job finds him at the helm of the Tedeschi Trucks Band alongside the equally adept singer/guitarist Susan Tedeschi, his wife and music collaborator. After playing on each others' individual albums, the two officially joined forces in 2011, releasing the band's debut album *Revelator*, which garnered a Grammy for Best Blues Album, several top prizes at the prestigious Blues Music Awards, widespread critical acclaim, and a top fifteen debut on the Billboard album charts. *Everybody's Talkin'*, a double live album, continued to reap the raves garnered the first time around, gaining entry on Billboard's list of best-selling Blues albums.

Trucks is an incessant multitasker, and he regularly shows up on lists delineating the greatest guitarists of our era. It's no surprise then that he's found himself performing some of the most prestigious gigs imaginable—onstage at the White House, the United Nations, the Grammy Award ceremonies, and the all-star tribute to blues great Hubert Sumlin, staged at the iconic Apollo Theater. In the process, he's shared the stage with legends like Mick Jagger, Keith Richards, Buddy Guy, B.B. King, Herbie Hancock, Wynton Marsalis, Tony Bennett, Stevie Wonder, and McCoy Tyner, to name only some.

As if Trucks and Tedeschi don't have enough on their plate already, the two also curate the Sunshine Blues Festival, a series of daylong Florida festivals whose list of special guests have included Dr. John, Walter Trout, Sonny Landreth, the Wood Brothers, and others. The concerts expand their roles as entrepreneurs—they already own and operate their own recording studio Swamp Raga located behind their home in Jacksonville, Florida—and add to their extensive list of career credits.

I spoke with Trucks by phone during one of his rare days off. Even so, it was obvious that work was still on his mind, and this brief respite from the road wouldn't last long. An amiable individual, his answers were frequently punctuated by laughter. Despite his impressive resume, he still managed to come across as remarkably unaffected and exceedingly down to earth.

Let's start by talking about your Sunshine festival. How did that idea come about?

It was an idea we had for a really long time. We really wanted to put a festival together where we hit the road and eventually do it nationwide if we can make it work. So we put some of our favorite bands together that we would want to go see, and this way we can sit out front and watch. We had a long list, and we just tried to piece it together. I remembered the Horde tour in the early nineties, when I went out with Aquarium Musical Unit and a bunch of different bands who I loved learning from and playing with. Now there's been a huge influx of different festivals. But with most of them, there are only one or two different bands I really want to see . . . [laugh]

So you're very selective.

Yeah, and so we thought it would be fun to do a festival someday where I would want to sit out front all day.

How did you coordinate all the artist schedules?

You just have to start early, maybe a year out or so in advance, and you have to put a wish list together and then start at the top [laughs] and work through it. And starting at the top doesn't always mean the biggest names . . . it's the people you really want on it. We were lucky. Sometimes it doesn't always work out. We were kind of testing the waters with this to see if it was something we can make work and make fly, and maybe turn it into something more.

So the goal is to eventually take this around the country?

We'd like to. The idea is definitely there, and we're actively talking about it and kind of feeling it out. It's a big undertaking, but I bet it will be fun.

You could do something like the Festival Express in the early seventies where the Dead, the Band, Janis Joplin, and others got on a train and traveled from one end of Canada to another. That would be fun.

Oh yeah. We talked about that too. We did a tour of Europe with our band where we did it by train—an eleven-piece band with twenty people in the crew. We took over a whole train car. It got rowdy a few times and I was thinking it could be fun. [laughs]

It seems like fun.

Yeah—fifteen bands going country to country or state to state.

It sounds like you're already having a lot of fun though. You play these incredible gigs . . . at the White House, at the UN, with all these incredible musicians. . . . You must be on cloud nine.

It's been an amazing run. When we put this band together we definitely had high hopes for it, but it's definitely exceeded what we hoped for. It's definitely an amazing start. Being able to play music you love to play with people you like being around is definitely hard to beat. There's a lot of hard work, and you're wrangling a lot of people and things do happen, but in the end, it's a good day's work. [*laughs*]

You seem like the ultimate multitasker. At one point you were gigging with your own band, you were playing with the Allman Brothers, and then Eric Clapton called and you went out on tour with him. How do you keep it all straight? Did you ever start a song and realize you're playing the wrong tune because you got your gigs confused? Maybe you start playing an Allman song when you were onstage with Clapton?

Luckily not! [*laughs*] When you get in that space and you're surrounded by great players, you learn the tunes and get them in your head. Once the band starts playing, there's this locomotion that happens and you get on board. [*laughs*] A lot of times a song will start and you have this one second where you go, "Oh shit, I don't know if I remember this one!" But once you get into it, it kind of plays itself. A lot of it is just muscle memory that's always there. But you definitely have to do your homework, especially when it's the Allman Brothers or Clapton. At one point, I was in three different bands that were touring full-time. I would have to listen to the records of whatever bands I was going to play with on the flight over and refresh my memory a bit.

So how do you manage your time? You also have a family and two small children. With all you do, isn't it a challenge?

For one, it helps being married to someone who understands what you're doing, because if Susan hadn't been a musician and understood what the road takes, I don't know if doing the three bands would even be possible. She understood the opportunities and understands it's not a 24/7 party. [*laughs*] When your wife and family are at home, and you're running all over the world, it's nice to know that the understanding is out there. So that helps. That's a big part of it. And when opportunities like that come up, you just have to take them. Those windows don't open often. So yeah, we really thought about it in '06 and '07, when it was nonstop. It was twenty-something countries and multiple bands, and that's when I decide to build a studio in the house. It was a matter of planning ahead and realizing, "This is amazing but I can't do this every year. We have kids and I want to be home sometimes." Even when they're flying out and visiting you, it's not the same as being home. So building the studio allows me to spend so many more months at home and be productive and work and make records. We've been fortunate, but you also have to be pretty proactive to make it work.

You and Susan worked on each other's records even before you formed the band together. But now that you're the co-leaders, so to speak, has that made a difference in terms of decision-making or direction? Do you have to run things by one another and always be in agreement? Is it a big change from doing things individually like before?

It was a big change, and it took awhile to adjust to it. You get so used to doing things yourself. The music business and the whole scene can be somewhat cutthroat at times, and it takes awhile to learn you're in all of it together [*laughs*] and that even if something may seem a little bit outside your comfort zone, it's actually in your best interest to have someone look out for you. I think for Susan, especially, it took awhile to kind of give in a little bit to being in the flow of a massive band and have someone else as a band leader essentially. Still, it's really been amazing for us personally and musically. It's been a huge amount of growth and it's made us closer, and it's an unbelievable band to be a part of.

So it's a good feeling. In a sense, it's a throwback to a time when people did things because they gave a shit [*laughs*] and wanted to do things. We're realists, too, and we've been on the road a long time, and so we look around and we don't see a lot of that. We don't see a lot of bands that are doing it for the right reasons, or artists who are doing it for the right reasons. So when you're a part of that it feels really good. That's part of the reason for doing this festival. We try to put like-minded people together who like doing it and feel like it's important work.

When you and Susan joined forces, you must have had to whittle down some of the players—people that were formerly in her band and people that were in your band. That must have been difficult, right?

It was tough, but when we decided to do it, we needed a break, a change. I had my band fourteen, sixteen years, something like that, so it was time mentally to try something different. So we kind of stopped everything and then restarted. [*laughs*] But it didn't feel quite the same. When you play with people that long, it's a difficult thing to make a move. Everybody was so close in the extended family, so there were a lot of straight, honest conversations, and there was a lot of understanding, even though it was difficult. But it's worked out amazingly well. I'm still in touch with everybody. When my old band and Susan's old band found good gigs, we felt really relieved. [*laughs*] We were just kind of hoping it would transition nicely, and it's been pretty great so far.

Some people find that working with their spouse can be a little weird at times. Do you ever take the band business home with you?

It's been a lot easier than I thought it would be. I went into it with my eyes open and believing it could cause a lot of added stress. But I think having a big band is almost like having a lot of kids. [*laughs*] Your attention is often focused on keeping things rolling, so you don't have enough time to be annoyed with each other. [*laughs*]

Very diplomatic, sir. Very diplomatic.

[*Laughs*] But also this group of people is so much fun to be around, and there's always an outlet, always a place to blow off mild steam if you need to. There are two buses on the road, so there are spontaneous parties starting here and there, and it's an unusually helpful situation to be in because there's always a great outlet. It's oddly healthy too. When we were at the Lockn' Festival last year, we played a tribute to Joe Cocker's Mad Dogs and Englishmen, and that was kind of the template for what we do. The difference is that, back then, the drug abuse made it harder and more experimental, and it led to a lot of problems in the end. [*laughs*] I feel like we've kind of sanded off a lot of those rough edges but it's still pretty free-spirited and it still gets crazy, but it never gets destructive.

You're probably learning a lot from their mistakes.

Well, that was part of the plan all along.

You've played with an amazing array of all-time greats. Have any of these musicians ever passed on any words of wisdom or, for that matter, any words of caution?

A lot of times it's just getting time to hang with people like that, and some of the time it's unspoken, and some of the time it's just really direct. I played in Gregg Allman's solo band when I was fourteen or fifteen, and he was really open about avoiding the potholes that he hit in a way that kind of seared into my brain. Some guys are really open about passing along life lessons, and sometimes it's just watching how someone goes about his business, rather than having real person to person conversations about their life. They don't have to say this is what you do and this is what you don't do, but it's pretty obviously implied. I think you have to keep your eyes and ears open. I've found that most of the true greats I've been fortunate enough to be around are really open and want to pass things along. It's not competitive.

Was it ever intimidating, playing with B.B. King or performing with Eric Clapton?

From time to time you have those thoughts, but those guys you're talking about are such open and sweet people that they make you feel like you've known them your whole life. There's none of that separation. And then you go through experiences that kind of steer you to that stuff. I remember when I first played a live show with McCoy Tyner and his band. This was a guy that was in the Miles Davis Quartet and played with some of the most badass musicians on earth. I got thrown in the deep end—it's like the jazz test—and so I hit the bandstand and they just start calling tunes that you've never heard. It's sink or swim with what you got. At first it's that deer in the headlights feeling, but then you just relax and you open your ears and you just play music and it goes. Then there's this wave of acceptance. "You're alright!" Something like that makes you feel like if there was any fear or any nervousness about sitting in with people you like, it's alright because I survived McCoy Tyner.

You recently made it clear that your intention now is to devote your energy to Tedeschi-Trucks exclusively. You must be pleased with the way things have transpired.

It's been an amazing run. When we put this band together, we definitely had high hopes for it, but it's definitely exceeded what we hoped for. . . . Being able to play music you love to play, with people you like being around, is definitely hard to beat. There's a lot of hard work, and you're wrangling a lot of people, and things do happen, but in the end, it's a good day's work.

40

·······································

Dave Rawlings

Man as Machine

Dave Rawlings is a man rife with contradiction. Although his partnership with longtime collaborator Gillian Welch has spawned six albums in twenty years, his name makes the cover of only one of them. He abstains from talking to the press, but on the rare occasion that he does, he's as gracious, amiable, informative, and talkative as the average artist is while enthusiastically touting a sequence of successes. The sole time he found himself at the helm of a band was less a solo venture than a communal ensemble. Likewise, his biggest foray into the musical mainstream was his participation in the best-selling soundtrack for *O Brother, Where Art Thou?*, a film made up of mostly obscure traditional songs from an era gone by.

"I would say on a whole David's probably undervalued by the world for what he's brought to the table," says Gil Landry of Old Crow Medicine Show, who's worked and toured with Rawlings on several occasions. "There is a Gillian Welch with Dave Rawlings, but not really. By that I mean his intrinsic value to those albums and songs can't be quantified."

Then again, Rawlings's career has always seemed somewhat out of step with the times. When he and Welch moved to Nashville in the early nineties after meeting at an audition for a country band at Berklee College of Music in Boston—which each happened to be attending at the time—male/female folk duets were decidedly out of sync with the changes taking place in Music City and the music industry overall.

"We were both transplanted here in the summer of '92," Rawlings remembers. "I don't think you can say we had a sense of what the larger music world was like. We listened to modern music in the late eighties and early nineties, but by the time we hit Nashville, we had kind of checked out. In a business sense, we came out of the new traditionalist movement in country music. At least that's what I call it. I think I read that somewhere. It was a late eighties and early nineties moment where you look at Steve Earle, Randy Travis, Dwight Yoakam, and Rodney Crowell all starting to emerge. Then you had Kathy Mattea, Emmylou Harris, and Mary Chapin Carpenter. There was this sort of folk influenced moment where there were women selling records. I remember asking, 'What are we thinking here?'"

That's not to say duos were entirely unheard of at the time, as Rawlings himself is quick to point out. Tim and Molly O'Brien and Norman and Nancy Blake, not to mention the Delmore Brothers, Hot Tuna's Jorma Kaukonen and Jack Cassady, and John Flansburgh and John Linnell, were all among the acts that convinced Rawlings there was at least some kind of market for partners and pairings. Nevertheless, the relative scarcity of that setup made Rawlings and Welch feel like they were the odd couple out.

"We moved to Nashville with three or four songs, and we just started writing together a bit," Rawlings recalls. "There was a market for folk-based girl things. They wanted to pair Gillian up with a Nashville style band and make a Nashville style record. I have some older demos of her, when her first publisher took her in, doing some recordings just like that, and they're awful. Because of our musical tastes, we hated that stuff. We didn't like those Nashville style records to begin with. We were more interested in bluegrass and old-time music. We spent most of the early nineties trying to emulate the Blue Sky Boys and the Stanley Brothers. We wanted to make music that sounded like that. Even if we were playing rock and roll, it would sound more ragged and more like Neil Young than whatever else we were hearing in the world. It felt a long way away."

"We were in a kind of acoustic cult niche," Welch adds. "We never wanted to form a rock band. What we were doing was something new that hadn't been done much before. We built our own little world to give us the maximum freedom. We took on that risk to be able to follow our own muse."

"We were on the extreme front edge," Rawlings says of the Americana movement that would later put their music in tandem with that larger trend. "We were both a little stubborn and opinionated in a big way. We knew exactly what kind of music we wanted to make. People would tell us, 'You gotta have a band,' and we would say, 'No, we're going to make it like this.'"

That's what they did, in fact. Beginning with 1996's *Revival*, the pair released a further four albums bearing Welch's name— *Hell among the Yearlings* (1998), *Time (The Revelator)* (2001), *Soul Journey* (2003), and *The Harrow and The Harvest* (2011). Each of those efforts found the duo sticking to basic precepts—that is, a penchant for archival folk that's timeless in its transition and paid little heed for modern amenities.

In 2009, Rawlings opted to finally put his own name on the marquee and release his first album under the banner of the Dave Rawlings Machine. (He's since released two more.) It found the two expanding the arrangements and adding other musicians to the mix. "Dave wanted to do something new," Welch remarks. "He just didn't know what, so he decided to create this rock band. He has more of a rock and roll voice, so this gave him a chance to kind of shine on top of the arrangements. He can do more with the Machine, and be more a part of the musical mix. It gave him a chance to explore some things that we had left by the wayside. And in the process, the Machine made those songs sound even better."

"I wasn't a fan of Americana to begin with," Rawlings says while speaking of Welch's albums. "We were just trying to do our version of duet music. We felt duet music hadn't really been explored. We added the harmonic sense that appealed to our ears. If you have something inside you that makes you happy and distinguishes you from other stuff, then give it some reason to exist. There was some stuff going on back then that I thought wasn't as good of a version as the older stuff we were replicating. Still, Gillian and I encountered a fair amount of resistance trying to do it that way in the beginning. There wasn't much we could point to that that indicated it was going to work. So Gillian went out with her guitar and sang in [A&M president] Jerry Moss's office, like they used to back in the day. He signed her on the spot because he knew he liked it. I give him a lot of credit to be willing to take that chance."

Rawlings says that by the time the second album rolled around, the intention was to add a third player—specifically famed bassist Roy Huskey Jr. "Sadly, Roy died," he says in retrospect. "It was less about playing with a bass player and more about working with Roy."

The other challenge was to find someone who could sit behind the boards, someone that understood their intents and could help them realize their musical vision. Rawlings and Welch met with fifteen prospective producers before finally deciding to align themselves with T Bone Burnett. "T Bone was the only one out of the entire group of people we talked to that even considered producing us as a duet," he says. "With everyone else, we would have ended up with some other kind of treatment. We had a meeting with one producer, and his first question was, 'Who are you thinking of having play the guitar?'"

Initially signed to A&M, Welch and Rawlings ironically found further impetus for pursuing their designs when the label folded and they opted to set out on their own. Their participation on the *O Brother, Where Art Thou?* soundtrack, which tagged Burnett as musical director and Welch as a performer and associate producer, marked another turning point in their trajectory.

"When Herb [Alpert] and Jerry shut down A&M Records, they were good enough to sell us our masters and we were able to start our own label, and that's when we were able to finally do what we wanted to do," Rawlings says. "That came right on the heels of having worked for quite a while on the *Oh Brother* soundtrack. Given how well that sold and how it helped spread old-time music, it gave us hope that we were on the right path. More than half of that soundtrack came from our record collection. Not many people outside of our world knew about that kind of music. There were huge holes in our collection, but we were pretty deep into the stuff we were into. It was such a shock to see the advantages that that soundtrack gave us. The movie was a great success and all of a sudden it was selling over ten million copies all over the world."

After Burnett produced *Revival*, he ended up walking out during the recording of *Hell among the Yearlings* after he and Rawlings had a falling out. Consequently, Rawlings found himself sidelined during the making of the *O Brother* album, despite the fact that he had scored the film. "It's weird," he remarks. "After T Bone had fallen out with us at the end of that second record, he decided he didn't want me involved in the soundtrack. I was scoring on the movie but he wouldn't let Gillian or I do anything on it as ourselves. He paired up Gil with Alison Krauss. We weren't involved as what we were doing at the time, which was our duo. It was an odd thing to say the least."

Nevertheless, the experience of working with Burnett would serve him well as he ventured further afield from the duo and began producing outside projects, including work with Old Crow Medicine Show and solo albums by two of the band's past and present principals, Willie Watson and Gil Landry. He also contributed to efforts by Bright Eyes, Ryan Adams, Dawes, and Robyn Hitchcock.

"I learned to make records by watching T Bone Burnett make our first two records," Rawlings reckons. "I never did any production or engineering prior to that. When we butted heads it was because as a producer, you have to have an opinion, and T Bone certainly did. But I also had an opinion about things. Give me three choices, and I'll tell you which is the best and why. I'm not going to say it's the best for everybody, but I have a vision, and I have ideas about how to create that vision. I don't think there's ever been much more to it than that. If something doesn't work, I'm pretty good at having three or four ideas about how to make it work. I never really mind tearing things apart and putting it back together again. I find that an enjoyable process most of the time. I think I have some personality traits that work well in the case of production."

"Dave's a problem solver," Welch says simply.

"If I get it to where I'm satisfied with it, a certain number of people in the world will agree," Rawlings continues. "I can't promise anymore than that, but I can promise that I will make a good record. I can't promise someone that I'll make a pop record that will sell five million copies or that it will be album of the year or anything, but if I can get it to where I know it's good, there will be an audience out there for it. I think you have to have a certain amount of confidence to be a producer, because people are going to disagree with you, and there are going to be discussions and arguments. But when things go well, those are all positives, because good ideas come from two viewpoints that are trying to find a middle ground."

"Dave's intensity and propensity for perfection is inspired and refreshing," Gil Landry suggests. "The world could do more with characters of his caliber."

Indeed, that last statement serves to sum up much of what is intriguing about Dave Rawlings. "I would hardly consider him a band leader," says Willie Watson, a member of the Machine who first met Rawlings when he took the initial assignment to produce Old Crow Medicine Show. "He just brings the right people together. I mean, the only thing that he does is start a song and we kind of follow it. Being in that band isn't like being in any other band; we really don't work out parts and there's not really any rehearsals ever. We just kind of play at the sound check. When I get out on the road and I hear all this rehearsal from other bands at shows, I just thank God I'm not a part of that. I could never do that again. When I think about the Dave Rawlings Machine, I love what a loose environment it is."

All Rawlings's charges agree that as a producer, he's a consummate professional and an absolute perfectionist to boot. Yet his way of working has less to do with taking total charge and more to do with allowing the musicians to find their own groove.

His initial encounter with the Old Crow Medicine Show helps prove the point. He became an early fan and mentor after they made their initial move to Nashville, and went on to produce their breakthrough albums, 2004's *Old Crow Medicine Show* and 2006's *Big Iron World*. Later, when Watson went solo, Rawlings and Welch invited him to record at their Woodland Studio, where Rawlings does most of his work.

"I first worked with Dave shortly after Old Crow Medicine Show moved to Nashville," Watson remembers. "He expressed interest in making our record, so right off the bat with that band, I got to have what I would call a real or 'official' studio experience. I learned right away that it was good to make records in a studio setting with real equipment, as opposed to making records in your living room like some other people were trying to do at the time. He was able to tell us what kind of record he thought we should make, and he definitely had a clear vision of the direction we could go. That's probably why Old Crow Medicine Show wanted to work with him in the first place."

"It's hard to appreciate what you do as much as other people might be able to," Rawlings concedes. "Music means so much to me, so when someone expresses interest in music I've been a part of, it's the greatest feeling in the world. That's why I do it."

It was little wonder that Watson opted to work with Rawlings again when it came time to record his first solo album, 2014's *Folk Singer, Vol. I.* "We were already on the same wavelength musically, but at the time, I was trying to write songs, so Dave steered me off that track and got me to focus on the old songs again, the same old songs I had a good time singing. Basically he was the whole direction for that record."

"I fall on the dictatorial side of things for sure," Rawlings maintains. "In the case of Willie Watson's record, I was insistent on not having Willie hear any of it because he sings really well when he's out there singing and not thinking about much. . . . A lot of the music I liked in the day wasn't like it was in the postseventies where the artist was in the control room all the time. After everything was done, and you did all the takes, and you say, 'OK this is the good one and do you want to hear it?' It's not so much about evaluating and changing things."

"I don't have a lot of options with my work or what I do," Rawlings continues. "I only know one way to make a record, but I think it's a good way and a considered way. So if someone is comfortable with that and we achieve results they like, then I've stayed true to it by default. If someone came to me and said we want to make this record, and we want to cut all the basics in one place and then we want the guitars to sound this way or that, I would

Kasey Chambers, AmericanaFest, Nashville, September 23, 2016

Tift Merritt, Folk Alliance International, Kansas City, Missouri,
February 2, 2017

Steep Canyon Rangers, 3rd and Lindsley, Nashville, September 21, 2014

Jonathan Byrd and the Pickup Cowboy, Folk Alliance International, Kansas City, Missouri, February 17, 2017

Graham Nash and Milk Carton Kids, Americana Music Awards, Ryman
Auditorium, Nashville, September 13, 2017

John Oates and Lee Ann Womack, Americana Music Awards, Ryman
Auditorium, Nashville, September 13, 2017

Amanda Shires performing at Americana Music Awards at Ryman
Auditorium, September 13, 2017

Ray Wylie Hubbard, Music City Roots, Nashville, September 14, 2017

The Falls, AmericanaFest, Nashville, September 16, 2017

Whitney Rose, American Legion, Nashville, September 14, 2017

Rusty Young, AmericanaFest, Nashville, September 15, 2017

Donna the Buffalo, Suwannee Roots Revival, Live Oak, Florida, October 13, 2017

Jeb Puryear and Tara Nevins of Donna the Buffalo, Suwannee Roots Revival, Live Oak, Florida, October 13, 2017

Woody Platt, Suwannee Roots Revival, Live Oak, Florida, October 14, 2017

Jim Lauderdale, Suwannee Roots Revival, Live Oak, Florida, October 15, 2017

Richie Furay, Moody Blues Cruise, *Celebrity Eclipse*, January 2, 2018

Steve Martin
at MerleFest in
Wilkesboro, North
Carolina, April 29,
2018

John McEuen demonstrates his musical prowess for the author in
McEuen's Florida home, April 8, 2013

have no idea. I'd say, 'Well that's awesome, you should do that, so let's talk about people who know how to help you with that.' It's just not the way I know how to do things."

"Working beside Dave, the times I've had the pleasure to, it was clear that he's a well-versed and passionate man who knows what he wants and has a good track record of being able to get it done," Gil Landry hastens to add. "He's distilled all the things I dig in a guitar player into his playing. His sense of timing and phrasing in my opinion is second to none, not to mention those harmonies he has. Personally, he gave me some solid advice on my first record deal, which I'll never forget."

It's that take charge attitude that's set Rawlings apart, especially as a producer. And while his methods sometimes seem unorthodox at times, they seem to have served him well. It was evidenced again when he went behind the boards with Dawes for their album *All Your Favorite Bands*.

"I fall on the side of having an idea to start with, but I'm flexible," Rawlings observes. "I'm willing to chase something if it sounds good. I don't stick to any particular vision. I've learned to have hunches and I've learned my hunches are reasonably good. For the Dawes record, I had a hunch about the particular treatment of the bass guitar. I thought it would work really well on this record and in that particular case it worked out great. Perfect. I ended up doing the whole record that way and that was a good hunch. For the drums, I had a few options as to how I was going to mike them and I don't think we used any of those."

Regardless, Dawes seems satisfied with the results. "One thing that doesn't get discussed when it comes to Dave Rawlings as much as it should is that, for my money, he's one of the best record producers out there," says Taylor, the group's singer and guitarist. "It's not just in the sense that he can get good sounds and has a great ear for arrangements, but he also knows how to recognize what people like about an artist. He knows how to draw that out. He knows how to adopt the language of a band and communicate on their terms."

"I'm pretty detail oriented and I'm a decent problem solver, and being a good creative problem solver is what it's all about," Rawlings points out. "If you want to get the sound of a good guitar part and you want it to sound a particular way, then you have to think of a few different ways to try that. So I'm pretty good at that. You just keep trying until it works out. You're going to fall down on your face a lot of times, but you just have to look at the averages."

"He knows how to get a band to really believe in themselves and then perform accordingly," Taylor adds. "Working with Dave was a truly joyful experience. He has such a deep knowledge of songwriting and records that whatever he says or suggests, you really trust. And it's always done in a way that inspires and never limits or stifles."

Inspiring perhaps. But there's also some surprise involved as well. "In the case of the Dawes record, they didn't hear any of the music we were recording for the first eight days or so," Rawlings mentions. "They were just out there playing and eventually we just got to the breaking point of trust where they said, 'We just got to hear something.' So I put the tapes together the way I wanted to and made a little mix tape. It was so satisfying to be doing this for a group of guys, where you take the best elements of the music and the band and the personalities and put their best foot forward, and then you play it for them and they're really happy with what it is. They might not even know how you edited it around or how you got to where you got. As I learned over the years when I was doing it with Gillian and me, if you do a good job, there's nothing more fun in the world than to edit things together and make something you never would have played, and never could have played, because you're not that human being. And it ends up being your favorite part of that record. There are times when you have to leave the mistakes in to make it a better record. I guess I've done that a ton of times, so I feel pretty good about the way I do it."

Rawlings is the first to agree that recording an album and not having the band hear the results is hardly the most orthodox way of making a record. Then again, this is yet one more reason why Rawlings is such a singular artist, maybe one of the most unique musicians in Nashville. He's thoughtful and well-considered, even when the results are yet to unfold.

"I know my techniques are not normal," he agrees. "But they

went in and they were playing really good, and it sounded really good. There is a thing about recording records when you are just in a room, and you walk up to a microphone and you play to that little space that you're in, and you try to make it sound good to that space. That's a great focused way of playing music. On the other hand, you can go in and play it a couple of times, and then you want to go into the control room and when you do go in, its going to sound different. So then you're going to hear something, and when you walk back into that room, you're going to adjust what you hear in that room for what you heard in the other room. When things are going poorly, that's a great thing to do. But if things are going well, a lot of times that makes things worse. Because you can't get back to that one place where you're seeing the big picture. So there's some value in what we did. It doesn't work all the time, but once we started working on the Dawes record, once we started going back and forth, we started hearing good stuff. It definitely took longer because there was more translation and there was more second guessing of things. You can't hear what you heard before because you hear it now. It might be close, but it's not a sure thing."

By his own admission, Rawlings doesn't exactly work at a frenzied pace. "We've never been the fastest on the writing front . . . ever" Rawlings admits. "I think we learned pretty early on the difference in value between a song that we were satisfied with and a song we weren't completely satisfied with. If we liked it and were satisfied, and people liked it, we could play it for the rest of our lives. If we didn't, that's not the case. If we had been so fortunate early on to toss off songs we weren't so fond of and still had people fall at our feet, we would write a lot faster. But that hasn't been the case."

"That's definitely a failing," Welch agrees. "I wish it was otherwise. People don't understand. We don't record anything unless both of us sign off on it. We're equally vested in this. I usually start the songs and he's the closer. I'll write about 80 percent and he'll finish it."

After nearly two hours on the phone, not counting a subsequent follow-up discussion, the overall impression Rawlings imparts is just how insightful—make that philosophical—he can be whenever he's given a topic to consider. His musings may take him off the subject at hand, but he returns to the point not only fully engaged and articulate, but also completely candid, especially when discussing his sometime tenuous creative trajectory.

"We might have a terrible run, but over the years it's led to our very best music immediately thereafter," he considers. "We get so fed up, we can't even tell why it's bad or why we taped some of this stuff. I'll never be able to tell you the answer to that, but then two days after that, we'll sit down and play something we'll never be able to play again, and then we're so happy we were able to put it on tape. It never happens without us being very warm after being very miserable. It's kind of like taking leg weights off if you're a runner or something. It's like being weighed down after playing stuff you don't like. All of a sudden we're playing something we like, and we're warmed up and fresh and we get something good from it."

He pauses and allows himself a lighthearted moment. "So there's a piece of advice. Write terrible songs and let yourself go."

41

·····························

The Dawes Pause

Looking Forward with a Nod to the Past

It's not always easy for a band to defy expectations. For Dawes, a group pegged as heralding the second coming of archetypical Laurel Canyon sound—the music that nurtured the likes of Joni Mitchell, Jackson Browne, CSN, and those other wide-eyed troubadours that defined the Southern California sound—breaking down their own boundaries has become a challenge they're eager to embrace. Indeed, while critics were convinced they had them pegged, Dawes has made it a point to evolve and expand, keeping their melodic intent even as they add new sounds to the mix. Over the course of their five albums—*North Hills* (2009), *Nothing Is Wrong* (2011), *Stories Don't End* (2013), *All Your Favorite Bands*, and *We're All Gonna Die* (2016)—they've imbued their sun-dappled sounds with reflection and rumination to put the music in a broader context.

In recent years, the band—brothers Taylor Goldsmith (guitars and vocals) and Griffin Goldsmith (drums), Wylie Gelber (bass), and Lee Pardini (keyboards)—have accelerated their trajectory, taking on new challenges while finding a closer connection to their growing legion of fans. Taylor, Dawes's primary songwriter, insists that the group is intent on finding new avenues of communication without regard to those who might be tempted to peer over their collective shoulders. His sole priority, he insists, is to drive Dawes forward.

"It's always good to stay busy," he insists.

Do you still enjoy being out on the road?

Absolutely. It's what makes it all worth it for us. I enjoy making records, but dancing around within a song with your band in front of a live audience is what we enjoy, and that's especially true for the kind of music that we make.

You guys have attracted quite an enthusiastic following, and that's especially evident when you see the band live. What do you think it is about your sound that inspires this sort of enthusiasm?

I don't know entirely. Obviously there are a lot of factors. We try to bring all we can to the table, and I feel like that makes it comfortable for other people to step up to the table as well. We're not necessarily a cool band per se. We're not intimidating, and that's what's allowed our relationship with our audience to be so much more genuine and authentic. People are there because we're a band they like, not because it's cool to say you're a fan of Dawes. I don't think that's ever played into it—at least not so far. I don't mean to put us down because we're really proud of the progress we've made, but if we can connect with the audience in a genuine way each night, then I think that's the thing that's most important.

The title song of your album *All Your Favorite Bands* has become of an anthem, a signature song that really sums up that kind of connection. It gets to the heart of why people really love rock and roll.

Yes, and that's what we were going for. The kind of music you listen to is one of the things you identify yourself by. It's kind of a reactionary experience when you tell your parents you love the Replacements or the Sex Pistols. There's a deeper conversation going on there. It's you telling someone who you are. It's not just a matter of saying that song's good. It's more a matter of it being a part of you. So when we identify ourselves by the music we listen to, or the art we subscribe to, that's what the title is talking about. I have friends who tell me that when REM broke up, it was more than just not being able to see them play live anymore. It was like a part of who they were as children was dying. I know that sounds dramatic, but it was like a chapter was closing in a very real way. That's something that fascinates me, and I'm right there with everybody as far as my favorite artists are concerned. So that was what that song was speaking to.

You may not consider yourselves a hip and groovy band, but you did get a lot of notice right out of the box, especially from the critics who picked up on Dawes straight away. You must be aware of that.

Yeah, totally. For people to respond to us early was so surreal, and to have them champion us so early in the way they did was just amazing. I don't mean to imply we didn't get a fair share or anything. We were luckier than anyone could possibly be when we set out. Folk rock—although that's not how we refer to ourselves—is not necessarily the record-selling monster that it once was. When I look out at the audience at a Dawes show, I want to speak to them. These seem like the kind of people I would like to get to know. I don't mean any disrespect to the hipsters out there. Many people would probably look at me and assume I'm one, and maybe I am, but at the same time you go to some shows and you don't feel so connected.

You're not wearing black leather trousers and sporting orange spiky hair.

Right!

Still, after getting the accolades you received early on, did that set an unreasonably high bar. Did you feel that you had to live up to certain expectations? Was it intimidating in any way?

It's never felt that way. Maybe it should have. Maybe we would have even taken it to the next level. We made our first two records, and there was a lot of buzz and anticipation about what could possibly come next. And then we made our third record and it was a little more idiosyncratic and impressionistic . . . not some aggressive rock and roll album. We're really proud of that record, and we play songs from it every night. But if there was a swing for the bleachers we needed to take, we didn't take it. We decided to keep plugging along and make the best music we can, and to keep all that noise out of our heads and try to operate in the same space that we did when we made our first record. I don't know if we or any band can live up to expectations. I think if we were to start making music that way, it would be pretty transparent and pretty unfortunate. I think people would see through it, and maybe wouldn't be interested anymore. We just want to be honest.

Still, that last album did seem a bit of a departure. It seems to veer away from the early template.

In some respects it does. But for us, it was about challenging ourselves. How do we put ourselves in the same state of mind that we did when we were making our first couple of albums? When we made our first album, it didn't take a lot. We hadn't been in the studio that much. Just hearing our acoustic guitars, bass, drums, and harmonies was enough to make us feel we were taking it as far as we could. And with each record, we wanted to add to the definition of what our band is. So if we got to the point where we were saying, "Oh, that worked, let's do it again," I think that would signal the fact that the release of Dawes records was getting tired and pointless. I think we needed it to inspire us. That doesn't mean it's going to be weirder and more out there. Maybe there will be a time when we feel an acoustic record is the logical next step in what this band wants to do or needs to do.

Still, it does have more of a tangled, experimental sound.

I think this record is an embellishment of our sound rather than an abandonment of it. They're still written from the same place. When we play a live show, all five records weave together really well. I hear these stories of bands that have new music, and they hate their old music and they won't play those songs anymore.

That couldn't be further from the band that we are. We're always thrilled to play songs from our first records as much as we are to play songs from our new record. We feel lucky and proud that we can include songs from our entire catalogue, and it still feels representative of who we are. We're lucky. Our latest record feels as definitive as the early records. People are cheering and responding to it all in the same way. We needed to make the record that we needed to make, as much as we needed to make every record we've ever made. The example that I think about is Paul Simon. If he kept making "Bridge over Troubled Waters" or "Mrs. Robinson," he wouldn't be in the conversation the way he is now. But because he made *Graceland*, he showed he had this broader range of what he can do. We can't compare ourselves to Paul Simon, except that we are trying to stretch ourselves.

It has to be gratifying that that record became your most successful album yet.

It feels pretty cool. It's so hard to gauge how well a record does now. People don't buy them anymore, and there are so many streaming networks that it makes it hard to gauge any particular one as a barometer. All we can go by is ticket sales, and we're doing really well out there. So in that sense, it's true. We've never had a record feel so good. So it's exciting to watch.

So how did you come up with that title, *We're All Gonna Die?* It does sound somewhat fatalistic, especially give all the losses we suffered last year. It's almost prophetic.

[*Chuckles*] Well, that was definitely in consideration when I wrote the song. But when I wrote it, it wasn't to that extent as when actually we recorded the record. I wrote the song just because I was fascinated by all the different places that you find that phrase turning up, whether it was in Disney movies or in a Steve Martin skit. The word is always "gonna." It's never "going to." There's an idiomatic quality to the phrase that goes beyond the literal meaning to it. Even that line has a history to it.

And it worked.

We strived to make a really beautiful song. To have a lyric like that cascading over itself would hopefully give a singular impression. When it came time to name the record, it was getting pretty heated in the world. So we decided it would make a pretty strong album title as far as grabbing people's attention and making them lean in. When we titled our album *All Your Favorite Bands*, that was also a weird album title. Yet it felt appropriate, and I feel like once people heard that song, they put it all into context. At first, though, people were confused. They thought it was a covers album, and so you had to hear the title track in order to hear how that song fit in. It was the same with this record. Reading the title *We're All Gonna Die* is one thing, but when you hear that song it's actually quite the opposite. It's a song about not getting hung up on the shit that doesn't matter and not to stress yourself out over these sort of lofty concerns. It doesn't matter that much. So it was about taking stock of what counts. I like to think there's a comforting feeling to the song, a juxtaposition between the title itself and the material.

42

························

Ruthie Keeps It Real

It's midnight in Vienna time, on the eve of Ruthie Foster's European tour with blues guitarist Eric Bibb. Foster knows she should be jet-lagged after her transatlantic flight earlier that day, but she's yet to feel it. "I'm actually OK," she reflects. "I'm feeling pretty good."

Indeed, she has reason to feel cheery. Two of her albums, 2009's *The Truth According to Ruthie Foster* and 2012's *Let It Burn* garnered Grammy nominations for Best Blues Album, while *Promise of a Brand New Day*, released this past August, has reaped critical kudos of its own. That's in addition to a string of career achievements that includes three consecutive Blues Awards from 2011 through 2013, an Austin Music Award for Best Female Vocalist in 2013, and a Living Blues Artist of the Year Award in 2010. All in all, it appears Ruthie is on a roll.

Nevertheless, Foster tends to underplay her accomplishments. "I wish I was more calculating," she admits. "It's great to be recognized, but my real goal is to work hard and bring my best to my audiences. Getting that recognition does makes you stand up straight. It's a good way to keep you in the game, so I don't want to discredit that."

As its title suggests, *Promise of a Brand New Day* elevates Foster to a new plateau. "I wrote a lot more for this album," she says. "I really wanted to go a lot deeper into the blues and genuine soul. Meshell was all about that. She knows a lot about that sound, so I threw everything at her that I had and she shared her suggestions."

Meshell is, of course, the extraordinary bassist Meshell Ndegeocello who produced, played bass, and assembled the musicians for the album, among them members of her own band, as well as guitarist Doyle Bramhall II and singer Toshi Reagon. "I had been following her for awhile and I know she had been following me," Foster explains. "We shared the same booking agency and that was kind of the catalyst, even though it took a year or so for us to finally connect. She'd go to my concerts and I'd go to hers, until we finally found a hole in our calendars where we could make it work."

Ndegeocello's participation in the project found both women exploring relatively new stylistic terrain. "She works in a totally different genre than anything I do," Foster says. "And I think she was breaking new ground for herself as well. But the blues is in her blood as much as it is in mine. She asked me where I wanted to go with this record and I told her I basically just wanted to say something meaningful. And she helped me with that in a way that kept the music close to both my soul side and my blues side. She wanted to put a record together that I could play live, and she kept that in mind as we went along."

Having just turned fifty last May, Foster's determination to make a social statement is evident in several songs that made the final cut. "I really wanted to get closer to that deeper meaning," she maintains. "I hadn't done much of that before, but I knew it was time to. I wanted to express things in my own voice. 'It Might Not Be Right,' the song I wrote with William Bell, addresses gay marriage, and the track 'Second Coming' brings a specific message about civil rights. Meshell was great about bringing songs to me and pushing me to write about who I am, as a black woman, as a woman who is involved with another woman, a woman who has a child and who's also a musician who spends a lot of time on the road. This album hit on a lot of themes having to do with real life."

That's a subject Foster knows well. Born and raised in the small town of Gause, Texas, ninety miles northeast of Austin, she descended from a long line of gospel singers, a family heritage that continues to exert a strong influence on her music. "They were Missionary Baptist," she reflects. "And that's where I gained my first musical awareness. From there it was blues and then country. But I experienced a very strict view of gospel while growing up, going back to my preteen years when I travelled from church to church in the central part of Texas as a guest vocalist. Surprisingly, the church congregation that I grew up with was very forgiving when it came to what I wanted to do. My grandmother, who was one of the church matriarchs, was OK with me singing a contemporary gospel song, and she supported me when I wanted to play guitar as well as piano. My mother was also very supportive. I was a very, very shy kid, but she encouraged me to sing and play blues in the local community center. She knew I would always remember my roots. And I do. I respect where I came from and it's all a part of my makeup. It all started there."

It's clear too that the life lessons still resonate. "It gets to a point where you are who you are and you get busy with living and not worrying about what other people think. It's hard to do that in the world we're living in right now. I've spent so much time in front of people, not necessarily hiding who I am, but just trying to develop my career. But I'm at a point right now where I can say, 'This is my life, and while it's not all that I am, it is what I do.'"

43

·····························

Mekons Blur the Line between
Past and Present

Some bands are considered timeless, if for no reason other than their music transcends the sharply defined boundaries of taste and trends. Others earn that distinction simply by slogging it out indefinitely and refusing to give up. Then there are those who keep their relevance intact by continuing to comment on the issues of the day, fueled by their determination to stay in touch with the changing times.

The Mekons qualify on all those counts. Formed by a group of art students from the University of Leeds, and borrowing their name from a villainous character prominently featured in an old British comic strip, the band—vocalists Jon Langford and Sally Timms, violinist Susie Honeyman, drummer Steve Goulding, accordion player Rico Bell, bassist Sarah Corina, guitarist Tim Greenhalgh, and multi-instrumentalist Lu Edmonds—has maintained their unerring trajectory ever since, spawning no less than two dozen albums, as well as the various offshoot outfits sired by Mekons members.

Not surprisingly then, the sound of the band continues to evolve, and while their insurgent attitude is still informed by their punk origins, their fascination with folk, Americana, country, and various sounds in between reflects a fluidity that's always been essential to their stock and trade. Part of the reason is due to the fact that two of the band's mainstays, Jon Langford and Sally

Timms, made the transition from the UK to Chicago, which also happens to be the home of their record label, Bloodshot.

I spoke to Timms and Langford around the time of the release of their album *Ancient and Modern*. As the title implies, it tidies up loose threads and makes a seamless transition between past and present. The album takes listeners back to the turn of the last century—the twentieth century to be precise—prior to the First World War, when the British were living in their isolated, idyllic environs, unconcerned by events elsewhere. For a band so well versed in contemporary commentary, it seems, at least at first glance, like an unlikely muse. But is that an unreasonable assumption?

I spoke to Mekon mainstays Langford and Timms to get their perspective.

The new album seems to draw on a specific theme, one that takes the listener back a hundred years or so with songs that take on a historical perspective. So did the songs come first or does the concept come first?

Jon: The concept really came first. I think we all kind of sat down and agreed on what we'd write about before we actually started writing. With this album, there was no fixed rule, and in fact with the Mekons, it's kind of the exception that proves the rule. Me and Lu actually sat down in my basement at the end of a tour and just started messing around. We actually did write a few little doodly tunes. Those were things we just kind of stuck in the back a bit, but when we came to sit down, we kind of had these things we were working on. They were like chord progressions and nothing else. I don't think any lyrics were written, so we sat down and things were just made up on the spot. So that gave us a little kick start so we could start working on and some of those we didn't use anyway. We went to this cottage in the middle of nowhere, and some of the best songs on the record came about very quickly and were kind of first takes. The opening track was this little tune we'd kind of been fiddling about with, and we expanded it. We were at this little cottage in Devon, and we wrote some words sitting around the dinner table and Tom sang it. [*Chuckles*] And then it was pretty much done.

So was the historical concept the idea from the beginning?

Jon: It was kind of a conceit on which to hang the songs on, but we just thought it was an interesting point in history, similar to what we find ourselves in now, what with the anniversary coming up of the First World War. One of the things that went through our heads was that the people who had fought in that war are all dead now. The last British soldier who fought in it just died recently. So it was sort of the dawn of the modern world. Back in 1911, it was sort of a similar time to what it is now. We realized the threads, as it were. The people were happy and elegant in their sort of Edwardian lifestyles, much like we're so comfortable in our consumerism and faith in our technology.

What seems so interesting about that is that the Mekons have always been a band that's so much in the moment, and one that's been unafraid to comment on contemporary events. And yet, here we have you shifting the era back over a hundred years. It seems a sort of drastic switch in strategy, both philosophically and strategically.

Sally: I think that's the point, that the moment now is the same as the moment then. What we're saying is that there's not that much difference between what's going on now and if you look back now to a hundred years ago; it's the idea that history is kind of repeating itself. If you go back a hundred years, you can see a period where it was almost an identical situation where it was a very, very shallow period of history, and that's what we feel this is as well. So we are commenting on the now and saying it happened before, so you can slip between the two things.

The Mekons have had a very curious trajectory. You started out at the height of the punk era and were very much a part of that era, and yet you've since transitioned to Americana and traditional folk. What instigated these changes?

Jon: We were never pressured about a Mekons "sound," especially when you think about bands of that era. If we were still doing "Where Were You," which was probably our biggest single for thirty odd years, we were more about the process of working rather than critical response or any notions of how a band should behave. We were never all that interested in developing some kind of sound or some kind of style. After the mideighties, we saw ourselves as a reflection and part of a history and a certain tradition of music making rather than simply being a part of punk rock or reinventing the wheel.

Sally: And I think, right at the beginning of the band's existence, the folk connection was always there. The places where we recorded were very old studios, and the producers would say, "Well, you sound like a folk band." It was a very simple three- or four-chord structure by people who maybe couldn't play that well and were self-taught. And we sang songs about real things, as opposed to romance or something like that. I think that's been there for some time, and I think there are definitely those connections going through, so even though the band initially fell under the punk umbrella, we were never what I would classify as a straight ahead punk band. But I would say the sound of the band has been rather consistent for the last twenty years or so, and the lineup has been consistent, but we've chosen to play different styles of music within than group of musicians. But it doesn't sound like a different band to me. It sounds like a band that's playing around with different genres of music.

It's interesting that you hail from the UK and yet Americana informs so much of your music both individually and collectively. So what draws musicians from the homeland to this indigenous American sound?

Sally: You can say that about pretty much every British band that's been around since the fifties and sixties. If you look at Britain or anyone in Europe—but Britain in particular—the influence of American music has always been huge. But I think with our band in particular, Country was something we came to after having been introduced to it by a good friend of ours. Jon, you liked Country in a lot of ways before anyone else.

Jon: We were into Jerry Lee Lewis and Jimmie Rogers and things like that. There was a time when the Mekons thought everything old was just crap and should be destroyed because that was sort of the punk way. And then we thought maybe what we're doing is part of a broader tradition along with the political elements and the kind of ranting was a kind of experimentation. So it was all stuff that had been done before, but we were just doing it in a different way. That's how it was in Britain after the Second World War. When I was a kid, there was still rationing. It was sort of a drab, black and white world. America never really got touched in the Second World War. Yeah, you lost a lot of men, but Britain got bombed to crap. It took a long time to recover. One of the things that helped guide the direction of culture after the war in Britain was a direct reaction to America. So we were kind of programmed to look toward America. After the war, America was kind of this gleaming beacon and in the ascendency. Things have very much changed now. [*laughs*] It's not surprising. I've lived here twenty years and I feel able, because I've got American kids, to be critical of America. But I'm also sort of fiercely proud about America's contribution to the culture of the twentieth century. The music that came out of America has had a huge influence on the culture of the world. It's been every bit as influential as your militaristic, imperialistic fucking snipes.

Well, perhaps . . .

Jon: I didn't mean you personally.

With all the projects you seem to juggle simultaneously, you are both supreme examples of dedicated multitaskers. How do you do it?

Sally: That would probably be best answered by Jon.

OK, that's to you then, Jon.

Jon: Yes, well . . . I've gotten to this sort of peculiar position in my life where I don't really have much choice. Time is very short.

What? You're hardly an old man.

Jon: No, I'm incredibly ancient. I think about what things I want to do in my life. That's why I'm going back to medical school. . . .

Ummm . . . really?

Jon: No, I'm just joking.

Well, one never knows. You are a bit of a renaissance man. That recent book of your original art was quite lovely. Perhaps the better question is, how you decide where to plant your material? You have so many different bands and guises . . . how do you decide which avenue to pursue?

Jon: When I write my stuff on my own it goes on my solo stuff, or it doesn't go anywhere. I may throw it all away. In the Mekons, we usually write together. Although we don't have many rules, the one we do have is that nobody does anything until we get together.

Sally: The ideas are formulated together somewhat, but the idea that people come with sort of half a written song just doesn't work. It's really a collaborative effort. It takes place when we're all in the room. For the last couple of records, we just rented houses in the countryside and moved into them for a few days and wrote the songs from scratch. And that's the way it seems to work in the studio as well. We have bits and bobs that we bring in there, but nothing that would qualify as even a semicomplete song.

So what is it that beckons the Mekons and brings them together? What tells you it's time to record a new album, and how do you go about gathering everybody together to make it happen?

Sally: It's like the migration of the wildebeest, what causes us to migrate from one side of the Serengeti.

Jon: There was some reason we were in England at that time. . . .

Sally: We were playing and we had a gap, so we thought we'd take advantage. When we go home we tend to stay put, so when we are called over to do shows, we like to take advantage and make a record, or at least start it, and so we book additional time to stay over.

Jon: I think we were on our way to Spain. . . .

Sally: Yes, you're right. We had a sort of four or five day gap between shows, so we had to think what we were going to do. So that's when we booked the initial session in Devon. Once we finish a record, the idea will always sort of be in the back of everyone's mind as to when we'll start on the next one. You know, we started this three years ago, so it's taken quite a long time to get it finished. It's also been finished for quite a while, but we had issues with (former record label) Touch and Go because they stopped putting out records, and so we had to find a new label. This has been the first time we've had to deal with this for a really long time. It's been quite a stressful process. Instead of having this long-term home where we just go, "OK, we're about to spend $5,000 on our next record," and "Yes, OK, as long as it's not more than that," we would go ahead. There was the freedom we had for being on a label for a very long period of time, with people who were really, really supportive, and we made sure we didn't spend tons of money. We were able to function in a way so that we always recouped and we made bits of money for everyone and we could kind of work within that structure and have this home where they were very kind to us. That was a great thing for a long period of time.

It's a great thing to be with Bloodshot now. We know them. We've worked with them. It's not as large as Touch and Go, but in some ways, especially musically, it's a more appropriate home for the Mekons.

Jon: We had to be somewhere where we didn't have to constantly explain what we were doing.

How do you account for the band's remarkable longevity? It's been well over thirty years that's you've been together.

Sally: Well, not all of us have been in the band that long.

No, but Sally, you yourself have been with the band for a good portion of that time.

Sally: Sarah is the group's newest member and she's been in it for twenty years. I think there are a number of reasons, and some of them are pragmatic. First and foremost, we don't force ourselves to work when we don't have to. Our own lives are allowed to exist; it's not like we're out touring four or five months a year and because there's no pressure to do that, we can make it fit around everyone's requirements. Another thing is, we actually really like doing it and we really like each other. So why not? As long as the band feels like there's something to be said, regardless of response, we probably will continue playing, even if it's in an empty room, although eventually I'm sure that would get strange. We've been in that position before, where no one was really interested, but we still carried on. There's been no period where this band has talked about splitting up. We've had a hiatus, but that's it.

Jon: I think the band's kind of gotten to the point now where we've managed to insulate it from any kind of commercial or real world pressures. It's just the choice we've made that we'll do whatever it takes, you know? It's not worth analyzing and thinking if there are reasons worth doing it. That's just not the point of it.

Does it help that you have so many outside projects and you can divert your energies elsewhere when need be, so that it doesn't become a matter of all or nothing as far as the Mekons are concerned? So if you don't get all your songs on the album, you have other places to place them.

Jon: We've all got our outlets for what we can do, and everyone else has their separate projects. Next year we probably won't do the Mekons. Lu is very busy with a project he's working on and other people have stuff that they're involved in, so it's quite possible that we won't do it again for another year or so. But there will come a point where something will come up, and someone will say, "Ah, right, we should do something then."

So the logistics of gathering everyone together, despite being spread across different parts of the planet, is something that can be arranged?

Jon: One of the major costs is airfare, but we have a lot of gigs that pay well and we'll have to drive between some of them. Some of them are subsidized, and we're socialists, so we subsidize everything.

....

Band of Heathens as a Band of Brothers

Unlike many outfits who take years to reap their just rewards, Band of Heathens worked their way into the spotlight fairly quickly. It wasn't that they had any grand designs early on, or even had any thoughts about becoming a band in the first place. What began initially as a series of Wednesday night jam sessions at a club in their native Austin—an event they dubbed "The Good Time Supper Club"—eventually coalesced into a band that quickly gained attention and soon climbed to the top of the Americana charts. They certainly had all the goods they needed from the very beginning, thanks to a pair of seasoned singer-songwriters in Ed Jurdi and Gordy Quist, each of whom had pursed solo careers prior to participating in those impromptu gatherings.

True to form, the group's initial albums were recorded live prior to releasing their eponymous studio debut in 2008. And while concert recordings continue to find a place in their catalog—and in their MO—Band of Heathens have shown a certain studio savvy as well. With the core outfit currently consisting of Jordi and Quist on vocals and guitars and later recruits Trevor Nealon on keyboards and Richard Millsap playing drums, they've earned all admiration that they've mustered.

I caught up with Ed Jordi on the phone from his home in Asheville and offered him the opportunity to delineate the band's unlikely trajectory.

Your band came together in an unusual way, recording solo albums before the band even started.

I think everything about out band, in terms of the way things are usually done, have been ass backward. We all were doing solo stuff and then this thing came together and took on a life of its own. You have moments in your life where things just sort of happen. We were all doing our own thing and just happened to start playing together, and it just sort of took off. It was a pretty unique sound, and we all agreed it might be something worth exploring. It wasn't like a discussion ever happened early on, but as we got into it we were kind of getting back what we put into it. We were feeling good about where it was taking us, so following that muse led us to where we are now.

Was there ever any second thoughts about putting your solo careers on the back burner?

The evolution was so slow and natural that that thought never entered into it. We were doing our weekly gig for like a year. That's all we did was play once a week in Austin while doing our solo stuff at the same time. So it was like, what if we do a week of shows in Dallas or Houston? So we started doing that and it was going great. We were doing the other stuff all along, and it was kind of like this is going so well and we're really having fun, and where the solo stuff was once a priority, let's make this a priority for a little while and see how it goes. We all felt there was room to do whatever we wanted to do on an individual creative level. Whenever you're playing in an ensemble, that's kind of what it is. It's kind of a balance of knowing what the group is doing while also being creatively fulfilled individually. The answer was yes to both of those things. So it was really a no brainer. Let's give this a shot for a little while and see what happens.

It seemed like the band started almost accidentally.

When it started, there was no plan to put a band together or make a record. It was really a jam. It was a fun thing to do on a Wednesday night. So at some point, when it starts giving back creatively to you and you're getting a nice return, you start to feel like, "Well, maybe we can start investing something into it."

That's really it. Just jamming and having fun and finding people who were really into it and having a great time. But at first we weren't really putting any creative capital into it. We're talking like a year or 18 months into it at this point, and then we started thinking, "What if we make a record and write some songs and see what it sounds like when we really start concentrating on it?" We did that and everyone thought, "Wow, this is great, this is cool." And that's really it. That's been the MO all along. See how it feels and take it from there.

So from the way you describe it, it sounds like a very gradual transition.

Yeah, and on another level, all of us, as individual songwriters, we still got to present our own material and we had a great band that everyone could play off of and with, and in effect do only a third of the work. For me, being in a band has always been the goal. Even when you're doing your own thing, you want to have a group of people around you that can play off of and with. As a music fan, that's the thing that always resonated with me. Watching a group of people onstage playing music together and interacting and having things happen in the moment. And so being a part of that interaction, that's the thing about making music that's special for me at least.

Your music was received really well at the outset. You garnered a lot of acclaim from the first note you released and instantly hit the highest peaks of the Americana charts. But did that in turn put a lot of pressure on you, knowing that you already had a high bar to maintain?

On a business level, it does, but creatively that's always been a very secondary thing to us. I never equated our albums going to number one with the quality of the work. Maybe it was an affirmation of the quality of the work, but the only judges of that are the guys in the band. Do we like it, and do we feel good about putting it out? If it's the best work we're doing in the time that we're doing it, then that's it. When we finished the new record and played it out, it felt like the best thing we had ever done. That's just my opinion, though. Everyone receives it differently, from critics to fans and everyone in between, and that's their right to have that opinion. But at the end of the day, all we can do is base it on the work that we're doing. Because otherwise, it's kind of unachievable. I have no idea how to make music that I think someone else thinks is great or going to be number one. It's such a nebulous field of reference.

Your name was actually the result of mistaken identity, was it not?

That's totally true. We were doing this Wednesday night thing and had been doing it for a few months, and we were calling it "The Good Time Supper Club," because it was kind of like an evening of different entertainers. We started it off and then some of our friends came down, and it became a big deal. Everybody started coming down just to see what was going to happen. Someone made some posters for the show and they started calling us "those heathens" or something like that.

How did they come up with that?

I have no idea. But it got to be known around town that on Wednesday night, you could see Those Heathens. So everyone just started calling us Those Heathens. It was just kind of like, "Well, OK, that's cool." At the time it was funny because there was a little bit of controversy about religion and how it's got its place in our society and how the conservatives were banging the drum about family values. If nothing else, it leveled the discussion in a tongue in cheek kind of way. So it just sort of stuck; it was kind of serendipitous like everything about this band.

What can we expect from a Band of Heathens concert these days?

That's a great question. I think in general the best way I can describe it is that we're a rock and roll band, so fundamentally you're going to get a rock and roll show. That being said, we're definitely into song craft. That's where everything starts and ends with the band, so we present these songs that we record and sometimes we do them the same way we do them on the record but most times not. We've changed a lot. I think the people that come see our band are just into the experience of being a part of the music, kind of going on a trip night to night, whatever that may be. Just watching us create on stage and just feeding off of that. Being a part of the moment.

45

Reverend Peyton's Big Damn Band
Go Back to the Roots

Rev. Peyton is the first to admit that the name of his outfit—Reverend Peyton's Big Damn Band—could seem like hyperbole, or worse, appear wholly misleading. "We've had so many soundboard people ask us over the years, "How many channels do you need? I don't know if our board is big enough!" He laughs. "I tell them, 'Your board is probably big enough.'"

Any confusion is only natural. For one thing, his so-called Big Damn Band is simply a trio. For another, Peyton is no reverend—at least not in the strictest sense. The "People have always called me 'Rev,'" he explains. "When we were naming the band, I had this tendency to identify things as a 'big damn' this or a 'big damn' that, and it became almost like an inside joke. So I came up with the name 'Reverend Peyton and His Big Damn Band.' We had no idea anyone was ever going to care. We didn't think about it in terms of marketing or anything. It just felt ironic to call this small band the 'Big Damn Band.' So I researched the name, and I just couldn't believe that no band had ever been called the Big Damn Band before. It was just too good."

For the record, Peyton keeps his own first name a secret. In fact, he insists that even his mother refers to him as "Rev."

Regardless, it wasn't only the irony of the name itself that some found confusing; it was their entire MO. On first hearing, it's unclear whether they're aiming to be a blues band, a jam band, a rock and roll band, a funk band, or an archival Americana band. Not that it matters, because in truth, the band offers some of each. While their new albums offer a predominance of bluster and boogie, its songs also encompass a casual country ramble, plenty of stomp and even more assertion. "We don't need another love song," Peyton insists on their song "Music and Friends." "The pop charts are pop tarts, with empty songs and empty hearts."

"Playing music that doesn't sound like a lot of contemporaries is our biggest strength," says Breezy Peyton, Rev.'s wife and constant collaborator. "The average music listener doesn't know where to categorize us. Sometimes it's frustrating from a publicity point of view, because it's hard to know how exactly to pitch us. But we don't really deal with comparisons and whether it fits into some specific mold. I hear all the time that we are someone's favorite blues, bluegrass, punk, or country band. I don't care what people call it, so long as they like it."

That stylistic mutability has also provided them with a wide array of performance possibilities. In past years, they've found themselves fitting in just as easily as featured guests on the Warped Tour (where they were named "Best Band") as they have while headlining at the Telluride Bluegrass Festival, WOMAD, the Cambridge Folk Festival, Glastonbury, and Bonnaroo.

"It's interesting," Rev. insists. "It's one of the ways we're able to do so many shows and keep it interesting . . . not just for the fans, but for ourselves. I remember one time when we played a bikers rally, and then we played a date on the Warped Tour, and then we played a Canadian folk festival . . . all in the same week! The only thing we might have had to adjust was the set list, but a lot of times we didn't adjust anything at all."

"The Reverend Peyton's Big Damn Band is a twenty-year-old bourbon in a room of vodka Red Bulls and PBRs," an observer once wrote. "Vintage yet timeless, exciting and still welcoming."

It's that depth and variety that's allowed Peyton and his band mates—Breezy on washboard and vocals, and drummer and backing vocalist Ben Bussell—not only to multitask with their approach, but also to find a fit with different audiences without alienating anyone in the process. That's quite an accomplishment, considering the fact the band averages some 250 dates a year.

"I think most of our musical evolution comes from playing so many shows," Breezy muses. "We're the tightest we've ever been and we've been exposed to a lot of great music along the way. What we listen to in the van encompasses a lot more musical genres than it did a few years ago."

"Sometimes audiences don't know what to expect, but that's what's so fun about it," Rev. admits. "A bunch of hardened bikers react to music in a different way than people at, say, Bonnaroo. You have to be able to read their reactions. For example, if you play straight honky-tonk country, there are only certain places you can play, and that's it. And if you play punk rock, there are only certain places you can play that and that's all there is there too. You're not going to be able to play just anywhere, because you're limited. On the other hand, I don't know if there's a type of venue in the United States that we haven't done—we've done blues festivals, folk festivals, punk rock clubs, hillbilly clubs, blues clubs . . . we've played with Derek Trucks and Susan Tedeschi. We've played with Flogging Molly. We've played with Clutch. We've done shows in tents, and we've done Austin City Limits. I feel really lucky in that way, because that's part of what keeps it exciting for me. If we showed up for every show and we knew it was going to be the same thing, same exact setup, same exact kind of crowd, then maybe it would be boring and maybe it wouldn't be so easy to keep it so fresh."

The critics seem to concur. "The band is amazing live," one wrote. "[Reverend Peyton] is truly one of the best guitar pickers I have seen. Seeing the fingerpicking style—where the thumb plays the bass line and the other fingers play the guitar part—was a real treat. You don't get to see many players like that anymore, but the truth is . . . you don't see many guitar players like Reverend Peyton."

It's to their credit as well that after a decade, the band still manages to retain their roots. Ask the Peytons about the source of musical inspiration, and the answer comes quickly. It lies in the place they call home—Brown County, Indiana.

"It's in the southern Indiana hills, near the border with Kentucky," Rev. explains. "It's a secluded, rural place that few folks are even aware of, but it's always influenced the content of my songs. I get messages all the time from my friends—'Man, why don't you come to Austin? It's really happening here.' Or, 'Man, come to Nashville, that's where it's all going on.' But I refuse to leave my home, and I refuse to sing songs that don't reflect this place that I'm from. It makes me feel good that we have so many fans from Brown County, so many fans close to home. I appreciate it. They know what we are and what we're all about, and they know that the songs that we sing are for real. Whenever I read that someone from far away didn't get where we're coming from, I figure they just don't know, because they're not from here. But the people that are from here know what life is like in this area."

Indeed, the Peytons' hometown pride runs deep. He knows true rural voices are rarely embraced by audiences outside of their hometowns, so he takes his role as a sort of ambassador seriously. "People are so used to hearing this characterization of what life is like out in the country, so I think when they hear a song describing what life is really like out here, they don't quite understand. My wife says I could work for the local chamber of commerce with all the good things I say about this place. Maybe that's true. Indiana is a little state, and so it is underrated. Oftentimes people that live in a small town like this say 'Oh, there's nothing to do here.' But when you get here, and you really look into it, you see there is plenty to do. I do a lot of traveling, and the further I get from home, the more I realize how lovely it is."

"We love having a home to come back to where we can have some peace," Breezy adds. "Brown County is a beautiful place, and it's home to some of the most interesting people in the world. We're surrounded by some amazing artisans, and that's extremely inspiring."

Indiana hasn't been the band's only inspiration, however. Far from it. Rev.'s infatuation with some early idols has also had a lingering effect on his music. "One thing I love about my heroes— Charlie Patton, Furry Lewis, Mississippi John Hurt—is that they didn't live by any set rules for what their music was," he maintains "They only put out stuff they thought was really great. In blues music—and in the modern world—that's something we seem to be lacking. Everybody's got a formula: twelve bars, and turn around, and shuffle. And that's it. But there's so much more to it. On this record I wanted to really push myself. It was like, "How much further can we take this? What can I do with finger style country blues guitar that's never been [done] before?" A lot of the songs on the record, particularly the first two—'Let's Jump a Train' and 'Pot Roast and Kisses'—allowed me to take a unique approach, and I'm really proud of that. When people hear those songs, they're going to think its two guitars. It's not. It's one 100 percent me laying it down live. Blues is the oldest genre of uniquely American music, and there's a lot more to make, but only if we keep pushing it and trying to make it sound fresh. We have to understand where it comes from, and also ensure that it remains in the here and now."

On that point, Rev. is especially adamant. "You can cover Son House all you want, but you're never going to do it as well as Son House, because he lived those songs. And that was one thing I figured out early on. If you're going to play the blues, then you have to write about stuff you're living. Blues is different in terms of its subjects. In certain genres of music, you can make up stories and write songs that are fiction, and it can work. But not in blues. Blues music forces you to open yourself up. And that can be a scary thing; when you take a song that's 100 percent autobiographical, and it's so incredibly personal, you run the risk of them not liking you."

No "empty songs and empty hearts" for him, then.

"I have nothing to hide," he declares. "People are so used to being lied to, they're not sure they're not still getting lied to, even when something is for real. I always considered myself to be a student of early blues, preblues—what I call country blues—a student who studied at that altar. Some people call it roots blues, because the label country blues confuses people. They think of Waylon Jennings as country blues. Waylon Jennings is great, but that's not necessarily what I do. Over the last few years I've come to figure out what I'm all about. . . . My goal is to play the guitar in a way that has never been done before. Of course, that's a tall order. People have been playing guitar in this country for centuries. It's something I literally work on every day. This new record has more of that than ever before. . . . Just one guitar—all me."

Clearly the band has come a long way from their earliest albums—their "field recordings," as Rev. calls them. Yet, while they've upgraded their technique and technology, the Big Damn Band still strives to maintain authenticity. "We put up the mics, and played our songs, and that was it," Rev. says, recalling those initial efforts. "When we first started making records, I was railing against everything in music that I thought was terrible in terms of what I thought sounded plastic and artificial, so that drove us to the extreme in the other direction. We were replicating field recordings on 1920s and 1930s microphones, and that was it. But I've learned over the years that we can make a vintage-sounding recording and also make it a good record. We've become less obtuse about it. For this record, we used forties and sixties technology, so maybe we're advancing." He laughs. "We're still thinking about the equipment and what we can use to create the sound we want, but we also want to make sure it sits well in people's iPods."

"Before I loved Rev. I loved country blues," Breezy reflects. "There are a lot of people in blues today that are talking about keeping the blues alive, but I believe the best way to keep it alive is to create new blues. Any artist can regurgitate music from another artist, but it's rarely better than the original. There are too few artists in blues that are making new blues music for modern times while still giving a nod to the old greats. I think that is Rev.'s biggest strength, and his true gift."

It's that desire to honor past precepts while still providing a sound that's still current and contemporary that's at the core of their MO. "I never want to sound like I'm in a museum," Rev. says. "That's never what I intend to be. I want to take country blues, roots blues, country-style blues guitar and play music for people that sounds like now, and doesn't come across as a museum piece."

To a great extent, Peyton's succeeded. However, there's no denying their well-worn template.

Fittingly, *So Delicious* was released by Yazoo Records, an archival label devoted to preserving vintage blues recordings. Rev. Peyton himself couldn't have been happier with the arrangement. "It was like a dream come true," he says. "I've spent my whole life listening to Yazoo releases. It's the number one place to find reissues of those classic 78 RPM records, and for them to believe in what we're doing, it's just so gratifying, so satisfying . . . it just really makes me feel like someone finally got it. That they understood where I'm coming from."

Getting people to understand is something both Peytons have

pursued for quite a while. And as Rev. admits, it hasn't always been easy. "I learned early on that not everyone's going to listen to music the way I do," he muses. "My level of passion borders on insanity. Not everyone has been studying music and pouring over it since they were twelve years old like I have. Not everyone has lived it that way. Most people listen, and either like it or they don't. Not everyone hears a hundred years of influences. And that's fine of course. It's OK. But it's nice when someone does listen to music that way and they're able to tell what we're trying to do."

As one who refers to himself as a reverend, and freely boasts about his achievements, even while inflating the size of his ensemble, Peyton is clearly self-assured. "I was really confident that I could take these songs, and take my vision for them, and move them forward and make the best record we've ever made," he says. "Maybe that's because of all the shows we've done on the road, or maybe it's because of the handful of records we've made. I don't know exactly where it comes from, but you know what? I know I can do this. All the songs were written and produced by me. That was kind of a scary thing. If it went well, it meant that I would look pretty good. But if it didn't go so great, I'd have no one to blame but myself."

While that may be the case, Rev. also credits Breezy with helping to make things work in terms of both the music and the mechanics. Anyone who claims that business and pleasure don't mix, or that spouses who work together wreck their chances of staying together, might take a lesson from the Peytons' partnership. "Breezy is my best friend," Rev. says confidently. "We have so much fun together. She always believed in me and the songs that I write and the music that we make together . . . even before I did. We never argue in a way that leads to anything serious. We might argue about something stupid, but we both know it's stupid, so it's no big deal. We help each other in every way. Her ability to run the business aspect of this is at the genius level. She's there at the exact places I need the help. And hopefully it's true for the vice versa."

Breezy concurs. "Rev. has developed so much vocally and lyrically since the beginning," she insists. "He is a true leader and he gives great direction for his vision with the new songs. I'm very lucky to be right there beside him."

Americana Abroad

Anyone looking for evidence of Americana's universal appeal need only notice the way it's been picked up overseas, in places far from the heartland geographically, but close in terms of sincerity and sentiment.

In Part 4, we conclude our look at Americana's burgeoning popularity by giving voice to some of the artists that have spawned interest in it overseas.

Indeed, there's no better proof that Americana is here to stay. . . .

46

Julian Dawson

Despite English Origins, He's Found
His Nashville Niche

Originally an integral part of the British folk music scene—he's performed with Richard Thompson, played in the band Plainsong with Iain Matthews, and appeared at the annual Fairport Convention reunion festival in Cropredy, which is where yours truly first caught him—Julian Dawson also has firm ties to Nashville, having first recorded there in the early nineties. In the years since, he's collaborated with Lucinda Williams, ex-Byrd Gene Parsons, Jules Shear, the Roches, Willie Nile, and Steuart Smith, whose most recent accomplishment includes *Covered*, the new album by Shawn Colvin. In 1996 he further engrained himself in the Americana Firmament by producing a comeback album by Charlie Louvin, *The Longest Train*.

Still, despite more than twenty albums to his credit, Dawson's yet to achieve the fame he so rightfully deserves. All that may change with the release of his new album, the aptly titled *Living Good*. A mostly low-lit endeavor due to its intimate execution, it reunites him with songwriter and producer Dan Penn, who he met during his earlier excursions to Music City.

"I've known Dan Penn since my second album recording in Nashville, back in the early nineties," Dawson recalls. "I first heard of Dan through reading Peter Guralnick's excellent book *Sweet Soul Music*, and I happened to arrive in town the night that Dan and Spooner Oldham were giving one of their very first live performances in the famous Bluebird Cafe. I got talking to Dan and his wife after the show and was bold enough to ask if he'd allow a fan to hear some of his legendary song demos. After inviting me to his house, he popped a cassette in my front pocket with a dozen then-unreleased tracks from his days in Muscle Shoals. He was then gracious enough to come in and sing a harmony on a song I'd written with Vince Gill on my album *Headlines*.

Dawson and Penn stayed friends over the years, and the two co-wrote several songs, in addition to Dawson's guest appearance as a harp player on a couple of Penn's own albums. Consequently, Penn returned the favor and produced Dawson and his namesake band's *Deep Rain* album in 2008. "His studio is full of fantastic vintage gear and he still has all the smarts that made him such a player in the sixties," Dawson recalls, obviously still in amazement. "I've had some great times and amazing experiences with Dan and his lovely wife Linda over the years. Then last year he suggested we record a solo album."

The album was recorded straight to analogue quarter inch tape, featuring little more than guitar and vocals. However, Dawson also couldn't resist calling on a few friends to assist in its creation. "I'd built up a group of fantastic Nashville based friends over the years and invited a few guests to add color to certain tracks," he says. "'A' list bass-player Michael Rhodes, husband and wife team Barry and Holly Tashian, multi-instrumentalist Jim Hoke, keyboard man Billy Livsey, guitar wizard Michael Henderson and the producer himself, with spontaneous vocal parts and harmonies. Nevertheless, it's my first 'solo' album after many band albums I've made over the years."

In some regards, Dawson is a renaissance man. In addition to his multitude of musical projects, he wrote a biography of famed session pianist Nicky Hopkins, which received glowing reviews. Nevertheless, he admits that he's become somewhat disenchanted with the multitude of same-sounding music offerings that pop up everywhere these days, and that it's starting to affect his own productivity. "I find that my response to the incredible overload of music in the Spotify and iTunes Internet era, is to write less than I used to, and then mostly when I'm moved by something personal in my own life. I also determined, as a reaction to all the gloomy, melodramatic CDs appearing everywhere from the current generation of singer-songwriters, to make my statement as positive as possible. This is not a helpful thing to do when looking for column inches from journalists, as the music media seems to focus more on extravagant back stories and well-trodden dramatic life stories than on the actual music."

That's not to say that Dawson has any doubts about his own efforts and intents.

In fact, it's quite the opposite.

"I've been doing this job now for a long time and feel pretty comfortable in my own skin," he insists. "At this point in time, I feel I don't have to prove anything to anyone. I love music just as much as I ever did, and have so far succeeded in maintaining a place in the new music landscape we find ourselves in."

We can all be happy he has.

47

....

The Dreaming Spires Share Their Search for the "Supertruth"

The Dreaming Spires' overriding influence doesn't differ too dramatically from other aspiring Americana artists in the UK. The Byrds, the Burrito Brothers, and other purveyors of Southern California's sun-dappled sound circa the late sixties and early seventies radiate from the two discs they released early on: 2012's *Brothers in Brooklyn* and its 2015 successor *Searching for the Supertruth*. "California is always on my mind," they coo on the aptly named "Easy Rider," a track taken from their sophomore set. It's no surprise really; brothers Robin and Joseph Bennett served their apprenticeship with two bands known for their California dreaming—Goldrush and Danny and the Champions of the World—while also having occasion to record with Gary Louris of the Jayhawks, Garth Hudson, Mark Garner of the Ride, Mercury Rev, and Saint Etienne. Along with current drummer Jamie Dawson, they create a sweeping sound that veers from the introspective to the anthemic while covering various bases in between.

The genesis of the band came about in a late nineties band called Whispering Bob, which received attention from John Peel and Bob Harris. However, their initial influences go back much further. "Our dad was a big Beatles fan, so we listened to them a lot as kids," Joe notes. "I knew the words to the whole of Sgt. Pepper by the age of six! When I began to discover music for myself as a thirteen-year-old, I got into REM, starting with *Automatic for the People* and working my way back rapidly to *Murmur and Green*. As a teenager living in Oxford at that time, you couldn't not be influenced by Supergrass and Radiohead. I learned to play bass listening to *I Should Coco* and *In It for the Money*, and then at seventeen I stumbled upon the Band. The way their three voices blend is so ragged and yet so beautiful, and Rick Danko's bass-playing style made a big impression on me. 'King Harvest (Has Surely Come)' is just one of the greatest grooves out there."

"Growing up in the same household, mine are largely similar," Robin concurs "That Beatles movie *Backbeat* came out when I was fifteen and sent me back to some of the source material— Sun-period Elvis, Chuck Berry, Little Richard. I remember Nirvana's MTV Unplugged opened my eyes to a more rootsy sound around the same time, and from reading interviews with the Lemonheads, I started to be curious about Gram Parsons. That may have been my gateway to Americana. I also found a box of old records containing Harvest, CSN&Y, and some others that changed the course of my listening. I wrote a script for a play when I was briefly at college, aged eighteen or nineteen, and it was all about a kid obsessed with Hank Williams. Sadly for posterity, I lost the script.

The band's 2015 album, *Searching for the Supertruth*, lives up to its title, given the meditative nature of several of its songs— the beautiful, caressing "We Used to Have Parties" in particular. "There's a few narrative threads running through, relating to our travels around the US and experiences with a dear friend of ours," Joe explains. "Plus, it's our quest for a greater meaning in life and our place in the universe . . . you know, lowbrow stuff!"

"A lot of them are continuing a narrative I started on the first album, *Brothers in Brooklyn*, about a close friend, Danny, who started out as the US tour manager for our old band Goldrush when we came to the States as backing band for Mark Gardener of Ride," Robin recalls. "He then became a friend and a songwriting partner. We struck up an amazing rapport that allowed us to churn out songs rapidly, including some that have been recorded by the Spires, such as 'If I Didn't Know You' from the present record. Around 2008 things started to go off the rails for him and I was stuck without my songwriting partner. So, after a couple of years writing more or less nothing, I wrote instead about what was happening to him and about our shared past on the road, and the songs just flowed. I felt that my friend would be helped by hearing the songs, strange as that may sound."

On a sonic level, I was trying to get a sort of consistent atmosphere across the whole record," Joe continues. "We created a lot of different drones and sound-beds under each track, which I hope give the album a certain discreetly epic ambiance, a restrained grandeur."

"It was special for us to record the whole album in our own DIY studio," Robin points out. "That was through necessity as much as anything! We certainly wanted it to complete the picture begun with the first album, and for it to be a step on musically."

So far things have been going well for the band, giving the Dreaming Spires reason to be optimistic about the future. They completed a visit to the States, which allowed them to perform at the Americana Music Conference in Nashville and to record some new material at Ardent Studios in Memphis. They also secured Stateside distribution via Last Chance Records, allowing their music greater exposure than they've ever had before. "There's always more you can do," Robin maintains. "But we try to enjoy the view along the way, and keep doing music that pleases our own ears first. When we write a good song or we make a good recording, we want people to hear it!"

"We just want to keep on reaching more and more people with our music," Joe insists. "We're now fifteen years and fifteen plus albums into this with all the various bands and projects we've been involved with, including Goldrush, Danny and the Champs, and our other projects like Co-Pilgrim and Dusty Sound System. It feels good to have such a body of work that we can be proud of."

Asked about their goals for the future, Robin is fairly succinct. "To keep writing better songs and avoid getting a 'proper' job," he responds. "I hope our love for our favorite music comes across from the record, and that people feel we've made something individual out of familiar elements."

48

....

The Sadies Look South

After more than two decades and a catalog of recordings that currently boasts upwards of twenty albums, the Sadies certainly have reason to tout their accomplishments. A band that's equally adept at purveying strains of Americana, rock and roll, surf music, twang, and traditional country, they can claim a broad musical palette, as well as a considerable level of achievement.

Still, the fact that they reside north of the border has tempered their progress so far. Like other Canadian combos—Blue Rodeo, the Tragically Hip, the Skydiggers, Blackie and the Rodeo Kings, and Spirit of the West among them—they champion a sound they've dubbed "Canadiana," one that's as roots relevant as any of their American cousins. Their 2010 album, *Darker Circles*, was shortlisted for Canada's prestigious Polaris music award and later garnered a Juno Award for best video. Sadly, though, due to setting or circumstance, their work has but been all ignored on the lower side of that northern divide.

Singer/guitarist Dallas Good explains that it's always harder for Canadian artists to get recognition in the States, at least compared to the acceptance that American artists receive in Canada. For one thing, visas are really expensive and difficult to get, so for many bands the possibility of doing several shows throughout the United States becomes a logistical nightmare. "I don't see it affecting Drake or the Biebs of course, but whatever," Good says. "I certainly don't blame the public for never having heard of me."

Indeed, if Good is overly concerned about the band's lack of awareness here in the States, he doesn't appear to let on. Between their ongoing efforts in the studio and a seemingly never-ending parade of collaborators—Neko Case, Jon Langford, John Doe, and Andre Williams are but a few of the artists that they've worked with throughout their career—Good and his colleagues (brother, vocalist, and guitarist Travis Good, bassist Sean Dean, and drummer Mike Belitsky) seem to have more than enough on their collective plate to keep themselves busy.

Good finds that the collaborations come about naturally, mainly because their circle of friends and associates is primarily made up of musicians. "We just remain diligent about being willing to do it and wait patiently until it makes sense," Good explains. "We aren't actively seeking new projects to work on with people, but we know it'll probably happen again as soon as it makes sense."

For the moment anyway, the band has plenty of priorities on which to focus their time. "We still haven't killed each other or even attempted to do so," Good says. Their album, *Northern Passages*, proved to be their most definitive effort yet. A combination of harmonious ballads and skittish rockers, it typifies what the band does best—that is, to create exhilarating music that reflects the influences they swear by—sounds that stem from the late fifties through to the late sixties, with ample doses of country and western, bluegrass, rhythm and blues, folk, instrumental rock, and psychedelia tossed in between.

"I don't think I'm very concerned about repeating myself," Good insists. "It's better than repeating someone else. We are still evolving. We may be a one trick pony but the trick is getting really good."

That's certainly how it appears. Good's hoping that audiences will concur. He describes a Sadies concert as one that boasts a fair share of surprises and a good show to boot. "We provide an environment that's conducive to having a lot of fun," he says. "It's scientifically enhanced. Factory adjusted. Like a Petri dish full of good times."

49

....

The Falls

Love, Life, and Life on the Road

The Falls' story seems like the stuff of soap operas. The Australian duo—specifically, Simon Rudston-Brown and Melinda Kirwin—met while the two were attending the Conservatorium of Music in Sydney. They immediately clicked both personally and professionally, prior to establishing a musical residency at a little hotel in Sydney and then heading to the United States to play SXSW. Just a few months after that, they signed a record deal with Verve Records and moved to LA to continue cultivating their career.

All would seem to have been going smoothly, had it not been for a turbulent love life that found them breaking up, making up, breaking up again, and then somehow finding the will to reconnect for the sake of their music. After making their debut with the *Hollywood* EP, they then returned with their first full length effort, *Omaha*, which was recorded in the city of the same name by local wunderkind Mike Mogis, the man behind the boards for recordings by Jenny Lewis, First Aid Kit, M. Ward, and Bright Eyes.

In the interim, the duo have toured with the Lumineers and Of Monsters and Men, and become staples on the festival circuit. Indeed, if their success seems to have come quickly, Omaha offers ample reason why. Although the songs bask in honesty and emotion, they're propelled by an energy and conviction that allows them to catch on immediately. They cite the Beatles; Bob Dylan; Crosby, Stills and Nash; Ryan Adams; Beck; and Neil Young as primary influences, but the outfit that swiftly comes to mind is

Fleetwood Mac, given their propensity for sharing their romantic ups and downs in a way that's instantly appealing.

"We've spent the past eighteen months traveling the length and breadth of the United States playing shows, writing songs, and just pretty much falling in love with this country," Rudston-Brown explains. "When it came time to decide which songs should make the album, it started to become clear how much the songs we had written had been influenced by our time on the road in America . . . by the landscapes and its people. However, the songs are also deeply personal—they're very raw, very real, and very honest, and I think we've written a lot about the feeling you get when you're away from home and missing the people you love."

While Hollywood reflected the sound they project in concert, Omaha finds them expanding their musical palette and opting for more potent possibilities. "When we recorded in the past, we were very conscious of not straying too far from what we do live, when it's just two of us on stage," Kirwin suggests. "On this record we wanted our sound to be bigger, darker, and more lush. That said, there are still a few songs on the album that are recorded the way the song was written, two voices and a guitar. Ultimately, we wanted to make a record that referenced our influences, without imitating them and to try to create something that is uniquely us."

In so doing, the two remain determined to share their own insights while hoping at the same time that the subject matter will also connect with others. "I think the coolest thing about being a songwriter is seeing how these songs that you write on your own in your little house end up reaching other people," Rudston-Brown marvels. "It's incredible when you find out that your songs have had an impact on someone else's life. It's very humbling to hear what they've meant to other people and how they make them feel."

"We try to write songs that are honest and heartfelt," Kirwin adds. "We can only hope that they provide comfort to someone in their darkest times and add a little more sparkle to their joyous moments as well."

50

Ireland's Arborist Details His Circumspect

Veteran singer-songwriter Mark McCambridge makes no pretence about being an upbeat guy. Under the guise of his nom de plume Arborist, he weaves a sound that's deep, deliberate, and well considered. "Most of the music I like has a slightly dark undertone," McCambridge admits. "It provides a certain comfort while negotiating the strangeness of being alive. I hope people get something similar from our music."

He needn't worry. With a series of supporting gigs for the likes of Low, Cat Power, James Yorkston, Echo and the Bunnymen, and Alasdair Roberts, and a full-length album titled *Home Burial*, Arborist covered a lot of turf in a remarkably short span of time. While comparisons to Leonard Cohen, Jason Molina, and the aforementioned Low seem inevitable, Arborist possesses a singular beauty that captivates all on its own.

"Music was always a big thing in my house growing up, though I wouldn't specifically say my folks were 'music fans,'" McCambridge recalls. "They didn't have an extensive record collection or play any instruments, but we had a piano from very early on and there was always music playing in the house somewhere, from Irish traditional to Pavarotti or Elton John, to Porter Wagoner and Tammy Wynette. When it came to my early teens, I had two main obsessions—the Pixies and the Smiths. Even now I still can't see beyond them, though I've stopped trying to write like Morrissey and scream like Frank Black. I think it's their otherworldliness that drew me in."

That's a quality that's obvious in Arborist's songs even on first hearing. They have a stately elegance and an elegiac quality that leaves a haunting, sometimes harrowing impression. Songs such as "Twisted Arrow" (which features a cameo appearance from Kim Deal, no less), "A Crow," "Kirkinriola," "A Fisherman," and "Border Blood" quickly get under the skin and refuse to budge from there. McAlister's impromptu solo appearance at the annual British BBQ that took place during this year's Americana Music Festival confirmed that impression even on his own.

"Many debut albums can simply become a collection of songs amassed to-date," he suggests. "But I was keen to avoid falling into this trap and preferred to concentrate on making a cohesive, flowing record. This meant leaving some strong songs out. However, I feel the album is better for it."

Not surprisingly, then, McCambridge is pleased with Arborist's progress thus far. "There have been some great live highlights playing alongside acts I've always adored, such as Low, Cat Power, and Mark Mulcahy, but 2015 really pushed things on for us," he says. "Having Kim Deal sing on our 'Twisted Arrow' that year was something I could've never imagined."

As far as the future is concerned, he's equally enthusiastic. "Everything to-date has been leading up to the release of our debut album early next year. Hopefully people will enjoy it and we can push on from there and recreate it live across the UK and Ireland and then . . . the world!"

Maybe he's not such a downbeat fellow after all.

51

···································

Jenn Grant Channels Her Mother's Inspiration and Her Own Determination

"My mother died in 2012, and her spirit lends herself well to *Compostela*," Jenn Grant responds when asked about her latest release. "I meet people again and again who tell me how this album has been a healing tool for them in some way. I've noticed it more than I ever have, and it feels like there is a vibration that is occurring between these songs and the listeners. I feel lucky to be a part of that."

That would seem quite an accomplishment by any standard, but one needn't rely on Grant's word as verification. Since its Stateside release in 2014, the album in question has garnered this young Canadian songstress a number of notable accolades — among them, a pair of 2015 Juno award nominations in the categories of Adult Alternative Album of the Year and Songwriter of the Year. In 2015, the Canadian Broadcast Corporation (the CBC) proclaimed it one of the thirty best Canadian albums of 2014, with the result that its lead single, "No One's Gonna Love You (Quite Like I Do)," spent six weeks on the CBC Radio 2 Top 20.

"I've been slowly building my career with each record since it began in 2007," Grant suggests. "But there was a shift with the making of *Compostela*. I began working with a new team, and I also took more care, precision, and thought with the making of this album. I spent a year taking the time to step away from it and going back to it—and to the songs—and in the end, the feeling that I wanted to achieve with this album feels complete. However, albums do not feel fully complete until they are released,

[and] songs feel unfinished until they are let go and can mean something to someone else!"

Grant knows of what she speaks. She dedicated an entire month to composing the material for the album, taking refuge in a camper near Lake Echo, Nova Scotia. The album title was inspired by the last words her mother spoke to her, "I will meet you in Spain," which she then took to mean "Compostela," a Spanish word that translates as "field of stars" or "star field." It's a phrase borne of the legend that the dust of the pilgrims who walk the El Camino make up the stars that form the Milky Way.

Indeed, the album is a star-studded effort, one that finds Grant teamed with such stellar special guests as Ron Sexsmith, Rose Cousins, Sarah Harmer, Doug Paisley, Kim Harris, and Toronto composer Jonathan Goldsmith, among others.

A native of Prince Edward Island in the Canadian Maritimes, Grant first started writing music while in her teens and took to the stage after receiving her degree in Fine Arts at the Nova Scotia College of Art and Design. In the eight years since and five albums since, Grant has attracted considerable critical acclaim at home, including ongoing Juno nods and inclusion on the Polaris Long List.

"My early influences were leaked to me from my parent's favorite records that played in our house as a kid," Grant recalls. "Willie Nelson, the Beatles, the Beach Boys, Patsy Cline. These were some of the voices I fell in love with as a child and still hold a deep connection to me as an adult." She goes on to cite First Aid Kit, Father John Misty, Rodriguez, Damien Jurado, Jenny Lewis, and Florence and the Machine among the artists she's currently enjoying.

These days, Grant looks toward to the future. "In order to really achieve what I want with this record, and for my future in this business, it's really important for me to tour internationally and continue to develop my live performance for my audience. Since its release, I've been able to tour *Compostela* in Canada, America, Australia, Europe [with a significant focus on Ireland], and the UK. This has been a huge step in my career. . . . I'm excited, thankful, and grateful for every opportunity to do what I love."

52

....

The Henrys' Unlikely Exposition

Credit the Henrys for dispelling the notion that all Canadian roots music more or less echoes the sounds that come from the opposite side of the border. While our neighbors to the north have an exceptional tradition of fostering authentic Americana — a style sown by their own rugged prairie roots as well as a heritage birthed below the 49th parallel — it's rare to find a band that's able to expand on that template and produce something so wholly unexpected.

Ironically, the Henrys aren't nearly as well-known as their Canadian brethren here in the States, something of an irony, considering the fact that their origins stretch back some twenty-one years and encompass six albums. It's also a curious turn of fortune in light of the fact that one of the Toronto-based band's acknowledged leaders Don Rooke has a resume that lists such luminaries as Margaret O'Hara and the Holy Modal Rounders. Then again, to this writer's ears, theirs is a sound that's not as instantly accessible as, say, some of Canada's other native sons, like the Skydiggers or Blue Rodeo. It's quirky at times, semiserious at others, often coming across like a chamber quartet caught up in classical intentions.

One reason for those eclectic inventions could be the participation of violinist and a Henrys mainstay Hugh Marsh, the musical mastermind behind Bruce Cockburn and Jon Hassell. Marsh's often unlikely arrangements take his charges' music to a certain fringe, a place where the avant-garde somehow manages to find common ground with more melodic intents. Likewise, the group's professed fondness for more exotic instrumentation — kana guitar (an antique koa wood slide guitar), pump organ, and other less common accoutrements—adds a certain fascinating presence to the usual guitar-bass-drums lineup. Taken in tandem with the words of vocalist Gregory Hoskins and contributions from bassist Andrew Downing, keyboardist John Sheard, pianist and string arranger Jonathan Goldsmith, drummer Davide DiRenso, and harmony vocalist Tara Dunphy, it creates a mesmerizing motif.

Quiet Industry illustrates that dichotomy to a great degree, with low-cast ballads like "As I Say I Do," "A Thousand Corners," "Dangers of Travel," and "Last One Here" sharing tracking time with ornate instrumentals such as "Invention of the Atmospheric Engine" and "Was Is." It's an odd juxtaposition at times, and when combined with such nocturnal laments as "Needs Must" and "The Almighty Inbox"—and an occasional abstract concoction along the lines of "Burn the Boat"—the overall effect is as impressive as it is intriguing.

In a review of their new album, Laurie Brown, host of the program *The Signal* on CBC Radio, remarked, "The words and music trade off moments in holding your attention, Brilliant production once again from the Henrys. I have used their CDs to buy two stereos in my lifetime. The sound is that good. Do your stereo—and your head and heart—a favor. Let them chew on the Henrys' *Quiet Industry* CD."

That would seem quite a compliment coming from an audiophile of a certain stature. Ultimately, though, the Henrys deserve wide recognition from the rest of us as well.

Appendix

Essential Albums That Trace the Transition

Hank Williams Sings (Hank Williams, 1951)
Moanin' the Blues (Hank Williams, 1952)
Elvis Presley (Elvis Presley, 1956)
One Dozen Berrys (Chuck Berry, 1958)
Modern Sounds in Country and Western Music (Ray Charles, 1962)
The Everly Brothers Sing Great Country Hits (Everly Brothers, 1963)
Blonde on Blonde (Bob Dylan, 1966)
John Wesley Harding (Bob Dylan, 1966)
Bright Lights and Country Music (Rick Nelson, 1966)
Gentle on My Mind (Glen Campbell, 1967)
By the Time I Get to Phoenix (Glen Campbell, 1967)
Buffalo Springfield Again (Buffalo Springfield, 1967)
The Notorious Byrd Brothers (Byrds, 1967)
Moby Grape (Moby Grape, 1967)
Sweetheart of the Rodeo (Byrds, 1968)
At Folsom Prison (Johnny Cash, 1968)
Nashville Skyline (Bob Dylan, 1969)
Pickin' Up the Pieces (Poco, 1969)
Hand Sown . . . Home Grown (Linda Rondstadt and the Stone Poneys, 1969)
Born on a Bayou (Creedence Clearwater Revival, 1969)
Green River (Creedence Clearwater Revival, 1969)
Willy and the Poor Boys (Creedence Clearwater Revival, 1969)
Music from Big Pink (The Band, 1968)
For the Sake of the Song (Townes Van Zandt, 1968)
Our Mother the Mountain (Townes Van Zandt, 1969)
The Band (The Band, 1969)
Shady Grove (Quicksilver Messenger Service, 1969)

California Bloodlines (John Stewart, 1969)

Rock Salt and Nails (Steve Young, 1969)

Rhymes and Reasons (John Denver, 1969)

Jesse Winchester (Jesse Winchester, 1970)

Stage Fright (The Band, 1970)

The Gilded Palace of Sin (Flying Burrito Brothers, 1970)

Burrito Deluxe (Flying Burrito Brothers, 1970)

Workingman's Dead (Grateful Dead, 1970)

Americana Beauty (Grateful Dead, 1970)

Despite It All (Brinsley Schwarz, 1970)

After the Gold Rush (Neil Young, 1970)

Idlewild South (Allman Brothers Band, 1970)

Magnetic South (Michael Nesmith and the First National Band, 1970)

Loose Salute (Michael Nesmith and the First National Band, 1970)

New Riders of the Purple Sage (New Riders of the Purple Sage, 1971)

Tupelo Honey (Van Morrison, 1971)

The Marblehead Messenger (Seatrain, 1971)

Deliverin' (Poco, 1971)

Aero-Plain (John Hartford, 1971)

John Prine (John Prine, 1971)

Welcome to Goose Creek (Goose Creek Symphony, 1971)

Diamond on the Rough (John Prine, 1972)

And the Hits Just Keep on Comin' (Michael Nesmith, 1972)

Garden Party (Rick Nelson, 1972)

High, Low and In Between (Townes Van Zandt, 1972)

The Late Great Townes Van Zandt (Townes Van Zandt, 1972)

Linda Rondstadt (Linda Rondstadt, 1972)

Will the Circle Be Unbroken (Nitty Gritty Dirt Band and guests, 1972)

Nervous on the Road (Brinsley Schwarz, 1972)

Exile on Main St. (Rolling Stones, 1972)

Seven Bridges Road (Steve Young, 1972)

A Good Feelin' to Know (Poco, 1972)

Eagles (Eagles, 1972)

Geronimo's Cadillac (Michael Martin Murphy, 1972)

Desperado (Eagles, 1973)

Pretty Much Your Standard Ranch Stash (Michael Nesmith, 1973)

Crazy Eyes (Poco, 1973)

Lonesome, On'ry and Mean (Waylon Jennings, 1973)

GP (Gram Parsons, 1973)

The Souther-Hillman-Furay Band (Souther-Hillman-Furay Band, 1974)

Grievous Angel (Gram Parsons, 1974)

Fire on the Mountain (Charlie Daniels Band, 1974)

Learn to Love It (Jesse Winchester, 1974)

The Blue Ridge Rangers (John Fogerty, 1974)

On the Border (Eagles, 1974)

Old and in the Way (Old and in the Way, 1975)

Blood on the Tracks (Bob Dylan, 1975)

Rose of Cimarron (Poco, 1975)

The Car over the Lake Album (Ozark Mountain Daredevils, 1975)

Red Headed Stranger (Willie Nelson, 1975)

Fly through the Country (New Grass Revival, 1975)

Old No. 1 (Guy Clark, 1975)

Hotel California (Eagles, 1976)

Indian Summer (Poco, 1976)

Blue Sky—Night Thunder (Michael Martin Murphy, 1975)

Texas Cookin' (Guy Clark, 1976)

Changes in Latitudes, Changes in Attitudes (Jimmy Buffett, 1977)

Wanted! The Outlaws (Willie Nelson, Waylon Jennings, Jessi Colter, Tompall Glaser, 1976)

Nothing but a Breeze (Jesse Winchester, 1977)

White Mansions (Various Artists, 1978)

One Road More (The Flatlanders, 1980)

How Will the Wolf Survive? (Los Lobos, 1984)

Southern Accents (Tom Petty and the Heartbreakers, 1985)

Shelter (Lone Justice, 1986)

Guitar Town (Steve Earle, 1986)

Copperhead Road (Steve Earle, 1988)

No Depression (Uncle Tupelo, 1990)

The Mavericks (Mavericks, 1991)

From Hell to Paradise (The Mavericks, 1992)

Anodyne (Uncle Tupelo, 1993)

What a Crying Shame (The Mavericks, 1994)

Trace (Son Volt, 1995)

Faithless Street (Whiskeytown, 1995)

A.M. (Wilco, 1995)

Index